The Medicine Way

A SHAMANIC PATH TO SELF-MASTERY

Kenneth Meadows, a former college lecturer and journalist,
has pursued his interest in the esoteric knowledge of ancient peoples for
rnany years. He has studied shamanic teachings directly under
Native American, British, Scandinavian and other European shamans.
He is a trained shamanic counsellor.

The Medicine Way

A SHAMANIC PATH TO SELF MASTERY

Kenneth Meadows

ELEMENT
Shaftesbury, Dorset ● Rockport, Massachusetts

© Kenneth Meadows 1990

Published in Great Britain in 1990 by
Element Books Limited
Longmead, Shaftesbury, Dorset

Published in the USA in 1991 by
Element, Inc.
42 Broadway, Rockport, MA 01966

Reprinted July 1991.
Reprinted December 1991.

Cover illustration by Martin Rieser
Cover design by Max Fairbrother
Typeset by Poole Typesetting (Wessex) Ltd
Printed and bound in Great Britain by
Dotesios Ltd, Trowbridge, Wiltshire

Library of Congress Catalog Card Number available

British Library Cataloguing in Publication Data
Meadows, Kenneth
The medicine way
1. North American Indians. Folk medicine
I. Title II. Series
615.882097

ISBN 1–85230–151–1

CONTENTS

Acknowledgements

THIS BOOK COULD NOT HAVE BEEN undertaken, let alone completed, without the help, support, advice and encouragement of a number of people who are dear to me:

My principal mentors, Silver Bear and Wolf Eagle and members of the Medicine Society of the Blue Feather who so generously have shared some of their knowledge and wisdom with me.

Harley Swiftdeer, who helped me make my first hesitant steps along the Medicine way, and United Kingdom apprentices of the Deer Tribe Metis Medicine Society for their companionship as I did so.

Wallace Black-Elk for extending my horizons with a vision of Lakota (Sioux) spirituality.

My friend and spiritual brother Tony Haggerstone who joined me along the Way and whose strength and wisdom have supported me.

Jonathan Horwitz, faculty member of the Foundation for Shamanic Studies headquartered in Newark, Connecticut, USA, for his gentle guidance as I embarked upon shamanic journeying, and Moon Wolf whose patience sustained me.

Leo Rutherford, principal of the Eagle's Wing Centre for Contemporary Shamanism, London, England, for providing me with opportunities to participate in revivals of many ancient medicine ceremonies.

Crow, on whose 'horse' I rode when I was given the commission to do this work.

My wife, Beryl, without whose tolerance and understanding I could not have kept going, and who became a traveller with me.

This book is dedicated to my children and grandchildren and all who come after me. May it help you to push through the barriers of bigotry, intolerance and ignorance and enable you to find for yourselves the healing balm that will make a Golden Age possible.

Above all it is dedicated to the Native American peoples in the hope that in some small way it may help to restore to them some of the recognition and respect that history over the last 400 years or more has so cruelly denied them.

Kenneth Meadows
(whose Medicine name is *'Flying Horse'*)

Preface

WHATEVER YOUR AGE, WHATEVER your work, whether you are married or single, male or female, of modest means or fabulously rich, something is missing in your life. You may not know exactly what it is. You may not be able to define it. You are aware only that the need to find that elusive 'something' has been with you for a very long time.

Some have sought it in fame. But when fame has come it has deprived them of the privacy and independence to enable them to live as they would like. So the high cost of fame is often loss of freedom.

Others have sought it in the acquisition of wealth and material goods. To the person struggling to make ends meet, wealth appears to be the one asset that would enable them to have everything the heart desires. Certainly money will buy many things. But not everything. Those with lots of money are not necessarily the happiest people on earth. Some indeed are uncertain about who their true friends are, who they can trust, and who truly want them for what they are and not just for what they have. So even lots of money cannot buy that elusive 'something'.

Others have sought it in religion. Religion, with its emphasis on spiritual and moral values, must surely bring peace of mind, individual fulfilment, and the acquisition of that elusive 'something'? But look around the world today. Isn't religion behind much of the turmoil in the world's trouble spots? Look back in history. Hasn't some of the greatest of man's inhumanity to man been caused because one idea of God differs from another? People of different faiths have often clashed because each has claimed that theirs is the only True God and everyone else's, an imposter. Even those confessing the same religion are sorely divided about basic tenets of their Faith, and millions have died because of it.

Some have looked to science. The march of science has made fantastic strides and has transformed the way millions of people live. In the course of a single lifetime we have progressed from horse and 'buggy' travel to flying through the air at great heights and at speeds faster than sound. A meal which might once have taken hours in preparation and cooking today takes only minutes at the touch of a button on a microwave oven. We can watch in our own homes events that are taking place at that moment in almost any place in the world. We have even watched man set foot on the Moon and have been following his attempts to reach for the Stars. Now such 'miracles' of science are so commonplace that we are no longer in awe, but take them for granted. Yet for all the wonder of its achievements, science has not satisfied the quest for that missing 'something'.

The hidden yet natural forces within yourself which have motivated you in that quest have brought you into contact with this book which itself is the culmination of one man's lifelong journey to discover the undiscovered — one man's Earth Quest.

For more than 40 years its author searched the libraries of learned institutions and combed publishing houses world-wide. He sought 'it' from spiritual leaders, from the mainstream of religious orthodoxy, from denominational teachers, and from those in a wide spectrum of sects and cults. He shared hours and even days with monks in their monasteries, with mystics and gurus, spiritualists and spiritists, theosophists and occultists, pagans and witches. He has been in contact with those who say they have been in touch with extraterrestial beings and even those who claim to *be* extraterrestial beings! But still the quest remained unsatisfied.

Each path of enquiry revealed something of value, provided some clue, some direction. Some paths were blind alleys, others narrow, confining and restrictive. 'What you seek is a Mystery that cannot be attained or even understood in this life. Accept what we say, believe what we tell you even if you cannot understand or comprehend it' was the general admonishment.

This voyage of discovery is like trying to find your way through a gigantic maze. Perhaps you have visited a labyrinth where you are hedged in on either side and where there is nothing to indicate whether you should take this turning or that? Or perhaps you have tackled one of those perplexing puzzles in which you are challenged to track your way through an intriguing complex of routes and where, as with an open-air maze, it is so easy to lose your way because the direction is changing all the time. Then, just as you begin to think you are making progress, up you come against another dead end, and in retracing your steps how often have you come right back to where you started?

This book charts a way through the maze which you have already begun to explore. It will help you to acquire the skills you need to continue your journey, and provide you with the means to overcome every problem and to meet every need and situation that may face you in everyday life.

It will not, however, be a journey without effort, but you can be assured of getting to the treasure if you are determined because the author himself has already tracked the route, persisting in spite of experiencing frustrations and disappointments, keeping on year after year through youth, into maturity and into the autumn of years until he found the centre where the treasure is. It is a journey that will take courage, because every step forward will be a step into the unknown. It will take determination, because some of the things you must collect along the way cannot be gathered instantly. And it will take persistence, because some of the skills you need to acquire to continue your journey need practice.

This book won't provide you with the treasure you seek. No book, no priest, no teacher, no guru, can do that either. But what it *will* do is enable you to discover where the treasure is and to have the ability to reach for it and to take it for yourself.

In a way, perhaps, this has helped to explain why you haven't known exactly what it is you are looking for. It is because you have been expecting someone else to reveal it to you when it is, in fact, much nearer to you than that, and you must discover it for yourself.

We are each looking for that which is totally fulfilling, but we don't know precisely what it is we are searching for. It gnaws at us emotionally like a kind of homesickness. We pine for a state in which we can be totally contented, totally at home, totally loved and in love, totally secure. Yet we don't know what it is that will give us that, nor where to search for it. We go through life seeking here and seeking there, and every time we think we have spotted it in one of its many guises, it has vanished again.

We are like the man who was searching under the light of a street lamp for the key to the safe where he kept his valuables. 'Can I help you to find it?' asked a kindly passer-by. They both searched and searched, but there was no sign of the key. Finally the passer-by enquired: 'Are you absolutely sure you lost it here?'

'Oh,' said the man, 'I didn't lose it here. I lost it in the house, but it's dark inside and it's light out here so I thought this would be an easier place to look.'

We may smile at the householder's stupidity, but most of us have been guilty of similar logic. It is easier to look for something under some kind of illumination provided by others, but if what we are seeking was never there in the first place no amount of so-called 'enlightenment' will lead us to find it. We search in vain. Yet all the householder had to do was to go home and turn on his own light and the key he wanted would have been within his capacity to find.

This, then, is a book for the Spiritual Adventurer by a Spiritual Explorer. It is a book of exploration that has been one man's journey of self-discovery but is also your journey to self-mastery.

Some people believe in Fate or Destiny, that coincidence isn't just an 'accident' but a preordained situation you somehow arrive at.

You were destined to pick up this book. It is no coincidence that it has come into your hands for contained within it are the answers to your hidden needs, those tremendous longings and deep desires that have been gnawing at your very soul. These desires are proof enough that the success of your journey of discovery and the attainment of the pearl without price is already assured.

Introduction

THIS BOOK EXPLORES A MISSING dimension in our understanding of life. It contains the basic principles of a remarkable system of personal development and life-enhancement based upon hitherto 'hidden' teachings of American Indians and on their correlation with the ancient shamanic knowledge of Northern Europe and Scandinavia and with the Taoist wisdom of the East, and adapted to the needs and circumstances of modern times. It is a system I have called the Medicine Way.

Perhaps no people have been more maligned, more misunderstood, more mistreated and misrepresented than the North American Indian. These once noble and courageous people have been despised, denigrated and defamed, and most of it unjustly. In comparison with today's city dweller, they certainly lived primitively — but they had a wisdom that enabled them to be in harmony with their environment and to have a respect for it.

They knew the Earth as the Mother who provided them with food, clothing and shelter and who, therefore, deserved their loving care and protection. When they moved their encampment they 'covered their tracks' by leaving the land as they found it, unspoiled and unlittered by human debris, or even signs of human occupation.

In comparison with people today living in centrally-heated homes and with all the provisions and benefits of a technological society, the American Indian of history does appear to have been 'wild' and 'uncivilised'. But to their children every man and woman was like father and mother. None went unloved or abused, and the elderly were honoured with the best of meat. They honoured and respected life in all its forms, and killed only out of need. Indeed, they even regarded animals and birds, trees and plants as their 'relatives' and therefore deserving of their respect if not always their affection. Murder, violent crime, theft, rape and child abuse were rarities.

Uneducated they may have been by today's academic standards, supported by no vast libraries, but as this book will indicate, they did possess a profound understanding of the mysteries of life, of the purpose of existence and of the natural world and the forces of Nature all around them — an understanding that eludes modern scholars and transcends the 'book knowledge' of learned professors. They had no scriptures or doctors of divinity, yet they enjoyed a personal relationship with the divinity they found all around them and even within them. They had no eminent scientists, yet they could control some of Nature's most powerful unseen forces.

When people from technologically more advanced nations came from across the seas proclaiming civilisation and morality and 'true' religion, they regarded the Indians' near-nakedness with shocked horror, steeped as the Europeans then were in sexual guilt and indoctrined with a belief that the naked human body was something shameful and wicked, its exposure a sign of godlessness and ignorance. Besides, they wanted the land and the Indians were in the way.

As the increasing deluge of settlers moved inland in the quest for material wealth, claiming ownership of the Indians' homeland by God-given 'right of discovery', the Indians were driven before them. In trying to defend and protect their communities the Indians had to fight not only the invaders but the onrush of brother Indian tribes so what came was not peace and goodwill towards all men, which missionaries proclaimed from their holy book, but violence; not truth but deception.

When, finally, the Indians were overcome, they were deprived not only of their freedom to roam, not only of their pride and dignity, but of their customs and practices which religious bigotry regarded as demonism. The spirituality of the Amerindian was outlawed. Yet throughout all the genocide, the cultural holocaust and the suppression of human rights, the American Indians never completely severed their shamanistic roots nor had them obscured entirely by repression or by an alien religion. These shamanistic roots reach right down into prehistory and to the secret wisdom of the ancients. The Indians had a priceless wisdom which mankind today, on the verge of a new Age of enlightened consciousness or the destruction of life and the planet, so desperately needs.

Before the Indians were finally overwhelmed by a period of great tribulation and suffering, Elders representing principal tribes met together and determined that some of the teachings were to be preserved by being conveyed down through the generations orally until they could be practised openly again. The spirit or essence of these teachings was, however, committed to the Sacred Fires and to the spirits of the Elements in a fire ceremony. During that sacred ceremony an assurance was given that they would be rekindled in another age. That time would come when the Earth itself was in trouble and the rekindling would include people who were not of Red Indian blood. That time is now. Part of that knowledge is about to be communicated to you through the pages of this book.

To the American Indian the word 'medicine' meant more than a substance to restore health and vitality to a sick or run-down physical body. 'Medicine' meant 'power' – a vital energy force that could be drawn upon and directed – and 'wholeness'. 'Medicine' also meant 'knowledge'. The 'Medicine Wheel' might be defined as, 'a Circle of Knowledge that restores wholeness and gives power over one's life'. The Medicine Wheel was developed by some tribes more than others, but to many it was the principal method of explaining life and a means to personal empowerment and life enhancement.

This circle of power – the Medicine Wheel – served many purposes. It was a map of the Mind. It was a chart to lead its user to the discovery of the Inner Self, to the divinity within, and to a knowledge of the true purpose of one's life. It was a working tool with which to fashion one's own self-development. It was a device for tuning in to the Earth's psychic energies and to the unseen forces of Nature. It was a working laboratory in which metaphysical tasks could be safely carried out. It was both a teaching aid and a learning package that uncovered the meaning behind some of the deepest mysteries of life.

Until recent years that knowledge and wisdom appeared to have been lost. It was, however, being guarded and protected, and now it can be made available, portion by portion, to the genuine seeker who has an open mind, a pure heart and a readiness to receive it. For the time has arrived in human history for a revival of the ancient wisdom – a revival that was foretold in the legends and stories of the Amerindians and of other cultures. It is a time when the Red Indian Race Spirit returns to help to turn mankind away from the path of destruction along which it is heading through man's folly, greed and arrogance, and to redirect it to the way of enlightenment and expanded consciousness.

Since this constructive way is not to be limited to a particular race, creed, nation or group but be generally accessible, some called the period of its accessibility 'the Time of the Rainbow Warriors'. According to the Inca shaman, Don Eduardo Calderon, the shamans of the coming Age – the 'wise-shapers' of tomorrow – will arise from peoples who were once the Red Indians' oppressors yet will become the true caretakers of the Earth and the needed teachers, guides and healers.

Shamans, medicine men and tribal elders, like Wallace Black-Elk of the Lakotas, Harley Swiftdeer the Metis Cherokee, John Redtail Freesoul the

Cheyenne-Arapahoe, Sun Bear of the Bear Tribe, and writers like Hye-meyohsts Storm, Carlos Castaneda, Lynn Andrews and Brad Steiger, have lifted the veil on some of the hidden knowledge and there is now a developing and insatiable appetite for it.

Traditionalists among the Native American people may be resentful that Medicine principles, so sacred to their own race and culture, should be made available to all who are ready to receive them. But what they may not have realised is that the Medicine Wheel was never an invention of the American Indian mind. It is a universal power source that was entrusted in ancient times to the Red race for safekeeping until the time arrived in human history when it would be needed to harmonise all esoteric traditions for the benefit of mankind. This was hinted at in many Amerindian legends.

Perhaps the most widespread of Amerindian legends is one about an ancient prophet-king of the Toltec Indians of Mexico called Quetzalcoatl (pronounced Ket-zal-kwatl). The word is derived from *quetzal*, the name of a rare and magnificent green bird, and *coatl* meaning serpent. So the name in English means 'Feathered Serpent' and implies a god-man who creates, sustains and is enduring. The legendary 'Feathered Serpent' prophesied that white men would come from the East in huge canoes with wings like a great white bird. He described the men as having one foot like a dove and the other like an eagle, and they would take away not only the land but the spirit from the Redman. The foot of the dove symbolised a religion proclaiming love and kindness, though few lived the religion they professed. The eagle's foot indicated the way they acted — like an eagle clawing and killing and devouring. In the story, 'Feathered Serpent' went on to say that many, many years afterwards other men would come and they would have both feet like a dove, and they would teach the Indians to be proud of their ancestors and to return to the knowledge the ancients had. And the Indians would get back their spirit, would rise up from the dust of despair, and would help to heal the Earth which at that time would be languishing in sickness. And, the story goes, they would help to build a better world in which love and trust and peace and harmony would rule.

This book is, in part, a small step towards the manifestation of such a vision. The knowledge contained in these pages has come orally through shamans under whom I have studied, through research and the application of shamanic principles of learning which they have taught to me, through gaining access to deeper levels of the mind which Jungian psychologists call the collective unconscious, and through direct teaching on inner planes which some call channelling. The teachings are not those of a particular tribe or group but rather represent a distillation of the essential truth of them all in the spirit of the wandering shamans.

Shamans are spiritually developed men and women who recognise that life is in all things, who are able to work with cosmic and natural forces and to experience different levels of awareness from physical reality. Shamanism is the study and practice of the techniques and principles of shamans. It includes utilizing altered states of consciousness and meditative techniques to contact inner sources, to experience different planes of existence and by so doing obtain information, effect desired changes, and heal and harmonise. Travelling shamans went beyond the limitations of their own tribal customs and traditions for they recognised that no single tribe or group of people had all Truth. So they sought it wherever it could be found, travelling from tribe to tribe and place to place, imparting wisdom and gaining new knowledge, weaving what they learned with what they already knew. They stimulated the inner senses of their listeners through their stories and the myths and legends they recounted.

Their counterparts in ancient Britain and Northern Europe were the Celtic Bards and the travelling Nordic Runemasters who encapsulated their esoteric knowledge in folk tales, fairy stories and mythic legends, some of which have been passed down to this day.

Let me stress two important features of Medicine Way teachings:

First, what sets the Medicine Wheel apart from many other systems is its lack of dogmatism. The student of the Medicine Way is therefore not faced with a set of beliefs or dogmas which have to be accepted before 'progress' can be made. Rather, you are encouraged to find your own perception of truth within a system which is itself but a map or a framework in which discovery can be made. Dogmatism arises from mistaking a map for the territory itself, or a menu for the meal.

Second, the Medicine Way is an exciting and absorbing adventure of self-discovery. You are not being led to become a Red Indian 'devotee'. There will be no call to dye your hair black or wear it in plaits, no invitation to daub on face paints, or wear moccasins! No appeal to give allegiance to a tribal leader or spiritual guru. The quest for Truth is lost immediately you transfer your power into the hands of another. The Medicine Way is about finding your own power – your own 'medicine'.

The Medicine Way is thus more than an entertaining and absorbing read. It is a fascinating and exciting experience, for the book is laced with intriguing practical exercises which enable you to discover for yourself the validity of some of the principles discussed. Furthermore, a series of 'adventure tasks' provide a powerful means of sharpening the senses, expanding awareness, and awakening dormant potentials.

Essentially, the Medicine Way is a path of discovery about yourself —
who you are, what you are, why you are as you are, and where you're
heading — and of learning to take control of your life and consciously
fashion your own destiny. On the Medicine path your consciousness is
expanded causing things to begin to happen in 'coincidental' ways. There
comes about a realisation of the true wonder of Nature and of the natural
world and a recognition that everything is alive and has its part to play for
the good of the whole. You will come to enjoy the moment, taking
pleasure in the Present, and you will possess an excited anticipation about
the Future.

Welcome, then, to the Medicine Way — an exciting and absorbing
adventure.

THE COMMISSION GIVEN TO 'FLYING HORSE' BY THE MYSTIC MEDICINE CHIEF 'SILVER BEAR'.

When you walk in darkness
It is no use carrying a lantern
Whose light cannot be seen.
For, then, every step you take
Will be a hesitation into the unknown
Where any tiny pebble on the Path
May cause you to trip or stumble,
Or the slightest impediment,
A cause for you to give up
And abandon the journey
To try, perhaps, another path.
So make a lantern,
Lit from the Red Indian fire
And whose light shines clear
For the way you've come
To be seen and marked,
And the way ahead to hold no fear
For others who come after you
To walk with an assurance,
Seeing by light from a torch you have left.
For those who walk this Path
Should not be left to grope in the dark
When light can make them aware
That the Path is beautiful
And the steps they take
Can be a choreography of beauty, too.
For this Path is the Beauty Way, the beautiful way,
Where all who will may Dance in Beauty
Around their own hearth fire
What they need to light the Way
Is a lantern that is bright.
So make one.
Lit from the torch you have been given.
The eight-rayed Torch,
The Flame Within
That illuminates the Eight Directions
And the Eight Dimensions.
Make one.
Be a Sun, Grandfather.

(This book is a component of that 'lantern'.)

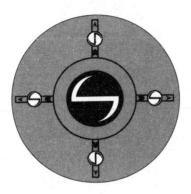

THE PREPARATION

CHAPTER ONE

The Earth is our Mother

TRY TO PUT ASIDE WHAT YOU may have read about 'savage' Red Indians and any impressions you may have formed from old Hollywood movies about barbaric natives who worshipped the Sun and communicated with evil spirits. Contrary to such misrepresentations, there is ample evidence that American Indians were, in general, a loving and gentle people of great character and strength of purpose, possessors of considerable courage and endurance, and with a deep reverence for life in all its forms.

Though there were hundreds of tribes, many languages, and different levels of development, they shared a common sense of honour and morality and a close affinity with Nature and the environment. They had a common attitude to life that was essentially both spiritual and practical. Indeed, the late Ernest Thompson Seton, one-time Head of America's Boy Scout Movement, who spent many years gathering material for his book *The Gospel of the Redman*[1] concluded that they were the most heroic, the most physically perfect and the most spiritual civilisation the world has ever known!

Christian missionaries of the time were not, perhaps, the best judges of a spirituality and culture that differed from their own, but some were sufficiently impressed with the inherent wholesomeness of the Indian to put their thoughts into writing for posterity.

The Revd C. Van Dusen, for instance, a missionary to the Ojibway Indians, in his book *The Indian Chieftain*[2] published in 1867, wrote: 'The Indian character in its unadulterated grandeur is most admirable and attractive. Before it is polluted by the pernicious example of others – the demoralizing and abasing influence of wicked whitemen – the genuine North American pagan presents to the world the most noble specimen of the natural man than can be found on the face of the earth.'

In an account of the picture writing of the American Indians published in 1893, Garry Mallery, who spent many years in close contact with Indians and was an authority of his day, said the most surprising fact about them which had not been generally recognised, was that they habitually lived by spiritual principles to a degree that was comparable only with the ancient Israelites under their theocracy.

In his book, *Picture Writing of the American Indians*,[3] Mallery said that this was sometimes ignored or denied by early missionaries because the aboriginal spirituality was not the missionaries' religion so it was either dismissed or pronounced to be Satanic.

George Catlin, a Pennsylvanian artist and author (1796–1872) who spent some of his life among Indians and wrote a detailed study called *Manners, Customs and Conditions of North American Indians*,[4] denied that they were in any way idolators or demon-inspired. 'They no more worshipped the Sun than the Christian regards the Cross as God' he wrote.

The Indian simply and practically realised that the Sun fertilised the Earth – the 'Mother' source of life – and so greeted it every day for without the Sun nothing could live.

Part of the misconception was due to the Indians' close affinity with Nature. The American Indian lived what might be described as a love affair with Nature. Earth was regarded as a living being – a Mother on whose garment all creatures moved, and from whom all obtained their subsistence. Earth supplied the substance of her physical body to provide the material from which the human physical body could be knitted together in the womb and be nurtured and protected from the time of conception until birth as a separate, individual entity. Like every mother, Earth provided all the physical needs of her children from the bounty of her own substance, and when any of her children died, their bodies returned to the Womb of the Earth from whence they came.

All creatures – whether they walked, ran, swam, crawled or winged their way in the air – were Earth's children, too. So were trees and plants who were 'alive' and had an awareness which, though it differed considerably from that of a human or animal, was no less 'real' all the same. Even rocks and stones were respected because they, too, were regarded as having a life of their own.

Since all these 'living' things shared life on Earth with humans they were truly man's 'relatives', born of the same Earth Mother and conceived also in the Mind of the Great Spirit – the Indians' concept of the Creative Source of all that is.

The Indian was thus a true naturalist and loved the Earth and the things of the Earth. Chief Luther Standing Bear, a Lakota plains Indian who was born in 1868, received a formal education from the age of eleven and spent his later years teaching and writing had this to say in his book, *Land of the Spotted Eagle*[5] published in 1933: 'The old people came literally to love the soil, and they sat and reclined on the ground with a feeling of being close to a mothering power. It was good for the skin to touch the Earth, and the old people liked to remove their moccasins and walk with bare feet on the sacred Earth. Their tipis were built upon the Earth, and their altars were made of Earth. The birds that flew in the air came to rest upon the Earth, and it was the final abiding place of all things that lived and grew. The soil was soothing, strengthening, cleansing and healing. That is why the old Indian still sits upon the Earth instead of propping himself up and away from its life-giving forces. For him, to sit or lie upon the ground is to be able to think more deeply into the mysteries of life and come closer to a kinship to all other lives about him ...

'Kinship with all creatures of the earth, sky and water, was a real and active principle. For the animal and bird world there existed a brotherly feeling that kept the Lakota safe among them, and so close did some of the Lakotas come to their feathered and furred friends that in true brotherhood they spoke a common language.

'The old Lakota was wise. He knew that man's heart away from Nature becomes hard; he knew that lack of respect for growing, living things soon led to lack of respect for humans, too. So he kept his youth close to its softening influence.'

This closeness to Nature enabled the Indian to be in continual contact with the inner world of the spirit that impregnates all things.

'We were lawless people, but we were on pretty good terms with the Great Spirit who is the Creator and Ruler of all' said Walking Buffalo, a Stony Indian who was asked by the Canadian government to make a world tour as a representative of the Indian people, and who visited London, England, at the age of 87.

'You Whites assumed we were savages' he told an audience, 'You didn't understand our prayers. You didn't *try* to understand. When we sang our praises to the Sun or Moon or to the Wind, you said we were worshipping idols. Without understanding, you condemned us as lost souls, just because our form of worship was different from yours.

'We saw the Great Spirit's work in almost everything – Sun, Moon, trees, wind and mountains. Sometimes we approached Him through these things. Was that so bad?

'Did you know that trees talk? Well, they do. They talk to each other and they'll talk to you if you will listen. Trouble is, white people don't listen. They never learned to listen to the Indians, so I don't suppose they'll listen to other voices in Nature. But I have learned a lot from trees – sometimes about the weather, sometimes about animals, sometimes about the Great Spirit.'[6]

Do you want to *hear* the voices of Nature? Well, are you willing to *listen*? Hearing such 'voices' may be regarded by cynical people today as imaginary, hallucinary or at best as some form of extra-sensory perception. The Indian was able to make use of other 'inner' senses of perception which extended the range of conscious awareness, as we shall discover later, and through his involvement with Nature the 'ordinary' senses were developed to a very high degree. Those of us living in big towns and cities today, and in communities much larger than those of the Indian, are not so close to the natural world and, as a consequence, our normal senses and perceptive capabilities are not adequately exercised and developed. We use only a comparatively small part of our sensory equipment.

Although there are some authorities who consider it is necessary to develop the psychic senses before one can make progress in esoteric work, this is putting the proverbial cart before the horse. The Indian was aware that the fine tuning of the 'ordinary' senses brought about an expansion of awareness and this gave a capacity and an ability which today might be called extra-sensory. Making better use of the 'ordinary' senses is the first step in awakening the inner — or so-called 'psychic' senses — but it does entail getting up out of our cosy armchairs and out into the woods and hills and open spaces of Nature.

So here is a simple exercise that can be performed to sharpen your senses and put you in tune with Nature — with what the Indians called 'the Earth Mother'.

EXERCISE NO.1:

Tuning Your Senses

Go out and find yourself a peaceful place among trees, on a hillside, or near a river or stream. If that's difficult because you live in a big city, there must be a park nearby where you can get away from the hurly-burly and pace of modern civilisation and where you can be surrounded by some natural beauty.

Look for a tree that has a fair amount of space around it, and one with a good, thick trunk. Sit with your back against it, so that the trunk supports your back and you can sit upright in comfort. Sit facing the direction of the Sun.

The idea is to spend a few minutes concentrating on each of your senses in turn:

Watch the sunlight dance on the leaves of the trees. Or notice the rich range of shades of green and brown. Explore the colours of flowers or shrubs, and the crinkly pattern of the leaves. If it's winter, examine the texture of the tree trunks and the arms and fingers of the branches. Watch the clouds scamper across the sky. Consider the weave of the grass near your feet. Just put all your attention into looking.

Then switch your attention to listening. Hear the whisper of the wind in the trees, the songs of the birds, the melody of flowing water, the hum of insects. Just listen for the sounds of Nature.

Next, concentrate your attention on your sense of *touch*. *Feel* the warmth of the sun on your cheek, the caress of the wind in your hair, or the kiss of rain on your lips. Take off your shoes and let your feet sink into the soft, springy soil beneath you. Feel your oneness with Nature.

Smell the scent of the grass, the sweet fragrance of flowers, the solid earthiness of the soil beneath your feet. Put all your attention into your sense of smell so that you breathe in the fragrance of Nature.

Then *taste*. Television commercials invite us to taste the freshness of certain foods, and that may be an exaggeration. But your taste buds will respond to the true freshness of Nature. Discover the taste in the fresh air that starts the saliva flowing — and that's no exaggeration.

Spend at least five minutes or so in putting each of your senses to work in this way, and you will experience a contact with Nature that you have, perhaps, not known before. Indeed, if you will spend a little time in this tranquillity, if only for half an hour or so once a week, within a few weeks you will recognise for yourself an opening up of your senses, a sharpening of your intuitiveness and creativity, and an awareness of the spirit of things. And one day when you perform this exercise you will become aware of the sounds behind those of the Earth, the 'hidden' sounds of Nature as the Indian was so readily able to do. When that day comes, as come it will, you will begin to understand the heart of the Redman.

Perhaps now, this brief insight into Indian 'spirituality' and communion with life, will help you to understand the attitude of the Amerindian when white men set foot on American soil some 500 years ago. The Europeans were warmly welcomed by the Indians and treated so royally that the early arrivals thought that since they were being treated like gods, the Indians must be ignorant enough to think they *were* gods!

The Indian attitude was to treat the stranger as the Great Spirit in disguise. It was a similar philosophy to the one contained within the pages of the Christian Bible and encapsulated in many of its stories. The difference was that the Indian actually lived out this philosophy whereas beliefs and actions were kept in separate 'compartments' by the European. When the Indians referred to the white men as 'speaking with forked tongues' they meant something deeper than the white men's apparent habit of appearing to talk out of the side of the mouth!

The early settlers did want to make treaties with the Indians, and offered gifts as evidence of their goodwill. But they were not content to share the land. They wanted it all, together with what it produced and contained. What could not be obtained by trickery and deceit was taken by force, by conquest and bloodshed. The fundamental difference was that Europeans believed they could own the land and do with it as they wished, while

Indians believed they were stewards and that no-one could actually *own* land.

In order to justify their actions, the settlers had to regard the natives as ignorant savages who worshipped demons and whose lives were enmeshed in superstitions and forms of devil worship. Indians were people who thus required to be conquered, subjected and converted if possible — or banished or wiped out if not. It was a classic example of the successful use of character assassination and de-humanisation as a psychological weapon of destruction.

Thus began the sorriest spectacle of genocide in recorded history — the destruction of an entire people and their way of life. When, by the middle of the nineteenth century, the Indian nations finally capitulated, Chief Seattle of the Duwamish people, speaking on behalf of tribes living in the Northwest region of the United States, delivered a message to President Franklin Pearce whose government had proposed reservations where Indians would be allowed to select their favourite valleys. His words are no less relevant today than they were then, and just as prophetic. His words were written down by a white settler who had learned the Duwamish language. Here are edited extracts of what he said:

'One thing we know that the white man may one day discover: Our God is the same God. You may think that you own Him as you wish to own our land, but you cannot. He is the God of man, and His compassion is equal for the Redman and for the white. This Earth is precious to Him, and to harm the Earth is to heap contempt on its Creator.

'When the last Redman has vanished from the Earth, and the memory is only the shadow of a cloud moving across the prairie, these shores and forests will still hold the spirits of my people, for they love the Earth as the newborn loves its mother's heartbeat.

'If we sell you our land, love it as we have cared for it. Hold it in your mind, the memory of the land as it is when you take it. And with all your strength, with all your might, and with all your heart, preserve it for your children and love it as God loves us all. One thing we know. Our God is the same God. This Earth is precious to Him ...

'We cannot buy or sell the sky, or the warmth of the land. We do not own the freshness of the air, or the sparkle of the water.

'Every part of the Earth is sacred. Every shining pine needle. Every sandy shore. Every mist in the dark woods. Every clearing. Every humming insect is holy in the memory and experience of my people.

'But to the white man one portion of land is the same as the next. The Earth is an enemy which is there to be conquered. He kidnaps the Earth for his children. He does not care. His appetite will devour the Earth and leave behind only a desert.

'There is no quiet place in the cities. No place to hear the waves of the spring or the rustle of insects' wings. The clatter only seems to insult the ears. The Indian prefers the soft sound of the wind darting over the face of the pond, and the smell of the wind itself cleansed by the midday rain, or scented with pinion pine.

'The air is precious to the Redman, for all things share the same breath – the beasts, the trees, the man. The white man does not seem to notice the air he breathes. Like a man dying for many days, he is numb to the smell of his own stench.'

Chief Seattle said that if he signed a treaty he would make one condition. It was this:

'The white man must treat the beasts of this land as his brothers. For what is man without the beasts? If the beasts were gone, men would die from great loneliness of spirit, for whatever happens to the beasts also happens to man. All things are connected. Whatever befalls the Earth befalls the sons of the Earth.'

In 1856, the treaties were signed and fourteen Indian bands moved into their reservations. Three months later, as settlers and miners for gold poured relentlessly into the treaty land, war again broke out. The spirit of the Redman was finally broken.

The American Indian was a natural man, a true Earth man, for he saw the Earth as a paradise to be savoured and enjoyed, and mankind as its caretaker. Today, the United Nations stands as caretaker and peacemaker of the Earth and comprises representatives of all races and peoples and nations – except the Redman. No Redman has a seat among all the peoples of the Earth but remains rejected, ignored, unrecognised. Yet it is to the spirit of the Redman that the peoples of the Earth must now turn if the Earth is to be healed from the sickness that has been inflicted upon her and if mankind is to find harmony and peace and be restored to its rightful role as caretakers of the Earth.

CHAPTER TWO

Ancient Origins

THE ORIGINS OF THE AMERICAN Indian peoples and the teachings that are at the very root of their culture may lie hidden in their myths and legends. Certainly among the stories of various tribes are hints of an ancient wisdom that was the foundation of all religions and was brought by 'wise men' who came from 'afar'. Some people have speculated that the stories refer to the survivors of lands now submerged beneath the seas as a result of a cataclysmic ecological disaster that changed the configuration of the Earth's land masses many thousands of years ago, whilst writers like Erich von Daniken make strong suggestions of visitations by intelligent and more highly evolved beings – space travellers from another planet.

Basic to Amerindian Medicine teachings is the idea that the human being has cosmic origins. They imply we come to Earth to learn through many lives and that there is a form of space travel which is a journeying of the Soul.

Some of the ancient stories refer to 'feathered gods' and, like most legends and biblical accounts of prehistory, seem implausible only if taken literally. For instance, the Indians who witnessed the arrival of European settlers in the sixteenth century told of giant white birds with mighty wings that came from a strange land across the waters, and which laid great eggs which hatched hordes of pale-faced men[1] They were trying to describe in terms of natural events with which they were familiar, the unfamiliar sailing ships and the dinghies in which sailors came ashore. We can discard, therefore, literal interpretations of men with feathered skins or even of men wearing plumed costumes. But were the stories of 'feathered gods' referring to beings who descended from the sky and who could transport themselves through the air like birds just as modern technology enables us to do today with aeroplanes and space vehicles?

European settlers must have been astonished to come across hundreds of man-made mounds, some of them massive and shaped like animals and birds. In southern Wisconsin, for instance, there are some 5000 animal and human effigy mounds including that of a giant bird with a wingspan of over 60 metres (200 ft) and a body nearly 30 metres (100 ft) long. In Ohio

*The Great Serpent Mound which writhes across the Ohio countryside in the
United States and is thought to be more than 3000 years old. Its purpose is
still a mystery*
**(Aerial photograph by courtesy of the Museum of the American Indian, Heye
Foundation, New York City, USA)**

there is a mound that writhes across the countryside like a giant snake and
is thought by archaeologists to be more than 3000 years old.

Modern archaeological research has discovered that although most of
the thousands of mounds throughout North America date from within
2500 years before Christopher Columbus 'discovered' America, others go
much further back than 1000 BC. Were some of the massive figure-like
mounds a means of communicating with beings from another planet? Of
were they, perhaps, a method of alignment with certain cosmic energies
and of bringing cosmic power from the stars down to Earth? Was it that
spacemen from another planet wore a feather or plumes of feathers on their
clothing just as American astronauts and Russian cosmonauts and military
personnel wear insignia on their clothing to identify where they're from?

Such ideas can be made to seem plausible when looked at through the
eyes of a Westerner with a background in materialistic science. But we

must try to understand them through the perception of an Indian to whom the stories were originally addressed.

Shamans of all races have worn feathers since the dawn of time and to them a feather is highly significant. They recognise that a feather gives out impulses of high-frequency energy, hence, a feather is symbolic of a message or messenger. The Seneca tribe, for instance, have a story of an ancient personality whom they call 'Heah-Wah-Sah', which means 'He from afar', and who brought a message of peace, brotherhood and good-will not dissimilar to that of Jesus Christ many centuries later. It is possible that 'Hiawatha', the poetic work of the nineteenth-century writer Henry Wadsworth Longfellow was derived from this legendary figure. Feathers were, therefore, a form of insignia implying not only someone who has something important to say, but also the powers to convey it.

The Cherokees, who at one time constituted the largest single tribe in south and southeast North America, called themselves 'The Ani Yunwiya', which means 'The Principal People', and this was because there was a history that their ancestors came from 'another place'. Neighbouring tribes called them 'Cherokee', which means 'people who speak the strange tongue'. Were the Cherokees descended from a people who came from another planet? Or were they from lands now vanished beneath the waves? Was their 'strange tongue' the language of those places? Let us probe further.

Of all the Indian languages, Cherokee was particularly distinctive because its rising and falling tones were spoken with hardly any movement of the lips, and although gutteral in places, it had a distinct beauty of its own. The language contained 'sounds of power' rather than words, so that when spoken it brought forth the spirit energy that was being called upon, for to the Cherokee, 'to speak is to be'. Similarly, the ancient runic sounds known by Nordic and North European shamans, and those of the ancient Hebrew alphabet, when sounded rightly were 'sounds of power'.

Like most languages, Cherokee had a number of dialects. Atali was the western dialect heard mostly in Oklahoma and Texas today, and Kituhwa was the dialect of western North Carolina. But it was Elati, an eastern dialect which is now almost extinct, that comprised what was called 'the language of the Ancients' or 'the language of the Stars'. Now the 'language of the Stars' was understood by some shamans to be a cosmic language. In North Europe and Scandinavia the runic sounds employed by the Rune-masters was similarly understood to be a cosmic language and not one devised by man.

Among oral traditions of the Cherokee is a teaching that man's original ancestors came to Earth some 250,000 years ago from Sirius in the Constellation of the Pleiades – a word which in the Cherokee tongue meant 'Ancestors' – and that mankind descended not from apes but from 'Star people'. Indeed, in some Amerindian cosmology, the Earth is referred to as 'the planet of the Children' which can be given the meaning 'the planet of the Star children'.

Another thing that singled out the Cherokee from most other tribes was the sacredness with which they held crystals. Most tribes had a reverence for quartz crystals, but the Cherokees were renowned for their ability to *heal* with them.

Quartz crystals figured prominently among the objects laid out on the medicine man's portable altar – and still do today. The healing crystals used by the Cherokee were crystal 'wands', perhaps 15 to 20 centimetres (6 to 8 inches) long. Because of their shape, size and thickness, the Christian missionaries mistook them for primitive phallic symbols for use in fertility rites. A similar misunderstanding was perpetrated by priests and monks regarding certain pagan forms in Britain, Europe and Scandinavia during the Middle Ages.

The crystal wand was – and still is – a powerful instrument, and the shaman knew far more about its properties than the most 'educated' men of that time. For instance, the shaman knew that crystal was a 'holder' of energy. It held it under control and in perfect balance. Quartz crystal was regarded as a sacred substance, holy 'ice' that had become petrified.

Among Cherokee teachings is a story that there were twelve skulls, each fashioned from a piece of solid quartz crystal. What was said to be unusual about these skulls was not just that their size was the size of a human skull but that the jaw moved and that they 'spoke' or 'sang'.

Harley Swiftdeer, a Metis Cherokee medicine man, explained that according to the oral teachings, the twelve skulls in ancient times were formed into a circle around the amethyst skull and that within this arrangement was placed eight crystal wands – one for each of the cardinal and non-cardinal directions. These crystal skulls, he told me, were very old and each was like a holographic computer which held information that had been programmed into it. That information included knowledge about the origins, purpose and destiny of Man as well as the so-called 'mysteries' of Life. The 'talking' skulls would one day be rediscovered and brought together for their collective knowledge to be available, but men and women would need to be sufficiently evolved not to misuse it. He told me that according to these ancient teachings there were twelve planets in the cosmos inhabited by humans and Souls could travel about as they evolved. There was one skull for each of these planets.

Far-fetched? Perhaps. Except that a crystal skull the size of a human skull and with a moveable jawbone came into the possession of a British explorer when, in the 1920s, he discovered a 'lost' city of the Mayan Indians deep within the rainforest interior of what was then British Honduras, now Belize, a country situated on the Caribbean between Mexico and Guatemala. This skull has been credited with strange powers.

British explorer Frederick 'Mike' Mitchell-Hedges (1882–1959), a member of the Maya Committee of the British Museum, was of the opinion that the cradle of civilisation was not in the Middle East as was commonly supposed, but in the West. He was convinced that the legendary Atlantis was a real civilisation which through some vast natural catastrophe had disappeared under the Atlantic Ocean. He believed that remnants of this prehistoric civilisation were to be found in Central America and that the most likely place was Honduras, where legends abounded about a 'lost' prehistoric city in the jungle. He organised a fully-fledged expedition to British Honduras and was granted permission to search for and excavate the unknown city should it be found.

In 1927 his party did find the 'lost' city deep in the interior. It was overgrown with foliage and suffocated by vines, so the party tried to clear the area by setting fire to the undergrowth. When the flames subsided, the stones and mounds of a once-great city emerged. It covered an area of some six square miles in the centre of which was a mighty temple. There were pyramids and mounds, houses and terraces. Underneath were subterranean passages and a huge amphitheatre large enough to hold more than 10,000 people. They called this 'lost' city, Labaanatum – a Mayan word which means 'the city of fallen stones'.

Mitchell-Hedges' adopted daugher, Anna (nicknamed Sammy), joined the expedition and it was she who discovered the skull buried beneath an altar in the temple ruins. In an affidavit attesting to the authenticity of the find, she said: 'We were digging in the temple, moving a heavy wall which had fallen on the altar. This took some time because the rocks were so heavy and we could only move about six a day. I came across the skull buried beneath the altar, but it was some three months later before the jaw was found, which was about 25ft (about 8 metres) away.' The skull was beautifully crafted and measured 124 mm wide (about 5 inches), 147 mm high (nearly 6 inches), 197 mm long (nearly 8 inches), and weighed 11 lb 7 oz.

For several years it was exhibited in the Museum of the American Indian in New York City, but it is now back in the possession of Sammy in Ontario, Canada. A second crystal skull, almost identical except that it does not have a detachable jawbone, is on exhibition at the London Museum. The London skull is thought to be a 'copy' of the Mitchell-Hedges skull.

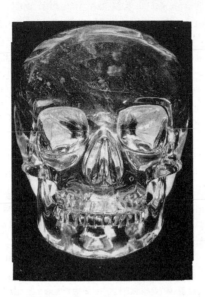

○ *The Crystal Skull discovered in the 'lost' Mayan Indian city of Labaanatum is life-size and fashioned from a single piece of quartz crystal. It has a moveable jawbone made from the same piece of quartz. It is thousands of years old and accredited with amazing powers*
(Photograph by Frank Dorland who subjected the skull to extensive scientific tests over many years)

In 1964 Sammy loaned the skull to Frank Dorland, an American crystal expert and an internationally-known art conservator, who put it to extensive scientific tests over a six-year period using specially-constructed, high-powered microscopes and cameras. Models of the skull were cast in plaster and epoxy, and cross-sections cut and measured with precision. During certain tests the skull had a distinctive glow, like an aura extending around it. On other occasions, sounds like the soft chanting of human voices emanated from it.

Dorland ran into innumerable dead ends when he presented the problem of the skull to conventional scientists. 'Many universities chose to ignore it simply because they could not come to grips with the fact that there may be knowledge demonstrated here which is beyond our civilised comprehension' said Richard M. Garvin in his book *The Crystal Skull*[2] Garvin goes on to stress that science is continually being presented with knowledge which present-day technology cannot understand. Since it cannot be understood, or goes against established ideas, it must be ignored or, safer still, rubbished as fraud.

Although it was regarded as Mayan, largely because it was found on a Mayan site, Dorland held the view that it dated back to an even earlier civilisation. Since crystal does not change with age or corrode, it cannot be accurately dated by Carbon-14 or other techniques, so there was no way of accurately determining its age. In any event, even if it could be dated that would tell only the age of the crystal and not when it was crafted into a skull.

In the autumn of 1970, Dorland took the skull to the crystal laboratories of the Hewlett-Packard Company in Santa Clara, California. Hewlett-Packard are among the world's leading manufacturers of electronic equipment and other devices. The skull was identified as female and tests proved that the skull and its jawbone were carved from a single chunk of quartz crystal. The workmanship was demonstrated to be truly exquisite. Strange sounds sometimes emanated from the skull, like chanting, and it earned the title, 'the singing skull'.

Although quartz crystal is extremely hard – it is only slightly softer than diamond – there was no scientific evidence of grinding or cutting tools having been used. If the workmanship was the result of patient handcrafting using sand and water to smoothly abrade the material, such technical precision would require an estimated 300 years of effort. Even with today's advanced technology it would not be possible to carve so exquisite an object, it was concluded.

Modern science has established that among the unusual properties of quartz crystal is its ability to hold under control 'electrical' energy and to oscillate at a constant and precise frequency. Not only can it hold energy (information) but it acts as a reflective device able to send out impulses or vibrating waves of information. This is why quartz crystal is used for the 'brain cells' of electronic equipment from watches and calculators, to radios, television, navigational equipment and the most advanced and sophisticated computers and space-age technology. No wonder the Indians regarded the quartz crystal as 'the brain cells of Mother Earth'.

Since the whole of the cosmos is comprised of 'electronic' energy with positive and negative force fields in a state of constant motion, and our own body cells are enabled to communicate with each other and with the mind/brain through impulses of 'electronic' energy, Dorland became convinced that energy waves from the brain can, in some way, activate a crystal which has electronic attributes and which can filter them and then, acting as a reflector, send them to the human power centres and psychic senses which are then stimulated by them. In other words, crystal can stimulate the inner senses and release inner knowledge that is somehow stored deep within the subconscious and unconscious mind and bring it into conscious awareness.

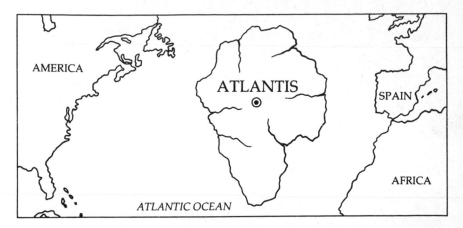

o*Fig. 1. The legendary Atlantis is said to have been a vast continent between the eastern Americas and western Europe*

Dorland and his co-worker wife, Mabel, thus became pioneers of bio-crystallography — the study of the interchange of energy between quartz crystal and the human mind. This new frontier would appear to add credibility to the belief that the crystal skulls contain knowledge of human origins and of the mysteries of life which has been programmed into them by an intelligent mind for the purpose of their being understood at some future time by human minds that could be attuned to their impulses.

Mitchell-Hedges was convinced that the American Indian and the ancient Mayan culture with which the crystal skull had been associated, had originated from antediluvian civilisation. In an article in the *New York American* of 31 August 1930, he described Central America as one of the cradles of mankind where had existed a people of an antiquity hitherto unsuspected who possessed knowledge that might well have been envied by modern man.

Mitchell-Hedges, who had personal knowledge of at least twenty tribes of Indians, believed that the remnants of that ancient culture were still preserved in part today in the myths, legends and esoteric teachings and in tribal rituals and ceremonials. He believed that Atlantis really existed until it was submerged under the Atlantic Ocean and that another legendary continent, Mu, occupied a gigantic area of what is now the Pacific Ocean before it, too, vanished under horrendous tidal waves. The peoples of both were said to be red-skinned.

In those days before the Flood, the mystery of man's origins and destiny would have been known together with the true purpose of 'the Planet of the Children'. Are those secrets locked within the crystal skull waiting for

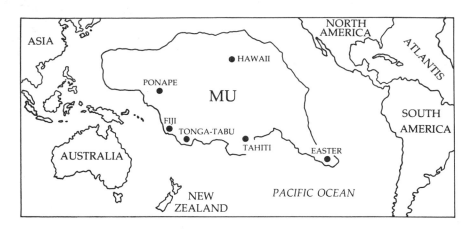

○Fig. 2. The legendary Mu is said to have covered an enormous area of what is now the Pacific Ocean. Easter Island, Hawaii, Tahiti, the Fijis and other islands may be what remains of a once great continent

man to regain the means of accessing into them? Do the answers to those same mysteries lie veiled within the esoteric teachings of the Medicine Wheel, cloaked by myth and legend and ritual?

Perhaps a reason present-day Americans have such a yearning for a sense of history is not so much that their own culture spans a comparatively short period of time, but that there is a subconscious guilt about the destruction of America's real heritage which may be more ancient than any other culture in the world.

Since 1975 archaeological discoveries in North America have further emphasised the need for a new evaluation of American history. Inscriptions have been found on buried portions of ancient stone buildings unearthed in the northwest region of the United States and elsewhere. Stone structures discovered in New England have been identified as Celtic and thousands of years old. The inscriptions have been confirmed as an ancient form of notch writing called Ogham. Transcriptions of some of these writings refer to the celebration of pagan festivals like Beltaen (May Eve).

According to Professor H. Barraclough Fell of Harvard University, a distinguished decipherer of ancient scripts, roving bands of Celtic mariners crossed the North Atlantic in their sailing ships some 3000 years ago and established settlements in North America — the land they called Iagalon, meaning 'the land beyond the Sunset'. In his book *America BC*[3] Professor Fell overturns previously held historical notions that no ships were capable of crossing the Atlantic until the end of the fifteenth century when Columbus 'discovered' the New World. The Celts, who occupied lands in the British Isles, Brittany, Spain, and other parts of Western and Northern Europe, were seafarers and built ships that were far superior to those of the Romans who later overcame them.

At South Woodstock in Vermont, New England, are stone slab structures which contain Ogham inscriptions whose uses appear to have included astrological observation and calendar regulation, and which provide evidence of a large Celtic settlement in this region of America.

Professor Fell says that these ancient settlements were established first in the northeast region and then as far west as Oklahoma, and lasted until after the time of Julius Caesar (100–44 BC). What caused these settlements and their peoples to suddenly vanish remains a mystery.

It would seem that these Celtic settlers not only lived peacefully in their communities alongside American Indian tribes, but enjoyed a close and harmonious relationship with them. Was a reason for this that the two races shared a common bond – a similarity in their basic philosophy and outlook on life? The Celts, too, had a caring attitude towards their environment and to other forms of life that shared the Earth with them. The Celts had a rich, shamanistic lore and an adherence to spiritual principles which bore a close resemblance to some of the tribal traditions of the Red Indian.

Such discoveries do indicate that the ancient culture of the Celts and that of the American Indian existed side by side in parts of North America for many hundreds of years.

Archaeology has opened up a chink in the prehistory of peoples whose roots can thus be seen to go back beyond the times of the Romans and the ancient Greeks to a period at least contemporaneous with the ancient Egyptians and possibly even further back. Americans need no longer feel deprived of a sense of history. Theirs is the most ancient of lands.

CHAPTER THREE

The Symbolism of the Skull

THE HUMAN SKULL, AS A SYMBOL, had a more profound meaning to the American Indians and to the Celts, the Norse and other ancient peoples than Death with which it is generally associated. To them the skull was an expression of consciousness and of the container of the most sacred part of man and being. It was revered as the house of the Soul and of the Intellect and Personality.

Like all esoteric symbols, the skull had a great many meanings. One was that there were 'unseen' realms, the entrance to which could not be obtained through the offering of material goods but entered only with the bare essentials of an individual's existence — by one whose 'flesh', or earthly personality, had been stripped away leaving only the skull — the individuality, the Soul, that outlives mortal flesh. The skull also implied Spirit journeying, or Soul travel to 'other worlds' which could not be entered by the vehicle of the physical body but could be experienced only through an altered state of consciousness which was the key to all the mysteries. The skull indicated that behind the outward, material, fleshly world of 'appearances' were other realms of conscious awareness. Only 'civilised' man regarded the skull as a sinister and gruesome symbol of death, but this was due to fear of death and a lack of attunement with Nature.

The crystal skull described in Chapter Two is thought to be capable of storing electro-magnetic thought-waves impressed on it by its programmers and of releasing them to humans who are 'sensitives', able to tune in to its very high rate of vibration and thereby 'read' portions of the information it contains. Under certain circumstances it can be done without the necessity of being in the actual physical presence of the skull, just as it is not necessary to be in the presence of a television transmitter in order to see a television programme being beamed out by it. For instance, by looking at the photograph of the crystal skull on page 15 stilling your mind and concentrating on the image for a while, your subconscious mind may have access to its store of information from the collective unconscious. This may come to you in silent thoughts, in words you 'hear' in the mind, or from impressions of symbols, colours or sounds.

LEFT LOBE
(Masculine)

Analytical
Logical
Linear
Specific
Time oriented
Verbal language
Judgmental
Beliefs
Logical thinking

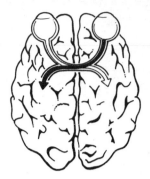

RIGHT LOBE
(Feminine)

Creative
Intuitive
Spatial
Holistic
Timeless
Symbolic language
Non-judgmental
Knowingness
Holistic thinking

○*Fig. 3. The visual fields crossover in the brain. The right visual field goes to the left side of the brain, and the left visual field goes to the right side of the brain. Comparisons indicate the different functions of the two sides of the brain.*

The Amerindians, Celts, Norsemen and other ancient peoples had a knowledge of the anatomy of the skull. They were well aware that the human skull contains a bone-like cartilage which separates the brain into two hemispheres, and this separation was of particular significance to them.

As modern surgery has discovered, the brain is divided into two hemispheres — the left lobe and the right lobe — and each deals with separate functions. The two hemispheres are divided by a fibrous cartilage which is shaped like the blade of a sickle and turns brittle as one gets older. Although there is a certain amount of duplication of function, in very general terms the left brain activity is concerned with what might be described as 'straight line thinking' — logical thought — and with the tendency to want to take things apart and to analyse, compartmentalise and categorise what is observed and experienced. It is also concerned with manual dexterity and with semantic precision. In simplistic terms it might be described as the 'organ' of the logical and reasoning mind. Right brain activity, on the other hand, is concerned with holistic thinking — with putting things together and with seeing them as a unified whole. It finds expression in creativity, poetry, music, song and dance. It might be described as the 'organ' of the intuitive or creative mind.

The left brain governs the right side of the body and is related to what might be described as 'masculine', active qualities. The Indian regarded the right hand as the 'giving' hand, the fighting or attacking hand of the body's masculine polarity, and the left hand as the passive 'receiving' hand, the defending hand of the body's feminine polarity. It is not without significance that it is considered to be a masculine tendency to want to take things apart to find out how they work, to dissect and analyse, and a feminine tendency to put things together, to unify, harmonise and create beauty.

In Western societies, left brain activity has been dominant for many centuries, though it is less so today in this period of transition from one Age into the next, and since machines have taken on much of the repetitive and burdensome work leaving more time for creativity. Until a generation or so ago, it was the man who had responsibility as the breadwinner, and male dominance was carried through all levels of society. The influence over many hundreds of years of monotheistic religion gave man pre-eminence over woman, and the structure of society was deliberately biased in his favour. In religion, divinity has been projected as a male God. When divinity was presented as wholly masculine and a God of judgement, aggressive and destructive forces were unleashed into the world because of the imbalance so created.

Where right brain activity has been dominant, the emphasis has been in favour of the woman, and in religion divinity was represented as a Goddess. The form of neo-paganism that has re-emerged today in which a Goddess is given pre-eminence is right-brain oriented.

Ideally, the capacity of both sides of the brain should be equally balanced. In religious outlook that means the concepts of God and Goddess being regarded as different but complementary aspects of divinity, neither of which exists without the other. Both exist as expressions of polarised forces within and without — of what the American Indians called the Great Spirit.

The Native American may have been perplexed by the civilised method of thinking 'in straight lines', the dominance of left brain activity. The European's attempts to solve problems by so-called 'logical' thinking seemed to create only further problems, and his attempts to explain Creation and the purpose of Life itself by rational thinking seemed to the Indian to be illusory and incomplete. The white man was of the opinion — and still is — that everything must have a beginning and an end, a start and a conclusion, whereas the Indian, observing no straight lines in Nature, perceived not beginnings and endings but only changes in a process of continuous evolution.

Spirit was eternally alive, so birth was merely a change in the way spirit was experiencing its aliveness and death was but a further movement along the continuous spiral of eternal life.

The cranium of the 'brain box' of the human skull is made up of eight plate-like bones that surround and protect the brain which is a bio-computer. To the American Indian this eight-bone structure of the skull was highly significant for it indicated design in accordance with the harmonic Law of Octaves which is an important and vital Medicine Wheel teaching as we shall discover later.

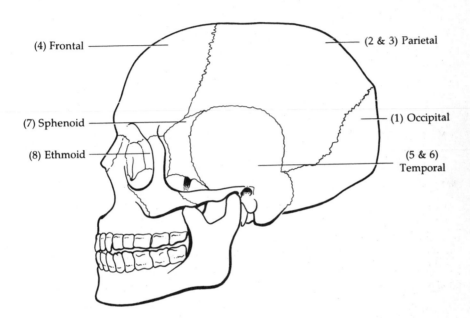

○*Fig. 4. The cranium or brain box which is the upper part of the skull is formed of eight bones: (1) The occipital at the back of the skull. (2 & 3) The two parietal bones that form the rear roof of the skull. (4) The frontal that forms the front roof of the skull. (5 & 6) The two temporal bones around and above the ears. (7) The sphenoid which forms the base of the cranium and has wings on either side that form the temples. (8) The ethmoid which forms the roof of the nasal cavities.*

This eight-fold structure of the human skull may have comparisons with the structure of the human brain itself and of the way the mind functions. For instance, a modern-day English shaman, Alawn Tickhill, in his book *The Apogeton*[1] likens the human brain to an eight-circuit computer and a holographic storage system. He describes four 'circuits' as governing the basic activities of human existence and labels them 'terrestrial', and the four others as dealing with what some people may regard as 'psychic' skills like intuition, telepathy, clairvoyance, clairaudience, healing and 'out of the body' experience, and he labels these 'extra-terrestrial'. The four 'earthy'

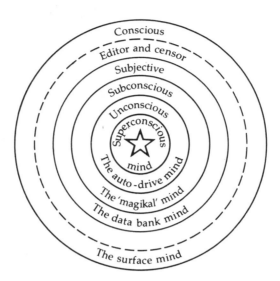

Fig. 5. The layers of the mind

circuits he relates to the Conscious Mind and the four 'higher' circuits to what he calls the Deep Mind. By transcending the Conscious Mind and opening up the four 'Deep Mind' circuits the whole range of conscious awareness can be expanded, he claims.

The American Indian was 'switched on' to these Deep Mind circuits for he acted with an instinctive awareness that everything around him was 'alive'. To him, animals, birds, fish, trees, plants and even rocks were animated by a subtle life force and had a form of consciousness, though very different from that of a human. The Indian was not only able to relate to them but, indeed, to communicate with them all! In addition, through the activation of these 'Deep Mind' circuits, contact was possible with the 'Source' at the centre of one's own being — the High Self, or the Spirit within.

Let us then examine the Mind. Let us imagine that the mind is a sphere. If we cut this sphere across its equator to see what's inside — just as we might slice an apple in half — we discover four concentric bands or layers of activity. The outer layer is the one that 'appears' on the surface. This is the Surface Mind, and because we are familiar with it we can mistakenly regard it as the whole mind — the entire sphere — though it occupies only a thin layer. The Surface Mind is the objective mind, the reasoning mind that deals with all the impressions it receives through the five physical senses as we go about our everyday activities. Since it is the part of our thinking with which we perform all our conscious and deliberate actions, let us call it the *Conscious Mind*.

Within the Conscious Mind is a mechanism that edits out what it considers to be unimportant or contrary to accepted belief patterns which are already stored at a deeper level. Part of the function of this mechanism is to prevent the mind from being overloaded with more information than it can handle. Let me give an example: you may be in a room with a clock ticking and a radio or television turned on, traffic noises from outside the building and the distractions of other people in the household moving about as you are trying to read this book. But the mechanism of your mind edits out the unwanted sound so that it becomes unobtrusive and you can concentrate on your reading. This Editor also functions as a Censor by rejecting any information that does not check out with established belief patterns – with what you basically hold to be true or possible – so that it does not get through to the Subconscious Mind at a deeper level where it can be acted upon.

For instance, when during those times that you have wanted to improve certain aspects of your life – move to a better home, perhaps, have a better-paid job, make more money, find a compatible mate, or whatever – and all sorts of reasons have sprung into the Conscious Mind to tell you why such a thing is not possible, that is your Editor and Censor doing its job of rejecting what is not in accordance with the belief patterns you have previously programmed into your mind. To make drastic changes in the way you perceive and experience life you need to change the programme.

Immediately beneath the Conscious Mind is a thicker layer. This is the band of the *Subjective Mind* which acts as a kind of databank or filing room where impressions from the Conscious Mind are stored away to be produced on demand as memories. The Subjective Mind contains your recall tapes which are an accumulation of all your longings and desires, of your experiences both pleasant and unpleasant, of your behaviour patterns which have been programmed in by your parents, teachers, priests perhaps, and by the society and culture into which you were born, together with all the anxieties and fears which from time to time since early childhood have affected your life.

It is from this layer of the mind that the psychoanalyst and the psychiatrist bring to the surface impressions and phobias which they consider may be at the root of deep psychological and emotional problems, bringing them to the attention of the Conscious Mind where they can be dealt with and hopefully overcome.

Indeed, impressions and memories of things we prefer to forget, and fears and anxieties which we have tried to repress, are filed away in the recesses of the Subjective Mind and can be responsible for nervous tensions, allergies, illnesses and even physical handicap. Illnesses considered to be psychosomatic have their origins in the Subjective Mind.

The Subjective Mind is at its most active when we are asleep and when the Conscious Mind is at rest. Subjective thoughts often express themselves in the form of dreams but are wrapped up in a symbolic way, for symbolism and imagery is the language of the Subjective Mind, not words. Once the language of symbolism is understood we can decode the message of the dream that has been brought back into waking consciousness.

Deeper down is the next layer — the *Subconscious Mind*. The Subconscious Mind is the 'magikal' mind which acts on whatever instructions it is given and in doing so will generally seek the line of least resistance. It is the allegorical 'genie' of Aladdin's lamp. It is Cinderella's 'good fairy'. It wears other garbs of allegory in the myths and legends of all cultures — in fairy stories, folk tales and in the scriptures of many faiths.

Hypnotism is an example of how the Conscious Mind can be put at rest and the Subjective Mind by-passed so that an instruction gets through to the Subconscious. Under hypnosis a new belief is programmed in and the Subconscious acts as if the new belief is true, even if it is not. For instance, if a subject is told that he is at the North Pole, the body will act as if exposed to cold, even though it might be a hot and sweltering summer day.

One can, however, give instructions to the Subconscious Mind and make use of its vast potential without resorting to hypnosis. It is done by translating instructions into the Subconscious Mind's 'computer' language — which is a language of symbolism and imagery — and by channelling that instruction through a point of focus as one might direct a laser beam.

Deeper still, beyond the Subconscious, is the *Unconscious Mind*. It is the physical body's auto-drive that works unceasingly from the moment of conception, in building and maintaining the body in accordance with instructions programmed into the genetic code and with those passed subsequently into the Subconscious Mind.

The Unconscious Mind never rests. It has been operating untiringly through babyhood, infancy, childhood, youth and adulthood, regulating the heartbeat and breathing, balancing the body chemistry, regulating the vital organs and self-repairing the human physical machine without our even being aware of anything taking place.

Still deeper, at the very core of the sphere of the mind is the *Superconscious* — the vortex that connects with the Spirit and with the Universal Mind which is the creative intelligence of the Great Spirit.

Of course, the compartmentation of the Mind I have just described is only a model or chart. In actuality the Mind cannot be divided into watertight compartments because the Mind is not physical and therefore has no form. My model of concentric circles reaching deeper and deeper into the centre of one's being is merely a geometric chart to help the reasoning mind 'grip' onto something more tangible in order to bring about an understanding of an abstract reality.

The skull can thus be seen as not only symbolic of the physical body and as the seat of consciousness, but also of the invisible Mind that is working within it, and as an indicator of the reality of interrelationship between outer and inner, higher and lower, physical and non-physical, seen and unseen, the mundane and the spiritual – of what the Amerindian called the Tonal and the Nagual.

Since the cranium of the skull is spherical it reminded the Amerindian of another important concept – the great Circle of Existence that contains all that is and was and is to be, and of the great No-thing from which all things are brought into manifestation.

The circle was sacred to the Amerindian for it presented a Way of Understanding. It provided a way of understanding the cosmos, the mysteries of life and death, the mind and the individuality of Self. With the circle the American Indian shaman was able to demonstrate how the cosmos worked, how natural and cosmic laws governed all living things, how to discover the relationship between man and other life forms on the planet and how to come into harmony with Nature and the Great Spirit and with one's own Spirit.

The circular cosmology of the North American was closely allied with the Mayan concept of the Zero. The mathematical concept of the Zero was known to the Mayan Indians long before it appeared in Middle Eastern, Egyptian and other cultures. According to Sylvanus G. Morley, an authority on the ancient Mayas, it was the Mayan Indians who developed man's first positional mathematical system involving the concept of Zero which he describes in his book *The Ancient Maya*[2] as 'one of the most brilliant achievements of the human mind'. The Zero was presented as that from which all other numbers came into existence. It was the 'nothing' that appeared to be of no value but was, indeed, the most potent of them all.

The Mayans often represented the Zero as an empty shell which early Christian missionaries and archaeologists mistook for a drawing of the vagina and therefore evidence of fertility worship and sex rites. It is interesting to note that in modern computer technology the Zero is represented by a similar symbol Ø.

Morley points out that the Mayans used only two symbols in their system of notation: a dot . which was given the value of one, and a bar —— which was given the value of five. The Zero did not feature in the system which was based on the number twenty rather than ten as with the decimal system, but was regarded as a concept of the First Cause from which

everything springs. By accumulation there was . one; .. two; ... three; ....
four; —— five; •⁝ six; •⁝• seven; and so on, with two bars ══ for ten,
three bars ═══ for fifteen and four bars ════ for twenty. This notation
system was sometimes referred to as the Twenty Count, and because a
child could understand it by simply using the fingers and hand – the fingers
were used to represent the dots and the flat of the hand for the bars – it was
also called the Children's Count. So the number three (...) could be
indicated by three fingers, seven (•⁝•) by the flat of the hand and two
fingers, fourteen (⁝⁝⁝⁝) by the flat of the hand twice and four fingers, and
so on.

The Twenty Count was the numerology system of the Sacred Skull.
Sibley S. Morrill, in an article in the June 1968 issue of *The Indian Historian*[3],
confirms that the jawbone was used to represent the number ten, and head
divisions represented the single digits one to nine. So if a jawbone were
added to the head variant figure for, say, seven it became seventeen.

Just as an alphabet encodes a language with which to communicate and
exchange knowledge – the English language, for instance, has a vast
vocabulary yet has an alphabet of just twenty-six letters – so numbers can
be channels of information as modern computer technology clearly demonstrates. However, we need to understand that the ancients' concept of
numbers was very different from our own.

Firstly, numbers were not regarded in a quantitative sense, such as two
hands, five fingers, ten toes, and so on, but as expressing *qualities*.
Secondly, numbers were also representative of resonant tones or wave
pulsations of energy. Today, computer technology is 'catching up' with
this ancient knowledge by making it possible to convert sounds into
numbers and numbers into sounds, so sounds can be 'manufactured' digi-
tally through circuits of energy streams. This is the very essence of
electronically-produced music. The Twenty Count represented powers
inherent in the cosmos and within the human being as a circuit of pulsating
energy streams – the signature tunes, as it were, of the forces that brought
the universe into existence and maintain it now. This notation system was
also used to describe the relationship of one thing with another within the
basic framework of the Medicine Wheel, and also for an understanding of
the special qualities of the 'give away' of those Powers of the cosmos and
of all things in existence. It could thus be related to a map of the mind and a
chart of existence.

In order to appreciate that numbers have special qualities rather than just
quantitative values, it is necessary for us to understand another characteristic of American Indian spirituality. Those of us brought up in modern
society are constantly bombarded with impressions that stimulate our urge

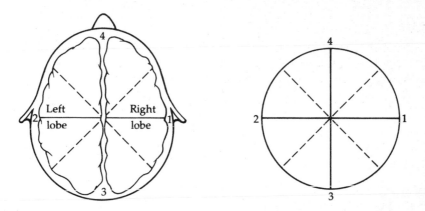

○*Fig. 6. The Medicine Wheel as a map of the mind*

to *want* things. Our television screens, newspapers, magazines, shops, stores, supermarkets, hoardings — almost wherever we look — feed our senses with an input of messages intended to trigger a desire to *get*, to acquire, to have, to possess. Success, achievement, even happiness itself, is measured by the extent of one's ability to consume. The 'successful' in life are projected as the haves, and the unsuccessful as the have-nots. That is the extent of our mind-conditioning.

The American Indian mind, on the other hand, was stimulated not by a desire to get, but by the need to *give*. This attitude of mind was encapsulated in an expression and a custom known as 'the give away'. The 'give away' had two main aspects. The first could be regarded as the giving away of a thing or condition which a person no longer needed or which had served its purpose. It included the banishment of any adverse condition, like an illness, for instance. The process of healing was itself a form of the 'give away'. The cyclical nature of the cosmos that is inherent in all Nature should always be borne in mind when considering the banishment of anything. Energy must go somewhere and the 'space' it had will become occupied by something else. So in giving away a negativity it should not be despatched to where it might affect or infect others, but 'sent' where it can do no harm and where it can be transmuted or transformed into its polar and positive opposite. In this way sickness is transformed into health, disharmony into harmony, greed can be transformed into generosity, envy into self-esteem and poverty into plenty. The second aspect was a giving away to another, or to others, a gift of something that would bring them benefit, to honour or please them in some way, and by so doing receive good things in return.

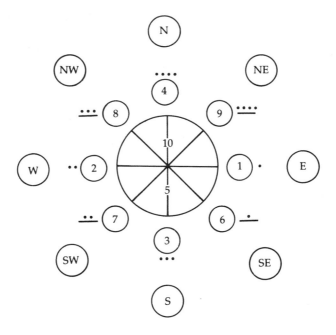

○*Fig. 7. The upper part of the Sacred Skull related to the numbers 1 – 10 and physical reality experience*

The item that was the subject of the 'give away' might well be something that the givers desired for themselves, or something of theirs which they valued or even treasured. In both aspects the 'give away' was part of the very substance of the giver, for whatever it was, the 'give away' was the power or *'medicine'* with which he touched others.

The Twenty Count was a way of understanding the special qualities of the 'give away', of the Powers of the universe and of all things in existence. It was a way of short-circuiting the world of form and of describing the indescribable.

Let us examine some basic concepts of the Twenty Count and see how they are placed in the cardinal and non-cardinal directions:

THE TWENTY COUNT

0	*Zero*	The eternally existing Nothing-ness that contains within it the potentiality of everything. The All That Is – the all-giving and all-receiving. The Wholeness of male and female energy. The Source from which all comes and to which all must return.

•	*One*	Grandfather Sun. The power of Light and of Fire. The power to see. Enlightenment. The power to *determine* spiritual energy. The power of the East where the Sun rises.
••	*Two*	Grandmother Earth. The source of all our needs. Bonding power. The 'marriage' of Sun and Earth that makes life possible. Earth is the great trans- formational power. The power of the West and of introspection. The mineral kingdom – the great *holders* of energy.
•••	*Three*	The 'moulding' power. The first 'child' of the union of Sun and Earth creating patterns of change. The Moon. The power of the South and of waters and emotions. The plant kingdom – the great *givers* of energy.
••••	*Four*	The second 'child' – the power of balance, align- ment, and harmony. The power of the North and of Air and the Mind – of knowledge and wisdom. The Stars. The animal kingdom – the great *receivers* of energy.
—	*Five*	The Sacred Five is the power of Love – the means of merging with all that exists around us. The primary matrix structure, i.e. a centre and four cardinal points. The power of Family. Humanity – the determiners of spirit. Five is placed at the south of centre on the path of Trust and Innocence.
•⎯	*Six*	Six is indicative of what has gone before to make us what we are now. It is the power of past experience and of personal history. It is the power of blood relationships and of ancestry and our ideas of self. It is assigned the Southeast direction – the place of the Ancestors on the Medicine Wheel.
••⎯	*Seven*	Seven is indicative of the actual process of life and a striving for perfection. It is the power of mystic potential as contained in our dreams and aspi- rations. It is assigned the Southwest – the realm of Dreams on the Wheel.
•••⎯	*Eight*	The Law of Cycles (Octaves) is expressed in the Eight. Eight is the realm of rules and laws and of our Karma. It represents also our Book of Life. Positioned in the Northwest.

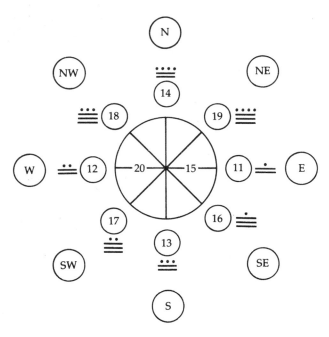

○*Fig. 8. The jawbone of the Sacred Skull added ten to the digits and so was related to the numbers 11 – 20 and to spiritual reality experience*

••••	***Nine***	The power of determined and purposeful movement. Designed change. The choreography of energy. Positioned in the Northeast.
═══	***Ten***	The Sacred Five and its mirrored reflection in the northern Centre – on the path of knowledge and wisdom – the realm of the High Self, where the Tonal and the Nagual are merged.

Through access to the High Self, the spiritual Self, we are enabled to raise our consciousness to the higher Octave of spiritual awareness and of communication at more refined levels of being.

•	***Eleven***	The power of access to the Collective Unconscious which makes recall of ancient knowledge possible – and to the spirit of the Stars (i.e. other suns). (East.)
••	***Twelve***	The power of organisational stability on a spiritual level. (West.)
•••	***Thirteen***	Thirteen is concerned with the shifting of energy from one dimension to another and also with

access to the spirit energy of plants. It is also the number of the Earth Mother. (South.)

Fourteen
Fourteen is concerned with the power of access to the spirit energy of animals. It is also the number of the Earth Father. (North.)

Fifteen
Fifteen is located in the eastern Centre – on the Path of Illumination – and is where the High Self can encounter and communicate with the souls of other humans.

Sixteen
Sixteen is concerned with the power of access to the Ancestors and with enlightened souls, inner plane guides, and with Master teachers of the universe. (Southeast.)

Seventeen
Seventeen is concerned with access to the realm of dreams and aspirations and makes possible contact with Dream Teachers and the interpretation of dreams. (Southwest.)

Eighteen
The power of access to the Law of Cycles in the northwest, to the realm of Laws, and to a knowledge of one's own Karma. (Northwest.)

Nineteen
Nineteen is concerned with the design of energy and with the power of making changes in the way one lives one's life. Access is also possible to knowledge of cosmic laws and with universal teachers. (Northeast.)

Twenty
The Sacred Twenty is located west of the Centre – on the Path of Transformation – and indicates the power of Oneness and Perfection and the Love, Light and Awareness of Wakan-Tanka. It is being back at the Source.

The Twenty Count can thus be regarded as twenty sacred powers within the great Circle of the Cosmos and 'gateways' to experience both the mundane and the divine, physical and spiritual, individuality and wholeness, and the realms of actualities, potentials and possibilities. The Medicine Way makes us receptive to these Twenty Powers as we work to bring our daily lives into harmony with our Highest Being and thus fulfil the true purpose of our lives.

CHAPTER FOUR

The Mind Machine

THE AMERICAN INDIAN REGARDED the circle as the principal symbol for understanding life's mysteries, for he observed that it was impressed everywhere throughout Nature. Man looked out on the physical world through the eye, which was circular. The Earth was round, and so were the Sun, Moon and planets. The rising and setting of the Sun followed a circular motion. The seasons formed a circle. Birds built their nests in circles. Animals marked their territories in circles. In the old days, tribes lived in circular homes called tipis and their communities were arranged with the tipis in a circle. Indeed, to the Indian, the whole of life appeared to operate in circular patterns.

When a shaman constructed the circle of the Medicine Wheel he was constructing a symbolic representation of the Universe and of the Universal Mind in which everything everywhere is connected and held in being by harmonic synchronisation. The Medicine Wheel was thus a model of the way the universe and the Universal Mind worked, for American Indian cosmology was not a science of materialism but of the Mind and the Spirit. Let us then consider what the Medicine Wheel is, and how it is set up.

To the American Indian 'medicine' meant power – a vital energy-force that was within all forms of Nature. It also meant 'knowledge' for 'knowing' gave the 'knower' power to do, to achieve and to attain. 'Wheel' is a word that had no equivalent in any American Indian tongue. The concept that Indians had was of a spiral or vortex of energy in motion. So 'Medicine Wheel' means a circle or spiral of generated power under the control of Mind that is multi-dimensional and multi-functional. It is a physical, mental and spiritual device that can enable its users to come into attunement with the cosmic and natural forces in which they are immersed and have their being, and find harmony with their environment and within themselves. It is both a map of the mind and a chart of Life that can enable its users to find their own path to self-discovery and self-mastery and a way of life-enhancement and fulfilment.

A basic Medicine Wheel is composed of a set of symbols. It can be constructed simply by placing small stones in a circle containing a cross whose arms are like the spokes of a wheel. The four spokes indicate paths to the hub at the centre which represents the Creator/Source and also, at another level, the Self. Eight stones are used to indicate the perimeter of the circle and to mark the four cardinal and four non-cardinal directions. These also represent Powers in the universe and within the human being, and serve as a reminder of the harmonic Law of Octaves inherent in Creation.

Eight other stones are used to form an inner circle, and these represent spiritual realities which encompass the Source at the Centre. A further eight stones form the arms of a cross – two being placed in each of the four cardinal directions between the inner and outer circles. These four arms represent the Four Great Paths – Love and Trust in the South, Knowledge and Wisdom in the North, Introspection and Transformation in the West, and Illumination and Clarity in the East.

A buffalo skull was sometimes placed in the centre as the seat of the mind and of consciousness and to provide a meaningful symbolic representation of the wisdom of Wakan-Tanka, the All That Is, being made available to the individual 'self', but for our purposes the centre is best left empty to stress the invisibility of the Source of power and of the Mind and Spirit.

The Medicine Wheel thus represents not only the 'little universe' of our own individual life and the product of our own individual mind, but the cosmos and the Mind of Wakan-Tanka – the Great Spirit in manifestation – for all that is in existence is seen as a manifestation of thought. In present day terminology we might then regard the Medicine Wheel as a 'Mind machine' which functions in accordance with certain laws and principles.

The Medicine Wheel I have just described could be laid out on the ground using 24 marker stones and would take up a fair amount of space if it were intended for use by many people. I shall explain later how to construct one for your own individual use using only five or nine pebbles or gemstones to occupy space no larger than a man's handkerchief. Since the Medicine Wheel is concerned primarily with the working of the mind and the exercise of the spirit, it can operate just as effectively with some people if drawn on paper or on some other surface or even just visualised in the mind's eye, but the use of stones makes it more tangible and easier to work with.

It was often within the circle of the Medicine Wheel that the Indians related to their children stories handed down to them from their ancestors which contained an essence of the ancient wisdom of the Medicine teachings. Such stories often made mention of the Great Paradox – that everything comes out of No-thing and to No-thing everything returns. Out of No-thing – the Great Spirit – came the Great Everything – Wakan-Tanka – whose name meant, 'The One In Whom Everything That Is Made Exists'.

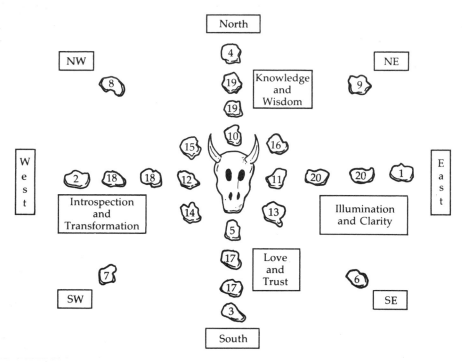

○*Fig. 9. Twenty-four actual stones were used to set up a full Medicine Wheel —
the Sacred Twenty representing all that has been, is, and ever will be, joined
with the power of Four which represents balance, alignment and harmony. The
eight outer stones represent the Sacred Powers of the Universe. The four stones
in the inner circle at the cardinal points (5, 10, 11 and 12) represent the Four
Winds, the Four Directions, the Four Elements etc. The four stones in each
cardinal direction indicate a path to self-realisation*

Every part of the physical universe and every living thing on the Earth
was seen as having its origins not in the material but in the spiritual and
mental, and while in manifestation each was in a state of continuous
change. The whole of Nature and of existence was thus regarded as a
'coming-into-being' and a 'going-out-of-manifestation' and its essence was
not material but spiritual and mental. Whatever was in being or was
coming into being not only had purpose but was directed by intelligence —
be it human, animal, plant or even mineral — and held together in harmonic
synchronisation. That directing intelligence was its spirit or essence.

The circle was thus a 'container' that represented the universe and the
totality of space, or the individual and everything around the individual. In
other words, when you construct a Medicine Wheel it becomes your

personal space – your own personal universe. In ancient symbolism the circle was a symbol of the infinity of space, without beginning and without ending, and when divided by a horizontal line it indicated the dividing of the infinity of space in order to provide the actuality of life in Time – in the Here and Now:

It also represented the power of the Formative/Receptive Force, the Feminine principle, without breadth or depth and the source of Form as expressed in the Sacred Law, 'Everything Is Born of Woman'. An upright line symbolised the power of the Active/Conceptual Force, the Masculine principle, which gives dimensions and thus a place in space:

The fusion of these two symbols provided a third – the encircled cross. The upright, equal-armed cross was an ancient symbol of manifestation in time and space. When contained within a circle it was a symbol of the limited and changing reality of physical things embraced within the infinity and everlastingness of spirit. The cross within a circle could also represent four expressions of cosmic power flowing to and from their source, or four qualities of elemental unformed substance, or four divisions of the mind, and much, much more.

The concepts I have just described could also be represented like this:

In the silence of the Void there was movement. The Origin. The beginning which paradoxically is also the ending. That from which all flows and to which all must ultimately return. The Supreme Unity.

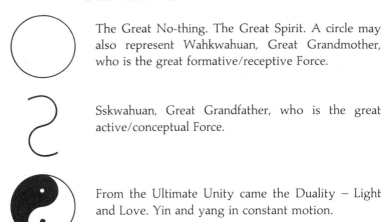

The Great No-thing. The Great Spirit. A circle may also represent Wahkwahuan, Great Grandmother, who is the great formative/receptive Force.

Sskwahuan, Great Grandfather, who is the great active/conceptual Force.

From the Ultimate Unity came the Duality — Light and Love. Yin and yang in constant motion.

Fig. 10

It was oriental philosophers who expressed the Duality in the form of what is known as the yin and yang mandala. This symbol of a circle divided into two tadpole-like halves one of which is black (yin) with a white eye-like dot, and the other white (yang) with a black dot represented a concept which the American Indian understood. The symbol represented the masculine/feminine, active/passive, positive/negative principle in all that manifests. Each eye-like dot represents the seed of the opposite — the seed of change — so there is mutual attraction, constant movement in a striving for union, constant change.

This constant striving for union which regenerates the creative energy that manifests in renewed life in all forms, was personified in most ancient cultures as the polarity of god and goddess. God and goddess were mental images of the divine powers behind Nature. They indicated the twin forces of Nature. These complementary aspects of Nature were not nebulous beliefs or mere superstitions but literal facts. The god and goddess were personifications of the forces behind those facts.

Since the yin and yang concept has become popularised in the West in recent years and these terms are 'neutral' in the sense that they are least likely to be associated with a particular belief system, I make use of them in this book to express the principles they represent.

Like all ancient peoples, the Amerindian did not regard the yin and yang principles as antagonistic opposites, like the God and Satan concepts of monotheistic religions, but as co-operating and equal partners in the entire process of continuous creation. They express the duality that came out of the Ultimate Unity that existed before the universe began. They represent the beginning of existence when positive, masculine yang and receptive, feminine yin came into being to provide the ever-present Life Force in all things that come into existence and are the polarities that provide the rhythm and movement of constant change and evolution.

As they may be described as the positive and negative ends of polarity there is an unfortunate tendency to interpret them moralistically: positive (constructive) yang, negative (destructive) yin; male (strong) yang, female (weak) yin; active (productive) yang, passive (non-productive) yin; Good (God), Evil (Satan), and so on. The two contrasting forces are at work in every aspect of life. The conscious mind, for instance, may be regarded as yang, and the subconscious mind as yin. Thought is yang, but feeling is yin. Here is a list of some yin/yang complementaries:

Yang	*Yin*
(which can be indicated by a solid line _____)	(which can be indicated by a broken line − −)
God	Goddess
Great Grandfather	Great Grandmother
Masculine	Feminine
Father	Mother
Initiating	Sustaining
Active	Passive
Projecting	Reflecting
Giving	Receiving
Extroverted	Introverted
Hard	Soft
Intellect	Emotions
Positive	Negative
Light	Dark
Dry	Wet
Objective	Subjective
Push	Pull

Let me try to describe yin and yang in the spirit of an American Indian's understanding. At the moment a singular unity becomes a duality, it is yin and yang. The physical universe came into being when the almighty One became Duality − became, in religious terminology, god and goddess; became in American Indian cosmology, Great Grandfather and Great Grandmother; became yang and yin. As a result yin and yang are manifested everywhere and in everything. In every atom. In every cell. In every molecule. In every creature whether it flies or swims or runs or crawls. There is nothing and there is nowhere where yin and yang do not exist −

except in Nothing and in Nowhere! Pause for a moment and think about it. It is not a stupid statement, or a piece of esoteric gobbledegook. What it implies is that at the very point of balance, at the very centre of being whether it is the centre of a flower or a seed or a bud, the point from which life radiates – at the very centre of balance, at the very source – there is No-thing!

Carry out a little experiment and demonstrate it for yourself:

EXERCISE NO.2:

Finding No-thing

Cut open an apple across its equator. In the centre you will find a five-pointed star – a pentagram. In the centre of the pentagram from which the apple has grown you will find – empty space! There is nothing there. There is No-thing. But that Nothing is really Something. It is the one thing that in order to manifest becomes yin and yang.

This is one of the most vital of realisations – that visible, material, physical *effects* derive from invisible power *causes*. So life is not the *result* of bodily function, as is commonly supposed, but the *cause* of it. And because of this, life does not end when bodily function itself ceases (at death), but rather it is the bodily function that ceases when life leaves the body.

The shaman looked out at the hot sun shining down and watched the vapour rising from lake or river and disappearing into invisibility in the sky, and he learned from that simple observation a great truth about life and about his own existence which modern man, for all his scientific achievements and academic knowledge, has overlooked because of its profound simplicity.

Of course modern man *knows*, because there is a law of physics to prove it, that water is vaporised by heat and converted into invisible gas in the atmosphere. When cooled it becomes visible vapour (cloud) and condenses back to water, falling as rain. A perfectly natural cycle which we all accept.

But the shaman *saw* what most of us fail to recognise. He saw an astonishing fact in the whole cosmic process, and the reason we fail to see it is because *it is invisible*. We fail to see the significance of the *invisible* segment of the water cycle just as we fail to recognise the invisible 'link' in the cosmic process of life itself. Yet it is this invisible 'link' that is the most vital, most powerful, and most dynamic reality of all.

What the shaman recognised was that there is an invisible element in the cycle of life, just as there is in the cycle of water I have just described. The water only *appears* to disappear as it changes to vapour and then vanishes into the atmosphere, apparently gone forever. But it returns again in due course as it changes back from invisibility to vapour and to water.

What the shaman had seen was a universal and unvarying cosmic law that no Force or Matter is ever destroyed or lost or comes to an end – it merely changes its form and the way it manifests. Nothing ends, but only follows a cycle of change. Everything that manifests comes into physical being and goes out of manifestation only to return to manifest once more in accordance with the Circle of Change.

This is the teaching of the Medicine Wheel, the Medicine Way. Every-thing comes from the same source of all existence – the Absolute Nothing, the Supreme Unity, 'God', or whatever name we want to give It. From this Supreme Unity, all things come into existence and to this Supreme Unity all things return. Life is that movement of coming and going. Life is a process of continual change – a turning of a Wheel. Indeed, change is the only aspect of life that *is* constant, for everything in the universe is in a state of flux, is in the process of changing. So nothing is ever 'final'. Every 'end' is but another 'beginning' – another turn of the Wheel.

The ancient wisdom taught that from the Duality, four Primary Forces vitalised all that exists in the manifested world. These four Forces and the four non-physical Elements with which Form is fashioned emanate from the Source but that does not mean that the Source is located either outside or confined to the centre of the universe. The Source is at the centre and everywhere. It is everywhere and nowhere. It is inside and outside.

The shaman recognised the cosmic Law that all power and energy moves along a circular path and returns eventually to its source. But when the power does get back it has undergone change. In fact, there is no actual 'beginning' and no real 'ending' for in this circular philosophy every beginning can be seen as an ending of what went before it, and every ending can be seen as a new beginning. This concept demonstrates another eternal truth:

LIFE IS CONSCIOUS CONTINUITY
WITHIN THE MOVEMENT OF CHANGE.

According to this concept, the Cosmos was separated from Chaos by Law being imposed, Light coming out of Darkness, and movement and Life taking place in the 'Deep'. Within the cosmos the forces express them-selves positively, though each has a dual nature and manifests as positive and active or relatively negative and receptive – masculine or feminine. This principle of duality, or polarity, is the Law of Spiritual Sexuality which governs everything, be it mineral, vegetable, animal, human or celestial. It applies even to the tiniest atom or particle of matter. So it is that there is an inherent attraction and impulse for uniting between the positive and active (masculine) and receptive and nurturing (feminine) energies of each of the Four primary Powers. Each affects everything, but the most subtle of all is the Life Force whose presence can be observed, though it can never be seen or measured.

The Indian shaman identified the Life Force as the power that makes a mighty tree grow from a tiny seed, that causes a beautiful flower to emerge from a small bulb and to release into the atmosphere a fragrance that brings pleasure. It is the power that enables each person to be aware of their own individuality. It is that which gives consciousness and awareness – our own individual 'separateness'.

Although the four primary forces influence all manifested things, one predominates in each of the four physical 'kingdoms' – mineral, plant, animal and human. So each of the four kingdoms manifests an essential *quality* of the Power that chiefly influences or governs it and of the formative Element with which it is primarily associated.

The Mineral kingdom of rocks and stones predominantly expresses *one* of these Powers and exhibits the qualities of cohesion, adhesion and aggregation. We might describe these cohesive qualities as essentially 'binding'. This inter-molecular Binding Force is the power that has centripetal movement – gravity, for instance, shows this. The Element which is associated with this force is EARTH.

The Plant kingdom predominantly expresses *two* Forces for it has, in addition to the Binding Force's quality of bringing existing particles into cohesion, the second Force's power of growth, of organisation and of generating new forms by attracting the required materials from the cosmic reservoir. This electro-magnetic Light Force is the Power that has wave movement. The Element which is associated with this force is WATER.

The Animal kingdom predominantly expresses *three* Forces and contains the qualities of both the mineral and plant kingdoms but additionally exhibits an even higher state of animation from a third Force, enabling the animal to experience sensation and the more sophisticated qualities of attraction and repulsion. For the first time, movement is possible under the direction of consciousness even if this is instinctive rather than willed. This Vibratory Force is the power that has oscillatory elliptical movement. Planetary orbits, for instance, show this. The Element associated with this Force is FIRE.

The Human Kingdom expresses *all four* forces but exhibits predominantly the most subtle of the four. One might describe it as 'egoistic' for it adds rational intelligence, determination of mind, morality, self-consciousness and free will, which are not yet within the experience of the 'lower' or less-evolved kingdoms. The Element associated with this Force is AIR.

FORCE	ACTION	TYPE	FIELD	ELEMENT	DIRECT- ION	PROP- ERTY
Vibratory Force	Reed 	Straight lines	Thought fields	Fire	NE–SW	Law
Life Force		Spiral	Bio-energy	Air	N–S	Life
Electro-magnetic Force		Waves attracting; repulsing	Organis-ational	Water	NW–SE	Light
Inter-molecular Force		Centripetal; centrifugal	Gravity	Earth	E–W	Love

○*Fig. 11. The Four Great Primary Forces*

The primary forces are unique expressions of the Source. The vibratory Force finds expression in *Law*, the electro-magnetic Force in *Light*, the binding Force in *Love*, and the life Force in *Life*. So the universe is constructed on the four great principles Life, Light, Love and Law.

Of course, what I have been endeavouring to describe is not a physical process at all, though it is an attempt to indicate how manifestation takes place. We need to understand that the shaman's perception of reality is quite different from our own. Our perception is conditioned by the Age in which we live. It is the Age of scientific materialism – the science of matter. Scientific materialism investigates and examines matter and looks for physical origins to explain a material universe. The shaman, as I have tried to show, considered the universe quite differently – that what is seen had its source in that which is unseen, the visible in the invisible. Everything in manifestation was considered to be a product of Mind which is invisible, directed by Spirit which is also invisible.

The Four Primary Forces were directed by Intelligences and represented on the Wheel by the eight outer stones which also indicate the dual nature of each. The directions are a means of coming into alignment with these intelligences and of obtaining knowledge from them. In the cosmology of the North American Indian these Four Great Powers were intelligences created by the Great Spirit in order to bring the universe into manifestation and to keep it in being.

CHAPTER FIVE

The Four Great Powers

VARIOUS CULTURES HAVE endeavoured to relate to the Four Great Powers by regarding them as gods. But the Amerindian related to them as Spirit 'beings' who expressed not so much the forces themselves but the intelligence of directing Mind that exercised those forces. These four Spirit beings were depicted in their principal role as, quite literally, the care-takers of the universe and associated with what the Indian called 'the Four Winds' of the four cardinal directions of East, South, West and North. Because they were regarded as expressions of the Mind of the Great Spirit, they contained within themselves the essence or spirit force of their particular power which keeps the universe and its life-support systems in existence, hence they were sometimes referred to as Spirit 'Keepers'. The four Spirit Keepers were said to reveal themselves through the language of symbolism, through an individual's 'inner' experience, and sometimes through visions or dreams.

The Spirit Keepers thus have similarities with the Four Archangels of Judaeo-Christian traditions and with the Four Guardians of the Quarters of Western mystical systems. But whereas the Western entities are formidable and fearsome figures and rather difficult to imagine, the Spirit Keepers are presented as approachable, helpful and co-operating. Indeed, the Indian did not distance himself from them but sought to establish a close and harmonious relationship.

In order to make this possible each Spirit Keeper was associated with a particular animal or bird species which best demonstrated some of the principal characteristics or qualities and thus helped to relate unseen powers to the realm of practical reality. This association was called a 'totem' and was an effective way of comprehending a non-physical power.

A totem is a symbolic sensor that serves as a connector between different levels of being, different life forms whether human, animal, vegetable, mineral or celestial, and different levels of the mind, whether unconscious, subconscious, conscious or superconscious. Totems are links also with formative forces that are otherwise beyond the range of consciousness and can only manifest within. Because totems express the qualities of something that is 'alive', they are more powerful symbols than geometric abstractions.

Neither the totems nor their creature counterparts were worshipped as gods. They were merely regarded as helpers and special messengers and a means of fostering an understanding of an invisible reality behind the representation. Response came not through an intellectual process but through the intuitive senses.

I shall purposely avoid allocating names to the Spirit Keepers since these differed among tribes who spoke different languages, but will refer to each as the 'Spirit' of the Direction with which it is associated. Since not all tribes used the same totems, I am making use of those which appeared to have been in fairly general use and, importantly, are ones which those of us from a different culture may readily relate to.

SPIRIT OF THE EAST   *Totem:* **EAGLE**

Colour: **YELLOW**

The power of the Spirit of the East is *illumination* that opens the spiritual eye and brings *enlightenment* and *discernment*. It is the power of new beginnings and of fresh new life, like the awakening of Spring after the dormancy of Winter, and the arising of Dawn whose light disperses the darkness and dispels ignorance. It is *awakening*. It is new light. It is *newness of life*.

Experience something of the power of the East for yourself. Get up early enough to go out into the open air where you can listen for the start of the dawn chorus as birds awaken from their slumber and herald the rising of the Sun in the East and you will know the joy of enlightenment. In Springtime, absorb yourself in the wonder of new life that is springing up from the earth all round you and contemplate on it, and you will recognise something of its tremendous power and vitality.

The totem of the East is the Eagle. The Eagle flies higher than any other bird and therefore 'closer' to the Sun, the source of light. Its closeness to the Sun — symbolic of the Great Spirit — is a reason for Eagle feathers being so prized by the Indian and used in headdresses and in other ways to indicate the wearer's desire to draw close to the Great Spirit, and to the High Self.

The colour assigned to the Spirit of the East is Yellow — the colour of the rising Sun, and of illumination and enlightenment.

So the EAST is the Path to work on to seek enlightenment, or in starting a new project, or when looking for a fresh new approach to a phase of one's life.

| SPIRIT OF THE SOUTH | *Totem*: MOUSE |
| | *Colour*: RED |

The power of the Spirit of the South is of rapid growth, and of exploring, experiencing and investigating. It is the power of *finding out*, It is the power of the fast-developing child, rapidly growing to youth and maturity. It is the power of blossoming and of unfolding as purposes become clear. It is the power that guides and grows. It is also the power of Trust – a trust in *feelings* and *intuitions*, the natural trust of the child, and especially trust in natural and cosmic laws.

Experience something of the power of the South for yourself. Go outdoors at noontime and breathe in the abundant glow of the light at its peak and feel its warm embrace. In Summer, absorb yourself in the joy that summertime brings and witness the abundance of life all around you as the things of the earth grow rapidly to full blossom.

The totem of the South is the Mouse which may appear to be a rather small and insignificant creature to represent so powerful a Force but remember in the stories of your childhood even the mighty elephant had respect for little mouse! The mouse has a very sensitive sense organ in the form of its whiskers and is able to perceive things 'close to' through touch. So the mouse helps in the understanding of the Spirit Keeper's association with the feelings and emotions, and stresses the importance of not confusing power with size – for even a tiny acorn clasps within it the power to become a mighty oak.

The colour of the Spirit of the South is RED, the colour of vital energy and of the life blood.

So the SOUTH is the Path to work on when seeking growth and development or when desiring to learn the lessons of change.

| SPIRIT OF THE WEST | *Totem*: **GRIZZLY BEAR** |
| | *Colour*: **BLACK** |

The power of the Spirit of the West is *strength* and *introspection*. It is the power of *looking within* to evaluate the lessons of growth so that realisation can develop. It is the power of growth to full maturity and of the consolidation of internal structures for the period of renewal that is to come. It is the power of *self-examination* and of the *transformation* of physical experiences into spiritual realities.

Experience something of the power of the West for yourself by watching the sunset and wrapping yourself in its blanket of softness as its colours cover the earth while it dips slowly and majestically below the horizon. In the Autumn absorb yourself in the golden glory of harvest-time and be aware of the bounteousness of the Earth.

The totem of the West is the Grizzly Bear, the strongest of the bears but also the fiercest, and most thoughtful about its decisions. In the Autumn the Grizzly eats well, strengthening its body to prepare for the sleep of Winter and the time of renewal. It is associated with introspection because of its characteristic careful consideration before taking action.

The colour of the Spirit of the West is BLACK, the colour of the formlessness from which all form comes.

So the WEST is the Path to work on to seek transformation or evaluation and to prepare for new action.

SPIRIT OF THE NORTH   *Totem*: **BUFFALO**

Colour: **WHITE**

The power of the Spirit of the North is the power of *renewal* and of the *quickening* of the spirit. It is the power of Winter when nothing appears to be growing but inwardly the Earth is gathering together her energies for the new life that is to come. It is the white snow of *purity* – not the self-righteous purity of the do-gooder but the purity that is a compaction of power that brings *concentration* and *clarity* of intent. It is the power that turns water to ice, the power that gives ice its strength to crush rocks into pebbles. It is the power of night when the physical is dormant but the spirit is active. It is growth wearing the cloak of rest, and new life attired in the shroud of death.

Experience something of the power of the North for yourself by going outside around midnight when the Moon is full and bathe in its silvery light while the Earth is shrouded in the blackness that absorbs all form. In Winter absorb yourself in its crisp purity and sense the activity of spiritual renewal beneath the physical appearance of barrenness.

The totem of the North is the Buffalo which, like the Spirit, gives totally of itself in order to sustain all that is in existence. It was sometimes represented as a White Buffalo, a rare animal with sacred significance which was associated with the legendary White Buffalo Woman who is reputed to have brought to the Red Indian people their most treasured possession – the Sacred Pipe.

The colour of the Spirit of the North is WHITE, and because white is the sum of all the colours it was regarded as the colour of perfection.

So the NORTH is the Path to work on for the perfection of any endeavour, to gain strength of Will, and clarity in one's intentions.

The Spirit Keepers were thus intelligences which directed and motivated the formative forces which brought matter into existence, for the shaman knew that energy had no mind of its own and therefore had to be directed in order to achieve anything. He knew that however awesome the power of energy, it could not of itself bring anything into being, let alone a universe and intelligent creatures. He knew such energy required intelligence to direct it and to put it to use, and he knew that spirit is the vehicle of intelligence. He knew it was spirit directed by intelligence and not blind undirected energy alone that brought things into existence. Matter, therefore, was spirit-directed energy condensed and shaped into form. It was the formative elemental forces and the Powers behind them that were the means by which matter was brought into existence. It was directing intelligences within the Whole that enabled the invisible to be made visible and maintained, just as the cells and organs and vital functions of the human body are maintained by internal, directing intelligences within, of which the human being is not even consciously aware.

The shaman saw the whole of physical creation as the invisible Great Spirit made manifest. That was why the Indian had such love and concern for the environment all around him.

The ancestors had taught that with the Great Spirit's breath when the cosmos was formed, came movement – AIR. On an earthly level, air blows at its strongest from the North in the Northern hemisphere and anatomically North is the upper part of the body so Air was assigned to the North on the Medicine Wheel. Out of Air, through inhaling and exhaling, came elemental FIRE which is light-energy in an expansive state and can be likened to the Sun, a great ball of fire from which light on Earth comes. Since the Sun rises in the East, the East was assigned the direction of elemental FIRE. As Fire energy cooled, it 'collapsed' into a fluid state, and so came elemental WATER. As movement was clearly in a Sun-wise direction, and anatomically the South is associated with the lower part of the body, Water was placed in the South on the Medicine Wheel. Finally, as formless substance appeared to stabilise, it 'solidified', taking on the properties of inertia. Elemental EARTH was placed in the West, the direction of the setting Sun and of completion.

Of course, these elemental substances are not *real* air, fire, water and earth as we know them physically. Rather, they are the *condition* of the formless substance which is in the process of becoming material substance. But each element has the qualities and characteristics of its physical counterpart and it is by these qualities that they can be comprehended and understood.

The formless source of these four primary elements was a catalyst which can be regarded as a fifth element, since the four elements are not only derived from it but contained within it. It was known in some Eastern traditions by the Sanskrit word 'Akasha' and in the West as 'Aether'. 'Akasha' means 'formless cloud' and was sometimes translated as 'spirit' by some schools of thought, but this is a definite misnomer and the cause of much confusion. Spirit is the life force and has intelligence and mind-power. A substance or an energy has no intrinsic intelligence or mind of its own, but does and goes as it is directed. This 'source element', this Akasha or Aether was so named because it is so ethereal, undefined and non-material. It is in every substance and in every form yet it is also in the space between every substance and every form, so it contains all within itself. No description or analogy can adequately describe it. I can only attempt to draw similarities which might trigger your own inner understanding. So let me give a couple of examples.

Aether may be likened to air. Sound, according to a dictionary definition, is a sensation on the ear caused by the vibration or movement of air. If we liken sound to movement, Aether is that across which or in which the movement or vibration takes place.

Let me try another example. Before I can communicate these thoughts to you – which are seemingly coming into my mind 'out of nothing' – I have to write them down so they are represented in characters and words which you, the reader, may recognise and understand. In other words, my thoughts have to be 'solidified' and put on paper in order that they can be seen and comprehended. Aether has a similar purpose in regard to the four elements as paper has for my words which were 'written', as it were, in the Aether.

In matter, the four elements are present in various proportions depending on the quality of the physical object itself. For instance, a physical object that is very solid and heavy, like iron or steel or rock, contains a high proportion of elemental Earth. A liquid will contain a high proportion of elemental Water although, because it has a certain inertia, it will contain also a proportion of elemental Earth. A gaseous compound will contain a high proportion of elemental Air, and so on.

My book 'Earth Medicine'[1] presents a system of personality profiling and self-analysis based upon the Medicine Wheel. It examines in detail how the way we individually perceive life, the basic 'equipment' of our personality, our strongest links with the natural powers that affect the inner-dynamics of our life, is determined to an extent by the time of year at our birth. As popular Astrology also indicates, we each have a strong association with a particular Element which helps to fashion the way we are. In American Indian cosmology, so important was this relationship considered to be that it was likened to belonging to a family or clan and a vital key to human understanding.

Let us look at these Elemental Clans and their principal characteristics:

ELEMENT OF FIRE   **The Elemental Clan of the HAWK**

The hawk is a magnificent bird, like the Eagle, but with rounded wings. Amerindians associated it with the Sun because of its ability to fly to great heights and thus be 'near the Sun'; also with thunder and lightning, dedication and understanding. The hawk thus characterises the radiant energy of fire, its habit of pouncing swiftly with the suddenness of illumination, and its powerfulness with the inherent transmuting energy of fire. It was sometimes associated with the mythical Phoenix, the bird which was able to rise up again from its own ashes – an indication of the ability of fire to purify and transform and to change matter back to its elemental substances and thereby provide the building blocks from which new forms may arise.

People associated with the hawk – especially those born between 21 March and 19 April, 22 July and 21 August, and 23 November and 21 December – are often guided by intuition and easily sparked into action, sometimes on exuberant impulse, and have a real passion for life. They often experience flashes of illumination to spark new ideas and projects, and the burning enthusiasm so necessary to activate ideas. They are usually clear-sighted, energetic folk.

ELEMENT OF WATER　　The Elemental Clan of the FROG

The frog is an animal that leads a double life for it is at home in either water or on land, and it achieves this state through a remarkable transformation process called metamorphosis. The Indian associated the frog with the Water element because water is a 'bridging' element – the process between the airy-radiant qualities of Air and Fire and the inertia of Earth. The frog characterises elemental Water through its adaptability and flexibility in undergoing change, and its ability to fit in with its surroundings.

The frog is able to live in two worlds – water and land – and Frog Clan people are similarly adaptable, whether they are perceiving through the ripples of emotion and feeling or through the objective reality of practicality. Frog Clan people include those born between 21 June and 21 July, 23 October and 22 November, and 19 February and 20 March. They are people with deep emotions, who like flexibility and malleable arrangements rather than rigid situations. Water is a healing element which rejuvenates and refreshes, and Frog Clan people are often natural healers, whether of body, mind or spirit. Frog Clan people have an affinity with water and can find calmness merely by being near water.

ELEMENT OF EARTH   **The Elemental Clan of the TURTLE**

The turtle not only reflects the stability and tenacity of elemental Earth, but also its sustaining nature. The turtle is characteristic of elemental Earth because of its solidity — its hard, protective shell providing comfort and security — and because of its persistence and tenacity. The turtle may appear to be slow and ponderous, but it has the determination to achieve its purpose. Remember the story of the tortoise and the hare? It was the tortoise who won the race because it kept going and was not easily distracted like the fleeting hare. Similarly, the turtle reflects the wisdom of having one's feet firmly on the ground and the need to attain stability and security by having 'solid' things around one.

Turtle Clan people are those born between 20 April and 20 May, 22 August and 21 September, and 22 December and 19 January. Like the turtle they are usually methodical and practical. They are people with a natural affinity with the soil and with plants and growing things.

ELEMENT OF AIR   **The Elemental Clan of the BUTTERFLY**

The butterfly begins life as a crawler and then, through a transformation process, learns to fly, carrying in its wings the colours of the rainbow. Tribes who chose the butterfly as a totem for elemental Air did so not only because of its great transforming powers, but because it characterised elemental Air through its constant moving and perpetual activity, always shifting its position from one place to another. The element of Air is the great transformer — its breath changing the atmosphere wherever it goes. The butterfly, too, transforms with its beauty whatever it touches. Butterfly people are usually great transformers and manipulators.

Butterly Clan people are those born between 21 May and 20 June, 22 September and 22 October, and 20 January and 18 February. They are similarly active, enjoying the variety of new places, new ideas, new things to do and new ways of doing them. Quick and lively, they are always busy, never wanting to stay still for long. Butterfly Clan people have an affinity with air, so will be invigorated by being out in the open and away from confinement of any kind.

CHAPTER SIX

Directional Technology

WE CAN NOW TAKE OUR knowledge of the Elements a stage further. I have explained how in the shaman's understanding the Great Spirit first expressed Itself through movement, just as a human being does. Motion is an expression of Aether, and our life on Earth began when we took our first breath of air when we were born. This movement and inhalation of air brings expansion and expression through the element of Fire which enables the individual Spirit to activate the mind and express itself through the personality. Our emotions express the way we feel about what we comprehend and they flow like elemental Water. Elemental Earth finds expression in our practical actions and regard for material realities. So the way we live and conduct our individual lives is an expression of the energies flowing through us. Your life is a 'dance' — a choreography of energy.

The Amerindian shaman regarded Man as a spiritual being — an individuated spirit that was a spark from the Fire or Soul of the Great Spirit. Indeed, the word 'human' means 'divine mortal' — 'hu' meaning 'divine' and 'man' meaning 'mortal' — an immortal spirit in mortal flesh.

The Indian understood that when the primary energies are expressed in accordance with the alchemical structure of the human being — the divine mortal — the inner dynamics are in harmony. If, however, polarities are crossed, there is discord both within and without. These polarities form the Basic Alchemy Wheel which opens up an understanding of the constitution of the human being when applied to the Medicine Wheel.

On the Medicine Wheel NORTH is the direction of RECEIVING.

Its polarity in the SOUTH is the direction of GIVING.

The WEST is the direction of HOLDING.

And its polarity, EAST, is the direction of DETERMINING.

When this is applied to the directional placements of the Elements — Air in the North, Water in the South, Earth in the West and Fire in the East — we have an insight into the human condition.

AIR is similar in nature to mental energy — ideas and things of the mind that come quickly and suddenly and then vanish without being seen.

Indeed, we talk of ideas coming into our minds 'out of thin air'. Thought, like air, is elusive. So Air in the North can be likened to the mind, to the intellect, to logic, to thinking, and everything concerned with mental effort.

FIRE – light-energy that comes from the Sun – can be likened to the Spirit because elemental Fire has qualities which are similar to the light of the spirit. Fire in the East can be likened to spiritual illumination and enlightenment, to principles and spiritual things.

WATER in the South has the characteristics of fluidity and motion. Elemental Water can be likened to the emotions which are our energies in a fluid state. So emotions and feelings and intuitive senses can be related to the South direction.

EARTH is inertia, stability, and solidity. So elemental Earth in the West has qualities similar to material, physical objects and the physical body.

These principles can be arranged on the Medicine Wheel like this:

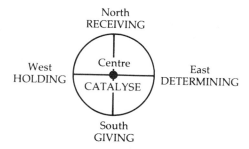

○*Fig. 12. The Basic Alchemy Wheel*

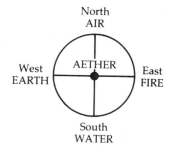

○*Fig. 13. The Wheel of the Elements*

○*Fig. 14. The Wheel of the Constitution of the Human*

In the centre is the SOUL through which the conscious entity expresses itself life after life through a physical body (West), through the emotions (South), and through the mind (North) using the driving energy of the Spirit (East) which characterises the permanent personality.

Let us pause here and consider what is meant by the Soul because there has been so much confusion through a misunderstanding of the difference between Soul and Spirit. Indeed, religionists are often so confused themselves that they use Soul and Spirit synonymously.

Our SPIRIT is our individuated life force with intelligence – an essence or 'spark' of the Great Spirit. The Spirit is immortal. It cannot be destroyed even by death. It is always-existing – our permanent Self. The SOUL is a vehicle for expressing the Spirit's individuality from life to life, recording and storing experiences, and modifying the personality as the being evolves. The Soul can be damaged. We can lose a part or parts of it through traumatic experiences – a bad accident, rape, incest, divorce, bereavement, for instance, are likely to damage the Soul. We can actually give a part of ourselves – our Soul – away to another quite unconsciously through the power or influence that person has over our lives, and we can have a part of our Soul 'taken' by another person, and again this is usually an unconscious act. Part of a shaman's function in tribal societies was to retrieve the part or parts of a person's Soul that had become separated in some way and to restore it or them to the individual and so 'make them whole'. In the perception of the shaman, much physical illness was caused by Soul loss and the resulting loss of power within the person's energy-system. Once the Soul had been 'healed' and restored, healing of the physical condition usually followed. This is a most fascinating aspect of shamanism.

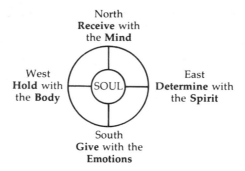

o*Fig. 15. The Wheel of the Life Energies*

We are now in a position to put all these Wheels together by superimposing one on top of another and see how our energy-system was designed to be expressed. This composite arrangement might be called the Wheel of Life Energies:

So the most *balanced* way to use our energies is to:

    DETERMINE with the Spirit
    RECEIVE with the Mind
    GIVE with the Emotions
    HOLD with the Body

Problems arise when we interchange these forces and as a consequence bring upon ourselves fatigue, imbalance, discomfort and pain. The most common way these energies are interchanged is by exchanging the South and the West *holding* with our emotions and *giving* with the body, and by exchanging the North and East, *determining* with the Mind and *receiving* with the Spirit.

Consider the consequences of these interchanges. By holding onto our emotions we are locking up our heart. We are often afraid to let our emotions express how we really feel because we think that by so doing we are making ourselves vulnerable. We think it best to express our feelings through *physical* things and modern society is fully geared up to help us to do this. Love, feelings and emotions are expressed through the provision of physical objects — television, videos, record players, perfumes, cosmetics, and all the 'goodies' of an affluent society.

Even 'love' can often become a purely physical, athletic act measured on 'performance'. Yet the most valid expression of love is the giving of oneself and the desire for the happiness of the loved one, without strings or conditions. True love is unconditional. Instead, we give with the body and offer a sexual love that is only a physical expression. We hold on to what should have been given — our emotions — which is our love energy in motion. Is it any wonder that by locking up our hearts in this way, heart disease has become the greatest single killer in western civilisation?

By *determining* with the mind we act according to logic with special regard to external appearances and by what is thought to be appropriate to bring about desired results, ignoring the possible consequences on others and on the environment. Whilst the material results might be achieved, the consequences of such actions bruise, injure and often deform the Spirit which receives the unbalanced energies produced, either by us or by the reactions to our acts.

Morality belongs in the Mind. Morality is part of the culture it is in. For example, it is moral in one society to have more than one wife, but not so in another society.

Principles and ethics, on the other hand, are expressions of the Spirit which has to do with the INTENT and WILL. Rules and laws are activities of the mind. Laws are fashioned by the mind in an effort to establish and safeguard principles and ethics — that is, to express the thought behind everything that is. When we obey a law in accordance with its intent, we are carrying out the spirit of that law (determining with the Spirit). We may, however, carry out the letter of the law — that is, by mental application follow it literally — yet act contrary to its spirit and intent (determining with the mind).

The results of this lie around us in confused, unhappy relationships, broken homes, crime and violence, moral bankruptcy, and in particular the disrepute of the law, government, law enforcement and justice.

Part of our problem is that when we suffer discomfort and pain or when there is disharmony and confusion in our lives, we don't treat this as a signal that it is we who are out of alignment — out of balance within ourselves. We have been conditioned to treat only symptoms and effects, rarely the cause, so we take another tablet, smoke another cigarette, have another drink, or seek escape in a television programme. It is like stuffing a fire alarm with rags instead of dealing with the fire that triggered the alarm.

How do we know when we are determining with the Spirit? We determine with the Spirit when we follow what our Heart truly wants us to do, for the heart is the voice of the spirit which is heard *intuitively*. We can't always be enthusiastic about some of the work we do, even if reason tells us that the task is necessary. It is when we find that we are putting ourselves 'heart and soul' into an activity that we are determining with the Spirit. Determining with the Spirit is uplifting and stimulating and makes us 'feel good inside'.

Medicine Wheel directions do not synchronise with those of Western esoteric traditions which put Earth in the North, Air in the East, Fire in the South, and Water in the West. There is a 90 degree discrepancy as if the circle has been turned a full directional 'notch' — which it has, in fact — and it does make a difference!

The encircled cross of Western traditions and the Medicine Wheel of American Indians are identical symbols, but aligned differently. It is not a question of right and wrong or of one being 'better' or more effective than the other. They are different orientations and the difference is important for not only do they bring about a change in attitudes but in the responses attained and the results that are achieved. For centuries the encircled cross has been the tool of the ceremonial magician, the experimental metaphysician, the occultist, the witch and the mystic. The Western way is sometimes presented as the way of the 'wise shaper' and that is a good definition, for the Wheel is aligned for the purpose of shaping and moulding. Western traditions put the emphasis on determining with the mind and of achieving desired effects in accordance with the will. They are essentially ways of gaining control and mastery over unseen forces of Nature and the elements, of directing energies in order to bring into physical reality that which has been desired or imaged in the mind through the intellect, and driven by the will that has been fuelled with emotion.

Air in the East means determining with the mind and the intellect and making decisions through the application of logical reasoning. Fire in the South puts the emphasis on the application of spiritual principles as a means of exerting power over things. Water in the West implies holding onto the emotions and desires and linking them to their polar opposite — the Will. Earth in the North puts the emphasis on the receiving of material benefits. It is a Way of logical, analytical reasoning. It is a Way of aims, goals and targets, of 'progress' from a 'lower' to a 'higher' grade, from one condition to something 'better'. It is acting in accordance with what is considered appropriate. It is using power in its aspect of might and for the purpose of exerting control over events.

Negative aspects of this approach have seeped through from inner levels and have found expression in the lives of those who do not have the vision or concern to take an holistic view of the universe. Manipulation, not only of energies and substances but of the minds of human beings, has been a by-product. Exploitation of the mineral, plant and animal kingdoms that share the Earth and its environment with us, have caused havoc to the planet and to its life-support system. It is vital that a change of emphasis is made moving strongly towards harmony, balance and beauty — to the Way with Heart.

The Medicine Way is a way for individual human beings to find harmony, balance and beauty within the environment around them and with forms and creatures that share that environment with them. It is using power in a different way – in its aspect as energy – with the emphasis on the spirit and on purity of intent for the good of the whole. Its essence is not that of control, coercion and subjection but the spirit of willing participation at all levels of being. Its purpose is to harmonise the individual with all the realms – mineral, plant, animal, human and celestial. This is why Medicine teachings which have hitherto been hidden within the oral traditions of tribal shamans are now being made generally available. This is why the ancient wisdom which appeared to be 'lost' is now being reclaimed and revived in many different ways, and through people of different races and cultures. It is to open up a new Age of enlightened consciousness – an Age of enlightened individuals and the acceptance of individual responsibility for what happens.

We have learned that the Elements of Air, Fire, Water, Earth and, of course, Aether, are the building blocks of the physical world and that without these unformed substances there could be no material universe. We are able to comprehend and relate to this physical world of matter only through the five physical senses which are our sensory devices. We could still be 'alive' and not see, hear, feel, taste or smell, but if we lost the use of all five, we would know nothing of physical existence.

The Elements relate to us and our five physical senses see overleaf.
The Elements were considered by ancient peoples to be the unformed substances that were at the foundation of all that came into physical manifestation and of the Earth itself. The human body, too, was regarded as not only composed of them but completely dependent on them. Even the mind was influenced by both their creative and destructive qualities. All were of equal importance and their properties functioned in the human being in ways similar to their function in Nature itself. So, ancient peoples saw a relationship between the driving energy of Fire and the dynamic power of the human spirit, between the ebb and flow of Water and the turbulence of human emotions, between the elusive presence and movement of Air and that of human thought, and between the fertility and self-renewing qualities of Earth and the functioning of the human body.

To the Amerindian shaman the elements were readily identified as powers of Nature and man was part of that ecology, impregnated by the physical environment that surrounded him, and related to it through the concept of elemental forces. Those of us brought up in a different culture and in an age of monetarism and scientific materialism, have been denied this respect for the elements which the 'natural' man living close to Nature enjoyed.

We have been insulated from the elements in our centrally-heated homes, and cocooned from the natural world in our travels in the tin shells

Air	Smell	Nose	Mind	North
Fire	Sight	Eyes	Spirit	East
Water	Taste	Mouth	Emotions	South
Earth	Touch	Body	Physical Body	West
Aether	Hearing	Ears	Soul	Centre

So we can construct another 'learning' wheel as follows:

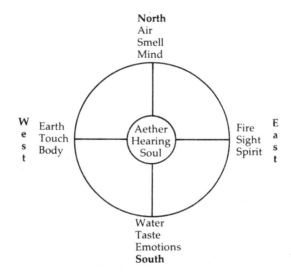

Fig. 16. The Wheel of the Senses

of our motor cars, railway trains, and aeroplanes. It is therefore less easy for us to relate to them so readily. The time and effort required, however, will be richly rewarded.

A knowledge of the properties and qualities of the elements was not only essential to the well-being of the 'natural' man, but an understanding of these powers and of their blending and balancing was a vital ingredient of the ancient wisdom and of the skill of the shaman.

Having looked at a number of teaching/learning Wheels, we can now move on to develop some of the principles they have demonstrated and endeavour to apply that knowledge to a 'working' Wheel. A 'working' Wheel is one that is performed by applying our own energy to experience it and by so doing gaining physical, practical results in our everyday lives as well as obtaining insight and understanding.

Working a wheel is like making a 'journey' in each of the four cardinal Directions in turn. Each of these four directions constitutes a path that leads to the centre of your own being where you can make contact with your own High Self, your Spiritual Self, the True Self that is at the very core of your being, and make connection with the Whole. Traversing each path will enable you to experience for yourself the energies of the Medicine Wheel and to acquire the knowledge to work changes that will put meaning and purpose into your life, bringing enlightenment and fulfilment. Each path is also a method of self-realisation and self-initiation into the mysteries of life.

If you will operate this Wheel by walking each path in accordance with the guidelines given, you will come to know a great deal of truth about yourself, discover how to rid yourself of many of the hangups and encumbrances that hitherto have held you back from making use of your full potential, and come to realise what it is you want to be. Each direction is a path of true initiation. Not the kind that confines you to a group or cult, or shackles you with rules and regulations, doctrines and dogmas devised by others, but one that admits you into the reality of your 'self' by your Self. Unlike many philosophical teachers, religious leaders, spiritual guides and gurus, the shaman seeks no followers. A Medicine Chief from whom I learned much was most emphatic on this point: 'Never try to follow me, look up to me, or bow down to me. You have asked me to be your guide, and this I will be because you have asked from the heart. As a guide I will be a friend and we can share our discoveries. But this is your path and you are on it to discover your own truth and to be empowered with your own "medicine" and only you can find it and become free and responsible.' When we parted after several days together he looked into my eyes and repeated advice I had been given earlier: 'Walk your talk, my brother. Walk your talk.' Walking the Medicine Way can never be just verbal adherence to a set of beliefs. It is a way of doing, a way of being and a way of becoming.

Let me make it clear that the teachings given in this book are not those of a particular tribe or group, but are an attempt to present the fundamental essence that impregnated them all in spite of geographical, historical and cultural differences. This fundamental essence instils a recognition of the holistic nature of the universe in which all things are interrelated, interconnected and immersed in the Great Everything called Wakan-Tanka. It is the spirit of the Redman which engenders a love of Mother Earth and a respect for all living things whether they walk, run, crawl, fly or just stand.

Part Two contains certain rites and rituals which are a means of gaining personal experience of the energies and forces involved. Let me make it clear that these are adaptations and not literal representations. They are purposefully designed to meet the needs of modern times and to be manageable, practical and effective for anyone, even if they live in a city rather than a rural environment. Ancient rites as performed in tribal societies were for people hardened by outdoor living in which they were constantly exposed to the elements all around them. Many such rites would not be suitable, and could even be dangerous, if performed by Western people today without proper preparation, training, and conditioning.

The exercises, rites and rituals given in this book make no great physical, emotional or mental demands on the individual, and are quite safe. They do, however, require the application of self-discipline, determination and commonsense. If they are carried out in accordance with the guidelines they will have effective, and in some cases, quite profound results. In other words, they work beneficially as you will discover for yourself.

ADVENTURER TASK NO.1:

Preparing Your Marker Stones

Adventurer Tasks were an essential part of shamanic training in self-reliance and self-development and not only extended practical skills, but developed the will, honed the determination, and strengthened fortitude. The Adventurer Tasks given in this book are simple but effective. Their purpose is a preparation for the exploration of unknown or unfamiliar territory. They will help to unfold your inner power centres like a flower opening its petals, and lead you gently into each stage of your progress along the Four Paths of the Medicine Way.

As I have already explained, the Medicine Wheel can be regarded as a device to enable you to tune in to the beams of energy that emanate from your own Source and to make connections at different levels with power sources within the holistic system of the universe in which we each have our existence. But before you can construct your own personal Medicine Wheel there is some preparation work to be done – your first Adventurer Task.

This first Adventurer Task is to acquire for yourself five coloured marker stones for setting up your own basic Medicine Wheel. Round, flat pebbles or small stones are best so they are easy to carry around. Four should be roughly the same size – about 5 or 6 centimetres in diameter (about a couple of inches). The fifth should be slightly larger. You can either look for a yellowish stone to represent the East, a reddish stone for the South, black for West and white for the North, or merely collect four stones that 'feel' right for you and colour-indicate them yourself. The colour affinity of the larger centre stone is green.

So, go out into your garden or take a walk in a nearby park or into the countryside with the express purpose of finding your stones. Meditate on the task before you set out. Intention is vital in shamanic work, so have it quite clear in your mind that you are going out to find five stones to be your helpers on the Medicine Way.

On your search don't pick up just any stone you see. Allow yourself to feel drawn to a particular stone. Then, hold it in your left hand and 'tell' it mentally that you want to make use of it on your Medicine Wheel, whose purpose is in furthering your own self-development and spiritual evolution. Wait to 'feel' the 'consent' of the stone. You will know intuitively whether to retain the stone as a helper or whether to dispose of it by putting it back in the area where you found it.

If the stones you have selected are already the right colours, lay them on the ground in front of you with the larger stone in the centre and the four smaller stones around it to represent the four cardinal directions of North, South, East and West. If you are not sure of the directions, use a compass. Each of the directional stones should be about 15 centimetres (6 inches) from the centre stone. Again, wait for a response. You will 'feel' that they are right or that one or more is 'out of tune'. Should this be the case, continue your search and repeat this procedure until you have a suitable replacement.

If it is necessary for you to colour the stones for yourself, lay the stones on the ground and keep moving the smaller stones around until you 'feel' the direction is right for each. Let your intuition be your guide. Then write in pencil on the stones which is North, East, South and West.

When you return home, wash the stones thoroughly and leave them to dry. If you are going to paint them, the kind of paint you use must be hardwearing so it won't rub off. The enamel paint used for plastic model-making is ideal and can be obtained in very small tins from a model shop or toy section of a department store. The paint can be applied with a small watercolour brush. The stones may be covered completely or simply marked with a blob or circle of paint to identify them. More than one coat may be necessary.

Later you can complete the outer circle of your Medicine Wheel by the addition of four more stones which preferably should be gemstones. I would suggest using quartz crystals for the non-cardinal directions. Choose ones that are 4 or 5 centimetres long (about a couple of inches) to give a nice 'balance' to your wheel. Though size is relatively unimportant, it is best for the stones to be roughly the same size. Alternatively, a small piece of jade or an opal for the Northeast, rose quartz or agate for the Southeast, azurite or topaz for the Southwest, and obsidian for the Northwest are most suitable. Quartz crystals, however, are fairly easy to come by. It is best to choose the stones for yourself rather than through someone else's choice. Have the purpose for which you require the stones quite clear in your mind before making a choice. If you are presented with a selection from which to choose, go for the ones you feel drawn to. Hold each in turn in your left hand and ask the question in your mind – for instance, 'Are you the stone for my Northeast direction?' – and wait for a response. You will either feel inclined to put the stone down and choose another or recognise intuitively that the stone is 'right'. Follow your intuition and not your reason or any sales patter.

Cleanse gemstones by washing them under a running cold water tap. Then put them in a glass of water on a window sill where they can catch the sunlight and leave them there for at least 24 hours. This will rid them of any negative vibrations they may have picked up on their travels.

You don't have to delay your Medicine Way workings until you have acquired all nine stones. A basic Medicine Wheel will 'work' with just a centre stone and four cardinal stones. The non-cardinal stones, however, will increase its effectiveness as a representation and its power as a 'connector'.

Before you use the stones for practical Medicine Wheel work you need to 'programme' each stone by 'telling' it that you require its help as an 'indicator' and 'connector' on your Medicine Wheel. 'Talk' to each stone in turn either aloud or mentally, along these lines: 'Please be my helper as an indicator of the (East, South, West, North, Centre) and to connect me to the powers of the universe and with the natural forces of the Earth, for our mutual benefit. Thank you.'

Some people may consider it foolish to suggest that rocks – which science and education have taught are inanimate objects – have life. Yet consider the remarkable things being achieved today with quartz crystals. As a result of the discovery that Nature has endowed quartz with a 'heart beat' when it is electrically stimulated and that it can hold its oscillations or frequency range 'true', television and radio stations in all parts of the world are able to transmit their broadcasts without confusion. A single telephone wire can convey hundreds of messages at once due to the unscrambling powers of crystals. The powers of earthquakes are registered by crystal-controlled seismographs. Navigators determine longitude at sea with crystal-operated chronometers.

Treat rocks and stones as if they are 'alive' and experience for yourself the difference.

Finally, you need a suitable container in which to keep your stones when they are not in use. A small bag or pouch made of soft but durable material is best. One can be easily made from a piece of chamois leather with a thong or stout cord for a drawstring, some strong thread and a stout needle. Little skill is needed in making one for yourself, but if you prefer something ready-made you may find what you are looking for in shops that sell goods from Third World countries or in large department stores.

Your Medicine Wheel can be set up in any room where you will be undisturbed for a while. It requires little space for it can be arranged on a flat working surface in front of you – on a coffee table, a dressing table or writing desk perhaps. Ideally there should be room for you to move around and switch positions so you can sit comfortably at any one of the four cardinal points, but do not worry if this is not possible and that the sitting position has to remain the same.

You will need to cover the surface with a cloth that can be set aside specially for the purpose. Black or white material is best so that no particular colour predominates.

The physical representation and your action in setting up a Medicine Wheel will help to strengthen the mental and astral imagery and bring about an alignment with the energies you will be working with, thereby triggering a response at all levels. As I explained earlier, a Medicine Wheel can be represented merely by a drawing or even visualised in the mind's eye, but I have observed people on a number of occasions who either 'couldn't be bothered' to make a physical effort or thought it wasn't really necessary and that some sort of meditative approach alone would suffice. I have tried short-cutting for myself, too. In all such cases the subsequent results have been disappointing and even non-existent in terms of practical results.

If you really want to experience the Medicine Way and to obtain positive benefits, you do need to engage your physical body and exert physical energy – not just your mind. I shall explain the setting up of your personal Medicine Wheel in the Introduction to Part Two which follows, but you will need to have your 'equipment' ready and have a suitable location prepared before you begin your 'journey' on the first Medicine path.

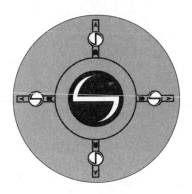

The Realisation

THE MEDICINE WAY

Let Light enfold me
That my inward eye may see clearly
The Path that lies ahead.
Let my mind be opened up
That I may recognise
The signposts along the Way.

Grant me the wisdom
That comes from understanding
The true from the false.
And guide my steps
So that should I falter or stumble,
Tripped by former beliefs
That blind me still
I may go forward with courage
And with the determination
Which persistence bears.

Let me be embraced
With the Love by which
The whole Creation is moved.
The very Essence with which
All things are held together
Dependent yet independent,
Whole yet individuated.
In which all are my relatives.

Let me know the way
That is the Beauty Way
The beautiful way
Where all who will
May Walk in Beauty
And where the end of the Path
Is but a new beginning
To my infinity.
And every new beginning
Another ever-present moment
In Eternity.

74

Components of the NORTH

Totem: Buffalo.
Element: Air.
Colour: White.
Kingdom: Animal.
Quality: Knowledge & Wisdom
Human Aspect: Mind.
Manifestation: Philosophy, Religion,
    Science.
Time: Future.
Heavenly Body: Stars.
Enemy: Certainty.
Season: Winter.
Number: Four.
The Place of Knowledge.

Gateway to the Mind

**Components of
the WEST**

Totem: Grizzly Bear.
Element: Earth.
Colour: Black.
Kingdom: Mineral.
Quality: Introspection
  and Intuition. Change
  and Transition.
Human Aspect: Physical Body.
Manifestation: Magik.
Time: Present.
Heavenly Body: Earth.
Enemy: Powerlessness.
Season: Autumn.
Number: Two.
The Looks-Within Place.

Gateway to the Body

**Components of
the EAST**

Totem: Eagle.
Element: Fire.
Colour: Yellow.
Kingdom: Human.
Quality: Illumination and
  Enlightenment.
Human Aspect: Spirit.
Manifestation: Art, Writing.
Time: Momentary.
Heavenly Body: The Sun.
Enemy: Death and Old Age.
Season: Spring.
Number: One.
The Far-Sighted Place.

Gateway to the Spirit

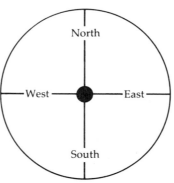

Components of the SOUTH

Totem: Mouse.
Element: Water.
Colour: Red.
Kingdom: Plant.
Quality: Trust & Innocence.
Human Aspect: Emotions.
Manifestation: Music, Song, Dance.
Time: Past.
Heavenly Body: Moon.
Enemy: Fear.
Season: Summer.
Number: Three.
The Close-to Place.

Gateway to the Emotions

∘*Fig. 17. Components of the Basic 4-Directions Medicine Wheel*

Introduction To Part Two

BEFORE YOU SET OUT ON THE practical work in Part Two, let me give you a brief guide to the journey we shall be taking along Four Paths of the Medicine Way so that you can see it in perspective. I must emphasise that the journey cannot be completed in a single session or in a single day. It requires a series of sessions over several days, or even weeks, for it cannot be hurried. I cannot set time limits, for on the Medicine Way you go at your own pace. You need to spend sufficient time on each directional path to absorb something of the qualities each has to offer. Practical work is given on each Path as a powerful learning aid. Just reading it will certainly be 'interesting', but like most shamanic work you need to *do* it to *know* it. Knowledge, realisation, illumination, comes from the actual *performance* of this work. Similarly, 'Adventure Tasks' are preparations for what lies ahead. Skip them and you will miss out on some valuable experiences. Do them and the range of your awareness will be gradually extended as your inner senses are awakened or enlivened from their dormancy.

The journey begins in the *South* because although we actually incarnate in the Centre, we grow in our mother's womb in the 'South' and are born there. You will see from the Chart on opposite page that the South is the direction of our Past and it is the Place for getting close to all living things. The special quality of the South is 'Trust and Innocence' which has to be applied in order to be obtained in greater abundance. That means approaching the teachings with an open mind, unhampered by any preconceived notions, theories and beliefs. This does not mean abandoning your beliefs — merely setting them aside for a while so you can consider new ideas with an unprejudiced mind and one that is free from making judgments or comparisons. 'Innocence' implies not looking at things with the cynicism and suspicion of the disillusioned adult whose dreams have not materialised, but with the hopeful anticipation of a child, expecting the best, and having an intrinsic faith that all things work together for one's ultimate good.

In the South you are going to identify with things that have caused you pain, discomfort and disappointment in the past and which somehow affect you even now. Then you are going to let them go from your life so that no longer will they cause you suffering.

In the South you are going to learn how to free yourself from those dependencies and attachments that have fettered you and discover how to release yourself from past mistakes that have locked you into a recurring cycle from which there appears to be no escape. By clearing yourself of the encumbrances of the Past you will then be free to begin to become what you want to be.

Before journeying to the West, which is the Looks-Within Place, you will pause at the Centre, the place of stillness where energy is generated from within. Your period at the Centre will be contemplative rather than active – a period of thoughtful consideration between directional 'working' Units. The 'working' Units in Part Two are assigned odd numbers, and the contemplative Units, even numbers.

In the *West* you will examine the qualities of Change and Death, discover how you can face your own death as an 'adviser' rather than an enemy, and come to recognise that every change is the death of what has gone before, so deaths are not endings but transitions to new beginnings. It is in the West that you learn not to fear death.

You will pause at the Centre again to contemplate a new topic before moving to the *East* – the Far-Sighted Place – where you will come to see things in their wider perspective and come to appreciate how everything 'fits together' like a jigsaw puzzle or giant tapestry. The East is the Direction of Enlightenment and Illumination, so it is here that you can seek a vision of your own true purpose.

There will be another topic for you to contemplate in the Centre before you move *North*, the Place of Knowledge and Wisdom. It is here that you will seek to bring into manifestation the vision you have gained about yourself and to turn ideas into actions that will bring about the changes you desire in your life.

Finally, you will complete your journey of the Medicine Way in the *Centre* where you can assume full responsibility for your own life. No longer a victim of circumstances, no longer ruled by 'fate' or 'destiny', no longer the puppet of others. You will have arrived at the end of your journey – the Place of Realisation. But it will not be the end – only a new beginning on the Medicine Way.

'Walking', or rather, 'working' a Direction does not mean that you are dealing with a physical area indicated by a coloured stone! Each marker serves as an orientation 'switch' to trigger a response on the inner planes. What you are truly concerning yourself with is the way the Essence of Being is expressed as seen from different viewpoints.

In working a Direction you should have your back to the direction concerned. A reason for this is that as a general rule you put yourself into alignment with the flow of expressions, qualities and effects of cosmic forces, natural powers and essences rather than facing or confronting them. It can be compared to swimming with the tide rather than against it or across it.

As the South path is the one we are going to 'walk' first, you should arrange your room so that you can be facing North and with the South behind you. If it is physically not possible because of space limitations, just *assume* you are facing North. Spread your cloth on the working surface in front of you. Place the green stone in the centre. The yellow (East) stone should be placed to its right about 15 cm (6 inches) away. Next, place the black (West) stone a similar distance to the left of the centre stone. The red (South) stone should be placed about 15 cm in front of the centre one. Finally, place the white (North) stone a similar distance behind the centre stone. (This is the 1-2-3-4 order on the 20 Count).

If you have the stones for the non-cardinal points these can now be placed in this sequence: southeast, southwest, northwest and northeast. If you have not yet obtained these stones proceed without them.

This simple set-up serves as a model of the larger version. If you were working with a larger Wheel you would physically move around the circle aligning yourself with the direction with which you were working. In the case of this smaller representation you simply move around the cloth, and if space does not permit you to do this, just move the stones around so that the one for the direction you are working is immediately in front of you. To begin with, this will be the red (South) stone. What is important is to have a clear mental picture that you are working an intended direction even if the physical representation is not in accordance with literal compass points.

Imagine the circle you have just constructed is the base or floor of a transparent dome. The other half of the dome lies 'underneath' it to complete a globe or transparent, invisible 'bubble'. It might be likened to a space capsule with you – or rather your consciousness – inside it like an astronaut about to be launched on a journey, not into Outer Space but to Inner Space.

In your mind's eye see the North, South, East and West markers as the outermost points of conduits running across the floor to the green marker which is a sort of central console. Imagine also that inside the dome is a pyramid whose apex point meets near the top of the dome and whose square base is so arranged that each of the four sides faces a cardinal direction. The top of the pyramid points upwards to the Sky, the Sun and the Stars, above, and is a reception point for directing in the masculine polarity of the Yang. Below is a mirror image with the tip of an inverted pyramid directed downwards to the Earth and to the female polarity which is Yin.

As a preliminary to any work with the Medicine Wheel, American Indians performed a simple aura-cleansing and atmosphere-purifying ceremony called 'smudging'. Liken it to washing the hands before a meal, or taking a shower to freshen up after a day's work, or opening a window to blow away stale air. 'Smudging' is a technique of using smoke from burning sage to clear away negative energies from the human aura and the immediate surroundings. 'Smudge' smoke has a pleasant aroma that is quite different from incense which, for most people, has religious or occult overtones.

Sage is a most important herb. It has cleansing qualities and disperses negative energies. The Amerindian medicine man also regarded it as a healing herb for clearing the respiratory passages. It was sometimes referred to as an 'ear opener' because, in addition to the physical ears which deal with sound vibrations carried through the air, the human being has 'inner' ears that hear the thoughts, one's inner dialogue, and also telepathic messages from other humans, from animals, plants, rocks and the 'voices' of Nature, and sage was said to open up these 'inner' ears.

Sometimes other herbs were added – cedar and sweetgrass. Cedar brings in positive energies and sweetgrass brings the blessing of a clear mind for it stimulates the brain. Sweetgrass is not easily obtainable outside the Americas, but lavender has similar qualities and can be used as an alternative.

A 'smudge' mix can be prepared by mixing a couple of pinches of cedar chippings and some lavender with a couple of heaped tablespoons of rubbed sage. Rubbed sage is readily obtainable from food shops and supermarkets. Native Americans use smudge in the form of a stick which is made by binding the natural herbs together so they can be held in the hand. These sticks can be obtained by mail order through specialist stockists.

You will need a container in which to burn the herb or in which to rest the smouldering stick after use. A large sea shell – the sort sometimes used as ash trays – a small earthenware bowl, the bottom portion of an incense burner, or even a large ashtray, are quite suitable. You will also need matches or a lighter to ignite the herb and something with which to fan it once it begins to smoulder and to cause it to produce smoke. Indians used a ceremonial fan of feathers, but a single feather will usually suffice, or even a piece of card.

Shamans taught that smudging ensured that an endeavour would be entered into with a heart cleansed of any bad feelings and a mind cleared of

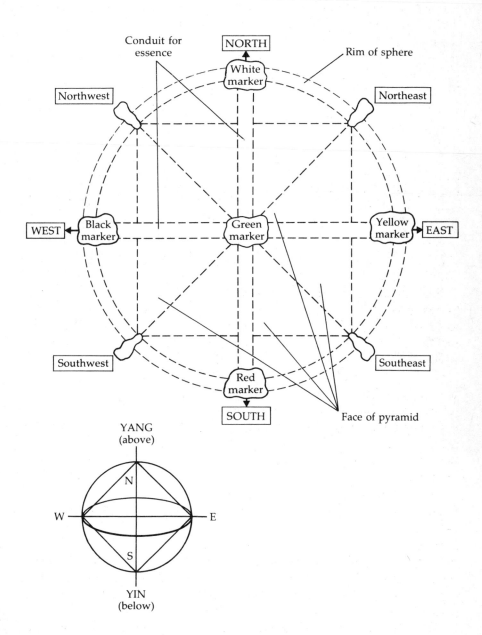

○*Fig. 18. The 'Inner Space' Ship*

negative thoughts. Once you have got together your materials, you can experience for yourself the truth of this teaching in this simple rite or ceremony:

RITE NO.1:

Smudging to cleanse the Aura and the Mind Space

Place a portion of sage or smudge mix into the receptacle you are using as a burner. Light it with a match or lighter and ensure that the mixture is well alight before extinguishing the flame. Hold the burner or herb stick in your left hand and fan the smouldering material vigorously with the fan in your right hand to get it smoking well.

Then fan the smoke towards yourself and breathe in the aroma of the smoke as you do so. The smoke is very gentle and its aroma is pleasant. Fan towards your heart, then towards your throat and up over your face and head and then down toward your legs and feet. Try and visualise drawing the smoke into the aura which surrounds you and interpenetrates your physical body. Repeat these actions four times.

Having smudged yourself the next step is to cleanse, clear and purify the area around you – your Mind space. To do this you fan the smoke away from you and into the direction you are facing.

Start with the East. Smudge the East direction four times and as you do so acknowledge the East and say, aloud or silently:

'SPIRIT OF THE EAST WHERE LIGHT COMES FROM.
GATEWAY OF THE SPIRIT AND OF THE ELEMENT OF FIRE.
ENLIGHTEN ME.'

Turn to your right and smudge the South direction four times, saying:

'SPIRIT OF THE SOUTH WHERE THE SUN IS STRONGEST.
GATEWAY OF THE EMOTIONS AND FEELINGS AND OF THE
ELEMENT OF WATER.
STRENGTHEN ME.'

Turn to the West and smudge four times, saying:
'SPIRIT OF THE WEST WHERE THE SUN SETS.
GATEWAY OF THE BODY AND OF THE ELEMENT OF EARTH.
TRANSFORM ME.'

Then face North, smudge four times and say:
'SPIRIT OF THE NORTH WHERE THE SUN RESTS.

GATEWAY OF THE MIND AND OF THE ELEMENT OF AIR.
INFORM ME.'

Turn right again to face East and smudge the area above your head four times, saying:

'GREAT MASCULINE FORCE BEHIND ALL THAT IS.
GRANDFATHER SKY.
EMPOWER ME'.

Finally, stoop slightly and smudge towards the ground and say:
'GREAT FEMININE FORCE BEHIND ALL THAT IS.
GRANDMOTHER EARTH.
NURTURE ME.'

Should you at some future time work with a group, you would smudge the others in turn, fanning the smoke upwards and over the head and downwards towards the feet four times. Always move in a sun-wise or clockwise direction when performing this rite.

Your aura and the area around you is now cleansed and purified. Put the burner and the fan down in a safe place where the smouldering herbs can safely burn themselves out. Then pause and become aware of the presence of your own Higher Self and of the powers of the universe that are around you and, indeed, flowing through you. Feel yourself immersed in these energies as if you were the smudge smoke.

Now be seated, facing North, with the red marker stone immediately in front of you. (Remember, by facing North you are actually 'sitting' in the South). Relax, and now create your own Mind space, sealing the aura by carrying out the following simple exercise:

EXERCISE NO.3:

Creating Mind Space and Sealing the Aura

Rest the palms of your hands on your knees, close your eyes and imagine yourself inside the globe of your own personal Medicine Wheel. Visualise the direct contact you have with cosmic forces flowing along the conduits to the centre of your globe which is the centre of your own being.

Now breathe in by pushing out the abdomen to take air into the deeper recesses of the lungs and count four seconds. Hold the breath to a count of four, then expel the air by pulling in the abdomen, also to a count of four. Then pause to a count of four before inhaling and repeating the cycle. Do this four times. This is called the four-fold breath and helps to clear the mind as well as relax the body.

Consider the globe around you as the clear outer envelope of your aura. Now, imagine that membrane covering as a hard plastic shield through which no unwanted influences or harmful energies can penetrate. Concentrate on this for a few moments. Then take four more four-fold breaths to confirm your activity. Your aura is then sealed, for the power of your thought will have performed the sealing. You will have built around you a shield that allows through only positive light energies but which will screen out negative or destructive influences. Now open your eyes.

Although this may seem simplistic, it is a technique that is in accordance with a cosmic law that energy follows thought. After you have practised this exercise a few times you will be able to perform it with little conscious effort. So practise it before you proceed to Unit One.

Unit One examines in turn each of twelve 'components' of the South. After you have read the portion dealing with a component, spend time meditating on the ideas and concepts presented. Have a notebook and pen by your side so you can make notes of thoughts and impressions that come into your mind. Complete also the Directional Quest and Give-Away before moving on to the next Unit.

I must stress that the meditation is not for the purpose of establishing mental agreement with what has been read. What you are being encouraged to do is to open up your inner senses and to establish contact with your own Spirit Self on the inner planes, for your own High Self is the true teacher. The thoughts and ideas presented are primers to enable this process to take place.

I cannot advise on a precise time to allow for each working. It may be as little as half an hour, an hour or much more. Do not hurry in an attempt to complete a whole Unit in a single sitting. Progress at your own pace. You will know when a period is enough.

The smudging rite should be performed before any Medicine Wheel sitting or working.

Attributes of the South

BEFORE EXAMINING EACH OF THE twelve 'components' of the South, try to sense – as you are sitting in the Place of the South – something of the power of the Spirit of the South. Make it your desire to connect with it, to feel its energies and to experience its qualities. This is a power that cannot be confined within an object or made the possession of a person. It is a power that by its very nature *moves*. Its might, strength and vigour can be absorbed because it is a power that flows through you and around you.

The South is the Path of Trust and Innocence and is sometimes referred to as the Way of the Child, so to walk it we need to reawaken the 'child' within us – that part of us that can establish relationships through exercising the faith, trust and innocence we once had as a child when we looked upon life with wonder and to the future with excited anticipation.

The South is the direction to help you to see things in clear detail and to begin to perceive your own nature. The ancient admonition, 'Man, Know Thyself' went much further than advocating a course in psychological analysis. It meant getting to know the Self for what it truly is – for the Self is the most sacred and precious thing any of us has. This was fully understood by the Masters of Wisdom whose admonishment that to love others you must first learn to love your Self implied the discovery of the highest aspect of your own being. The journey in the South is where the process of finding your True Self begins. In the South you are going to rid yourself of the encumbrances that obscure your True Self and prevent you from seeing your own Self in its true light.

Twelve 'components' of the South which we are going to consider are:

1. *Quality*: Trust and Innocence.
2. *Totem*: Mouse.
3. *Element*: Water.
4. *Colour*: Red.
5. *Kingdom*: Plant.
6. *Heavenly Body*: The Moon.

7. *Human Aspect*: Emotions.
8. *Time Period*: The Past.
9. *Season*: Summer.
10. *Numbers*: Three (....) and Thirteen.
11. *Enemy*: Fear.
12. *Manifestation*: Music.

1. *Quality of the South*: TRUST AND INNOCENCE

The Amerindian sometimes referred to the South as 'the way of the child' because it was associated with the child who was growing in body and mind towards maturity, yet still retaining an attitude of trust and innocence, unblemished by the cynicism, arrogance and insensitiveness of the world of the adult. You can align yourself with the special quality of the South by refusing to allow yourself to be tainted by the cynicism or arrogance that stem from a belief that you 'know it' already, and by refusing to be stained by guilt and embarrassment.

The Spirit of the South helps you to acquire things of a spiritual and lasting value and, like a child, to grow quickly towards maturity. But this spiritual maturity can come only through adopting an attitude of trust and innocence. Then will follow an understanding of one's true identity and an acceptance, as a spiritual 'adult', of control over one's own destiny.

The quality of Trust and Innocence required is not the misplaced trust and innocence of naïvity and immaturity, but the kind which makes learning an adventure, finds excitement in discovery and joy in the awareness that new knowledge brings. It means not allowing the illusory fears, false values, double standards and guilt complexes of adulthood to spoil and mar your progress.

It means trusting your own instincts and not being swayed by what others may think or say.

Observe the way the young, innocent child enjoys the sheer experience of living and how quickly and readily it learns from every new adventure, and you will begin to appreciate the meaning of the quality of the South.

You need to regain some of the wonder and excitement you had as a child and to apply it to the process of living. Then you will have acquired a zest for life that comes from being aware that life is intended to be a wonder-ful experience to be savoured and enjoyed, not just tolerated or suffered and endured.

Take time now to absorb yourself in the quality of the South.

2. *Totem of the South*: MOUSE

According to some Amerindian stories, there was a time long ago when animals and humans talked together, understood each others' ways and even helped one another. Perhaps the animal stories of our own childhood in which animals talked like humans contain an element of some race memory in the mind of the authors.

For a very long time animals in the wild have suffered a great deal at the hands of humans and show an understandable instinct for survival by being frightened as soon as a human approaches. Only domestic animals are treated with some respect, but many of these are so pampered that they have been deprived of their dignity as animals.

Animals can 'speak' to us if we will listen. They speak, not by using human words as in the children's stories, but by their habits and manners, though they can also communicate thoughts telepathically. Each species of animal accomplishes what is necessary for it to achieve by applying a particular attitude or approach. If we wish to assume a similar attitude or approach in human terms we can do so by learning from the animals. This attribute was a feature of self-development among the Amerindians. Let me now use the mouse as an example.

The mouse is an animal associated with the South. The mouse may appear to be a rather unsuitable creature to have as a totem and especially as a teacher, but to the Indian every animal had something of value to impart and mouse was certainly no exception. So don't underestimate little mouse, neither be afraid of him, for he can have much wisdom in store for you. Mouse personifies the characteristics of becoming aware of things through getting close to them – by feeling and by touch – for the mouse is very sensitive to its surroundings through its special organs of touch: its whiskers. A mouse perceives by its closeness to things and by its feeling towards them, and the South teaches us to do the same.

As we discovered earlier, the power of the South is in growth and trust. It is a power that teaches us to grow rapidly spiritually while learning to trust our intuitive feelings. Our feelings and our intuitive senses should have developed alongside our physical growth, but in modern societies we are often advised not to trust our feelings, and intuition is regarded almost as a superstition. Actually, intuition is no such thing. It is an inner teacher that ignorance has denied us or bigotry has stifled. Little mouse is teaching that feeling and intuition often precede discovery. Think about that.

The power of the South emphasises the importance of examining your own feelings and emotions and being guided by them. That does not mean being controlled by them, but letting them flow – not holding on to them and bottling them up.

Study what you can about little mouse. Go to a good reference library and consult books which contain information about the habits and characteristics of the animal. Apply what positive attributes you discover to the human condition. There is often much truth contained within children's stories in which mouse figures as a character. Authors of such stories often write inspirationally, unconsciously drawing not from their own memory bank of life experience but from deeper levels of the mind — from what the pioneer psychologist Carl Jung described as the collective unconscious.

3. *Element of the South*: WATER

We can learn more about the Spirit of the South and the way its essence is expressed through the Element with which it is associated in American Indian cosmology — Water. As we discovered earlier, an element is not the physical substance which bears its name, but rather the essence or spirit which characterises that physical substance. Physical water is fluid and fluidity is a characteristic of Elemental Water. Water flows downwards from one level to another and if poured into a container will immediately assume the shape of its mould. Elemental Water is like that, immediately assuming the 'shape' of the Thought Form which provides the matrix of what is to become a physical manifestation.

Water is the great 'in-between' — the medium between solidity and radiance — for physical water can be solidified into ice or transformed through fire into vapour and then radiant energy. Elemental Water, too, is in-between the radiance of Fire and the mobility of Air on the one hand and the inertia of Earth on the other. Without the flowing, penetrating movement of water, the Earth would dry up and become barren, and nothing would grow. Without the flow of emotions human beings, too, become 'dried up', brittle and barren.

Our emotions and feelings are an expression of Elemental Water. Emotion is energy that can be felt, that touches the heart — the Spirit — which is why it is frequently mistaken for love. The association of water with emotion is reflected in such sayings as 'floods of emotion' and 'waters of compassion'. Love must be allowed to flow, too. It should not be bottled up or it will stagnate and even turn sour. So your love must flow. Let it move gently in the direction of those you care for. Don't try to contain it. Let your true feelings find expression. Look for ways of letting your loved ones know you care about them.

Don't confuse loving with liking. Love is essentially a spiritual force, not a mental and physical activity. Contrary to popular belief, you don't have to 'like' someone to express loving concern for them. Love desires only what is in the best interests of the one or ones to whom it is being expressed. It desires only their good. That is what Jesus meant by his admonition to love one another. For love is a healing balm that soothes and comforts, harmonises and bonds. It is one of the Great Powers of the cosmos. Liking, on the other hand, has to do with the mind. It implies being pleased with the object of one's liking. It is finding something or someone agreeable, congenial, compatible. We choose the things we like and to be with people we like, which is an activity of the mind. Love is of the heart so you don't need to 'like' someone to show love towards them. Love is essentially an activity of the spirit.

Applied to the emotions, water suggests depth of feeling but its negative polarity would be ineffectuality. People who display negative aspects of water in their actions are sometimes referred to as 'wets' or 'drips', suggesting a formlessness that lacks directing or channelling power. People who are 'soppy' are reflecting a negative quality of Water in a stagnant state for they have allowed themselves to be absorbed and saturated by their own emotional energy and are projecting that clammy experience outwardly. The negative aspects of water can be destructive, erosive and divisive for it can dilute, dissolve and break down whatever it penetrates. In its positive aspect, water is life-giving, nourishing, refreshing, soothing and protecting. These positive and negative qualities can be applied to the 'water of emotions' too, for emotional effects can be healing and restoring, comforting and calming, and they can be disturbing and upsetting, violent and destructive.

The ancients regarded water as a feminine aspect of the Source of life and associated it with fertility. To them a spring mothered the stream and the stream gave birth to the lake, so water was understood to be an expression of the yin process.

Water is used by a shaman as a great healing agent. It dissolves and carries away impurities to where they can do no harm – usually being returned to the Earth for transmutation to the original elements from which they came.

4. Colour of the South: RED

Colour is a way of making connections at all levels for colour has a powerful influence and can affect us positively or negatively, physically, emotionally, mentally and spiritually. Changing the colours of the decor in our home or at work can bring about a marked change in the way we feel in these places. We may enjoy doing certain tasks in a particular room rather than another and that may be due to the atmosphere created by its decor as well as the direction the room faces. Some colours or shades of colour are restful and relaxing, others are stimulating and exciting to our energy-system.

Red is the colour usually associated with the South on the Medicine Wheel because it is the colour of oxygenated life blood and therefore represents life, vitality, health and vigour. In its positive aspect, Red is the colour related to strength, courage, physical energy and sexual potency. Red is the colour of passions so it can be volatile and in its negative mode is associated with lust, anger and malice. Red is warm, the colour of the South where the Sun is at its peak at midday in the Northern hemisphere.

Red-skinned people reflect something of the qualities of the South, for they, too, are warm and have an apparent child-like simplicity and a trusting nature. American Indians indicate this in the way they learn best — through play and in singing, dancing and chanting. Indeed, singing, chanting and dancing are ways of attuning to the powers of the South.

5. *Kingdom of the South*: THE PLANT KINGDOM

If you refer to the Basic Alchemy Wheel on p. 58 you will see that the South is the Realm of GIVING. It is the Place of the GIVERS, and the Plants are the great givers of energy. Plants and trees give themselves to the planet. They give themselves as food and shelter to the creatures of the Animal and Human kingdoms. They give beauty, harmony and balance to the soil in which they are rooted and to the whole environment in which they live.

Plants can do almost anything an animal can do, except more slowly. According to Professor Malcolm Wilkins, of Glasgow University's botany department, plants can count, tell the time, ask for water and respond to sound. Furthermore, they have a memory, a nervous system, colour vision and a sense of taste.

You can learn much about the Spirit and the Soul from the Plant kingdom. Plants 'recognise' their true parents as the Sun and the Earth, and rely on them with the trust of an innocent child. Each plant begins life as a seed of the plant that lives before it. It is nurtured in the darkness of the womb of the Earth until the Sun activates the nutritive substances within so that it can sprout and penetrate the surface of the Earth to absorb the sunlight, grow, develop and reach maturity to seed itself and ensure the continuity of life, living in trust that the Sun and the Earth will care for it.

The South is the direction to learn about the Plant kingdom, not just by 'book' learning, though that can help you to identify different plants, trees, shrubs and flowers, but by coming to know the Plant kingdom through being a Spiritual Adventurer. You need to come to recognise that plants and trees are living things and once you come to develop an affinity with plants you will find that they will respond to you. You might even discover that you have acquired 'green fingers'.

Notice how plants thrive in a happy and harmonious atmosphere, but seem to wither and die in a negative or turbulent environment or one where there is pain and suffering. The condition of house plants in any home can tell you much about the people living there. So can the front and rear gardens.

It is to the Plant kingdom that we turn to discover the *Great Healers*, for plants and trees are the restorers of harmony and balance to the Mineral kingdom which is 'below' them in evolution and which they control, live on, transmute and express at a higher level of vibration. Because of their ability to communicate with Nature and their close observation of the natural environment, the American Indians had an extensive knowledge of what is referred to today as 'folk medicine'. Indeed, the folk medicine which forms an important part of what has become known as 'Alternative Medicine', particularly in the United States, embraces much of what were the natural healing remedies of the Indians. Regretfully, as with other things, little credit was ever given to the Indians. It was centuries before serious attention was given to native American curative skills and then, according to V. J. Vogel in his book *North American Indian Medicine*,[1] 'an astonishing number of Indian drugs were found to be of enormous value'. Dr. Frederick Banting, the discoverer of insulin, credited Indian healers with the 'pharmaceutical spadework' which led to it.

In 1787 a German physician, Dr Johann David Schopt, published a list of more than 300 vegetable remedies in use in the eastern United States, many of which were reputedly learned from native Americans. Furthermore, more than 200 indigenous drugs in use by one or more of the principal tribes have been listed in *The Pharmacopoeia of the United States of America* since it first appeared in 1820 and in the *National Formulary* since it began in 1888.

The fact is that American Indians had a profound knowledge of their native flora, though much of it was obscured by those who labelled such healing remedies as 'irrational'. A similar attitude has been taken by orthodoxy towards 'Alternative Medicine'. Let me take one example. Because chemical analysis of flower remedies developed by the late Dr Edward Bach, a renowned London physician and bacteriologist, failed to trace a physical substance in the remedies other than water and a preserving liquid, they were largely ignored by orthodox practitioners. The healing agent in each remedy, however, is not a physical substance but the unseen life force of the plant itself. The remedies are produced homeopathically, relying on energies whose potency increases as dilution increases.

Again, those using the materialistic approach fell into the trap of believing that if a thing cannot be seen or measured it cannot exist. But the Indian understood the power of life force in all living things, particularly with the Plant kingdom, and worked with it.

We are here concerned with exploring something of the inner nature of the Plant Kingdom and its value in healing, and an insight into the Bach remedies may help to further that understanding.

Dr Bach gave up his Harley Street practice in 1930 to carry out full-time research into a method of restoring physical health through the application of remedies which he had discovered in the Plant kingdom and which were prescribed *according to the patient's state of mind* – be it fear, anger, depression, jealousy or lethargy – rather than to a physical complaint. 'Treat the patient, not the disease' became the dictum of what became known as the Bach Flower Remedies, a method which is now established in what I prefer to call *Complementary* Medicine, as a natural way of healing through the personality and harmonising its expression within its physical vehicle – the body – by the use of the essences of wild flowers, trees and shrubs.

The Bach Remedies make use of the characterised life force of the plant – its essential energy – rather than its physical material as is the case in herbal medicine or with drugs. The plant's characterised life force is extracted in a particular way and stored in preserving liquid. Dr Bach categorised the most common inharmonious states of mind or moods affecting mankind like fear, loneliness, uncertainty, over-sensitivity, despondency, over-concern, and so on, and discovered a remedy for each of them.

These remedies treat the psychological cause – that is, the unseen cause – with an unseen energy (the very essence of the plant) and once the psychological condition is neutralised the physical effect will disappear and harmony will be restored. Shock, for instance, whether through an accident, a financial crisis or an emotional upheaval, might manifest as say, pleurisy or even cancer. Self-pity might manifest as backache or even facial spots, depending on the reaction in the individual. Red Chestnut was found to be effective for anxiety; Larch for feelings of inadequacy; Sweet Chestnut for anguish; Wild Rose for apathy; Olive for physical and mental exhaustion; Gorse for chronic depression; Holly for anger and bitterness, and so on.

Dr Bach discovered what native Americans had known for thousands of years – that physical disorders are caused through a way of life that conflicts with Nature. It is the turbulence brought about in the psyche at a subtle level that manifests as physical disorder. The condition may be erased and healed through the contact made with the natural world, whose characterised life force brings the psyche back into harmony. Look into the Bach flower remedies.[2]

Let me explain a little more about *flowers*. The reason that flowers enhance the atmosphere and pleasure the senses is that their vibrations are intended to be food for the *Spirit!* That is why it feels good to have flowers around you. That is why receiving flowers brings joy to the heart of any woman for they bring an instant reaction of the Spirit (women are usually more receptive of subtle vibrations than men). Flowers are associated with love. Why? Simply because flowers are a physical manifestation of divine love, and because flowers have great soothing and harmonising qualities.

The scent of flowers can be considered to etherialise the rock, soil and mineral substances which the plant has transmuted through itself and raised to the highest level of vibration. Flowers represent the perfection of the cycle of birth, change and death, for the seed is the result of a flower's death — a death that leaves an impression to forever carry on, for the seed contains within it the memory of the original spark of Creation. The essential purpose of plants is to express a thought in the Mind of the Great Spirit *in one place*. They do not move, but express most especially the qualities of the place where they are.

Get to know *herbs*, too. Learn how to use herbs in cooking. They will not only enhance your meals and make them more enjoyable but improve the chemical balance in your body also.

Consider herbal remedies when your body is out of balance. A medical herbalist makes use of whole plants in dispensing remedies to restore health and this is another area of Complementary Medicine.

Trees can be great teachers, too. Indeed, trees are magnificent. They purify the atmosphere, breathing out the life-giving oxygen that sustains us and breathing in the carbon dioxide which is our waste product. Trees can be likened to the lungs of the Earth. A tree is so stable, solid and 'down to earth' yet it reaches up to the heavenly realm. Make friends with trees. A tree has so much to *give* you, so much to tell you, if you will let it.

Find a copse or a spinney or some woodland near your home. If you live in a city, go to a park where there are trees. If necessary travel out of town to a country spot where you can spend some time among trees. Feel how enjoyable, how peaceful and relaxing it is just to be among trees. Open up your senses to them. Put aside your inhibitions, ignore your fears about what others might say and go and hug a tree! Put your arms around it and rest your forehead on its trunk. Think lovingly towards it and you will soon come to realise that a tree is indeed a living thing.

Trees have a 'High' Self like humans have, but theirs is more readily discerned as being like a Group Soul. It, too, exists in another dimension and has a benign influence on the world. The Group Soul may embrace just a few trees or very many and could extend over a large area. Chopping down whole rain forests has a debilitating effect on the whole planet and is like depriving a human being of part of a lung. Billions of years of evolution on this planet has made the Group Souls of plants and trees more highly evolved within their own path of evolution on this planet than is man.

Here is an Experiment you can perform while you are working the South Direction.

EXERCISE NO.4:

Communicating with Trees

As soon as convenient, go out and find yourself a tree which you can sit against quietly and undisturbed for half an hour or so. If you have a garden with trees, or can find a secluded spot in woodland, perhaps, all well and good. But if not, a tree in a public park will suffice as long as it is away from noise and distraction.

Choose a tree that is good and solid, like an oak, a pine or silver birch, and sit on the ground with your back firmly pressed against its trunk. Once you are comfortable, close your eyes and relax. Don't think about anything in particular. Just let go.

Before long you will feel any tension and uptightness drain from you. You will feel a comfortable warmth – a sort of glowing sensation – and it will be accompanied by a feeling of stability and security, the calmness of *well-being*. That comes from the tree.

Now extend that sensation to all that is around you. Appreciate the rich, earthy smell of the ground beneath you. Breathe in the fragrance of the grass, shrubs and trees. Listen to the sound of Nature. If you are fortunate enough to have found a spot away from any sound of civilisation, you will sense a feeling of actually being a *part* of Nature rather than being separated or isolated from it. Drink it all in. Savour it. Extend all your senses.

When you feel it is time to go, slip off your shoes and stand barefoot if possible so that you make contact with the Earth. Feel it beneath your bare feet and enjoy the sensation for a few moments. Then, before leaving, put your arms around the tree trunk and give it a hug, thanking the tree as you do so for the magikal moments you have just enjoyed in communion with Nature.

If you practise this a few times you might one day experience the tree 'talking' to you. Trees *talk*? Surely, your Surface Mind will be telling you, that's *ridiculous*. I thought so, too. 'Trees *talk*?' I must have expressed my own disbelief when I put that question one day to Silver Bear who had spoken to me as if they do. He answered quite simply, 'Go listen to the trees.'

I went to a nearby forest, found myself a secluded spot and set aside my own cynicism, deciding to approach in 'Trust and Innocence' and work the South Direction with my back against a tree. I closed my eyes and as I sat there with my mind stilled I experienced a sensation of travelling backwards. It was like being on a train with my back to the engine and everything receding away from me. I opened my eyes because the sensation was quite peculiar. I was immediately aware of how tall the trees were ahead of me. Their uppermost branches were dancing in the soft breeze and I observed that they were tracing circles in the sky as they were being moved by the wind, yet their trunks, of course, remained firm and unmoved, rooted in the same spot.

'You are That which turns and moves without leaving where You are.'

Those words came into my mind with a sudden impact. They were not my words. It was not 'my' thought. 'What on earth does that mean?' I asked myself. Then thoughts came tumbling through my mind as if inspired by the trees as their tops circled and swayed.

'You are always where you are Now, though You, too, move in circles as you respond to the currents of energy in which You are immersed. You are constantly moving and tracing Your circles of energy as you dance in the winds of change, just like us. And just like us, you are always where you are – Here, Now.'

The trees were talking to me and likening my spiritual life with their life. The Real Me – the Real You – stays always rooted in the ever-present Now like a tree rooted in its place on the ground. The tree experiences travelling in circles by moving its branches in the air. Our lives travel in circles moved by the Spirit. Part of the purpose of life is to *experience* – to see and be seen, to listen and to be heard, to touch and to be touched, to love and to be loved. And the Spirit is the guide.

It was an overwhelming experience, but not an isolated one. A few days later I returned to this very same spot and tried again. When I opened my eyes I became aware for the first time of a small tree among those tall trees just ahead of me. Fancy my not noticing that tree before. 'What are you trying to tell me, little tree?' I asked almost instinctively.

Then into my mind came these words: 'You are like me – the little tree. You have been here before and never even noticed me. And you have not noticed the Real You before. The Real You has been obscured by everything else that looms so large around it, just as you let all these tall trees obscure me so you didn't even notice that I was here.'

I observed that the little tree had green leaves. It was winter and all the trees around it were now bare. So it was an evergreen, always in leaf when other trees are dormant. Just at that moment the sunlight sparkled on the moisture on its leaves and they twinkled and glistened like diamonds as the globules of water captured the sunlight.

'Your Real Self is loaded with precious jewels, too, and they will sparkle and glisten and come alive if you will let the light of the Sun get at them, too.'

Can trees talk to us? I would no longer put such a question to my Indian mentors. If you are open to being taught by Nature, go listen to the trees.

Then in the Plant kingdom there are also the *grasses*, which form a carpet for our feet and a blanket for us to lie on. The soil is the skin of the Earth Mother and the grass is like the hair which grows on your arms!

Take off your shoes and socks or tights and enjoy the soft caress of grass under your feet. Stroke it with your hands with the soft, gentle touch of a lover, and the Earth herself will respond to you because she feels through the plants which grow on and in her.

Do all these things and you will be making your connections with the Plant Kingdom.

6. *Heavenly Body of the South*: THE MOON

The Heavenly Body associated with the South is the Moon. The Moon is closely linked with Water because the Moon cycles have such a powerful effect on water and more than 70 per cent of the Earth's surface is water. Water is present in everything. Even in the driest desert there is some. There is no life without it.

As the Moon's magnetic influence on the Earth causes the rise and fall of vast oceans, so this gravitational pull affects living things, including ourselves, for the human body, too, is composed of more than 70 per cent water. Even the brain is a mass of semi-liquid pulp and is affected by the Moon's tides.

We live our lives within a vast invisible force matrix of energy patterns which affect or influence our growth and development. Some of these energy patterns are harmonious and therefore helpful but others are disharmonious and even destructive. Some influence growth and development, others have a contrary effect and are involved in breaking down and dissolving.

The Moon has a tremendous effect on the Earth, on ourselves, and on all living things during its orbit of approximately 29 days round the Earth. This cycle is a measurement of Time – a month or 'moonth', a single revolution of the Moon round the Earth. The gravitational power of the Moon, combined with the movement of the Earth, causes the rise and fall of massive expanses of water in the oceans and the fluctuation of the tides. It influences the flow of sap in trees and plants. It affects body fluids in the human being, including the rhythm of the blood, the female menstruation cycle and gestation. It affects the fluids of the brain.

The gravitational effect varies in accordance with the Moon's distance from the Earth. The Moon follows an elliptical orbit, so it appears at its largest when it is closest to the Earth, when its power is more than 25 per cent stronger than when it appears at its smallest. There is also a variation in its height in the sky because the Moon's orbit is not parallel with the Earth's equator, so it appears to 'wobble' and be higher in the sky at some times than at others.

By becoming aware of the pulse of the vibratory force field and gravitational pull of the Moon and of the electro-magnetic force of light reflected to the Earth through the phases of the Moon, we can synchronise our own activities with the ebb and flow of these invisible and visible energy forces and thus become attuned to and work with lunar power.

There are four stages of the varying degrees of reflected light from the Moon – four phases which indicate the way the unseen Forces are working.

The first stage is the *Dark Moon* when the Moon is not visible because it is rising in almost the same place as the Sun. This phase lasts for four days and is followed by the New Moon when a thin crescent appears. The second stage is when the Moon is *Waxing* and appears to be getting fatter. This mode lasts for eleven days. The third stage is the *Full Moon*, the period of greatest light, and this lasts for three days with the night of the Full Moon falling on the third day. The fourth stage is the *Waning Moon* when the Moon appears to be getting thinner until it is reduced to a narrow crescent. This stage lasts for eleven days.

These four phases indicate the way the light energies are working. The *Dark Moon* is when they are at rest or withdrawn. This is a time for exploring possibilities, for meditation and contemplation, but not for action.

The Waxing Moon is when the energies are fast-flowing and moving towards us. So the New Moon is a good time to start a new project or launch a new idea and to push forward with it as the tide of energies continues to build up. The Waxing Moon is also the time to plant things that grow upwards towards the light. It is also the time to work on those things that we want to attract and bring into our lives.

The Full Moon is when the Influences reach their climax and culmination, so it is the time for completing things, and for bringing things to perfection. With the Full Moon, Nature reaches a crescendo of activity so it is a time of fulfilment.

The Waning Moon is the mode of outgoing activity when the energies are flowing away from us like the ebb of the sea tides. So this is the period for getting rid of things and for letting go of circumstances that have fulfilled their purpose. It is the time for giving out to others the benefits that we have derived from our experiences and from our own efforts. The waning Moon is the time to plant things that grow downwards.

The Dark Moon is the time for resting from such activity and considering the lessons learned from them. And so the cycle begins again.

My book, *Earth Medicine*,[3] explains in detail how to harmonise with these Influences and operate these modes.

The cyclic pattern of the Moon's modes produces the pattern of the rhythms of planet Earth. The eleven days of the waxing Moon is like an in-breathing, the three days of the Full Moon of holding the breath, the eleven days of the waning Moon is like an exhalation, and the four days of the Dark Moon is like a pause before the next inhalation. To put ourselves in harmony with the Moon's cycle has the effect of putting us in harmony with Mother Earth and synchronising us with the Earth's pulse.

7. *Human Aspect of the South*: THE EMOTIONS

Because of their fluidity, the human emotions are likened to water, and both Water and the Emotions are components of the South. A dictionary definition of the word emotion is 'agitation or disturbance of the mind'. According to this definition, emotion is mind-energy in motion — the energy of the mind taking in or giving out impressions through feeling. Or to put it another way, an emotion is mind-energy that can be *felt*. It is mind-energy that touches the Spirit — the heart — and we are consciously aware of it through feelings.

Emotion is thus a powerful driving force and it is also an urge for expression. Like water, it can be stirred up and become murky and out of control. When in this condition it can be debilitating, even destructive, and the mind can no longer see clearly through the screen of distortions and confusions. Like water, it can roar and rush away affecting everything in its path unless it can be controlled. We either control our emotions and direct them or they control us.

Emotions are linked with the Past – which is another component of the South – and with attachments to people, to objects, and to conditions. Emotions have an affinity with the colour Red – the colour of strong energy expressed on the physical plane. To prevent ourselves from being tossed to and fro on a sea of emotions, we need to free ourselves from past attachments which limit and inhibit us – which cause us emotional pain in the Present and which promise further suffering in the Future. That will be the purpose of the Adventurer Task at the end of this Unit.

8. *Time Period of the South*: THE PAST

The South direction emphasises past activity. Keep in mind that you are on the Medicine Way in order to obtain knowledge and encounter experiences that will teach you self-mastery and lead you to the enlightenment you seek. So on the Path of the South you need to review your past 'close-to' – to put it under close scrutiny so you can see how much you are shackled by past conditioning, what may be holding you in a rut from which there appears to be no escape, and to discover how you can free yourself from them.

Most emotional traumas we suffer have their origins in the experiences of the past. By holding on to the past we ensure that they are continually repeated. The solution can be found in a recognition of the ever-present Now! The past is what has already been, the present is what has become, and the future is what is becoming. By disposing of the garbage of the past we can change the direction of the Now and the essence of the future.

9. *Season of the South*: SUMMER

The season attributed to the South is Summer because it is the season of rapid growth and therefore can be likened to childhood and youth. Learning is at a faster rate during childhood than during any other phase of life. If you are persistent and determined in your efforts to progress along the Medicine Way, it will be noticeable how you have 'grown' and how much new knowledge you have acquired in a comparatively short period of time, just by completing the South Path indicated in these pages.

10. *Number of the South*: THREE (....)

Each direction on the Medicine Wheel is allocated numbers on the Twenty Count. The numbers one to ten are concerned with the 'outer' manifestations and eleven to twenty with inner realities.

In American Indian symbolism the number three was regarded as the result of the union of masculine and conceptual 'one' with the feminine and receptive 'two'. 'Three' was the 'child' of the union of 'one' and 'two' so it had a youthful quality about it – the unsophisticated nature of a growing child, the characteristic of childlike wonder which has been so strongly emphasised on the Path of the South. Three has the freshness and spontaneity one might associate with youthfulness – and how much we desire to retain youthfulness as we grow older!

Three is also regarded as the number of family relationships – father, mother and child. It is related to one's relationship with divinity – that is, as a 'child' to a Father god and Mother goddess. A triad of a godhead is found in most cultures – Sskwahuan, Wahkwaahuan and Wakan-Tanka of North American Indians; Osiris, Isis and Horus of the ancient Egyptians; Father, Son and Holy Ghost of the Christians; Vishnu, Siva and Kali of the Hindus, and so on. Among the ancient Northern peoples the world tree of their cosmology had three roots and there were three Norns or 'Fates'.

Thirteen has the quality of acting as an 'inner-opener' – that is, making knowledge available from the 'inside' rather than from external sources. Thirteen is closely related to death and rebirth and to change through the transition from one level of existence to another. Because of its mystical qualities and its value as a key to the mysteries it was deliberately maligned in mediaeval Europe and associated with bad luck and misfortune by those who wanted to keep people in ignorance and superstition. Thirteen helps the development of the Spiritual Self, or High Self, is associated with the spirit energy of all plants and the receptive-creative Yin, the female force of life which is why thirteen is also found to be related to Mother Earth.

Plants absorb negative energy – carbon monoxide for instance – and emit it to us as positive energy (oxygen, for instance). Furthermore, plants have a direct affinity with the human emotions since both are components of the South. Plants can therefore be our allies in healing emotional wounds. Plants, and especially trees, can do this by taking the pain (or negative energies) from us and dispersing them in the Earth to be trans-muted back to the primary elements. They can also strengthen us by allowing us to draw on their own spiritual energy to soothe away what may have been troubling us.

In applying numbers to the Medicine Wheel, think of them in a qualita-tive rather than a quantitative sense. In writing a figure 3 (....) and 13 (....) you are expressing all the qualities and concepts of the South direction which have taken me several thousand words to describe. Such was the 'computerised' technology of the ancients and of the Medicine Way.

11. *Enemy of the South:* FEAR

Every step in learning is a journey into unknown territory and sometimes we fear the unknown simply because it is the unknown. On the Medicine Way you are on ground that possibly may be unfamiliar to you. So in the South, in entering the unknown, you are facing your first main enemy — FEAR.

There are two types of fear — reality fear and illusory fear. Reality fear is fear of the real. It is a positive kind of fear because anything that is a possible threat to your survival is a real fear.

Illusory fear is the kind of fear we suffer most of the time. Whereas reality fear is about the present — the immediate threat, the instant danger — illusory fear is about what might happen in the future ...... IF ..! The fear of what might happen if you can't find the money to settle a bill. The fear of what might happen if you don't achieve your sales quota, or complete all the jobs expected of you at work; what might happen if you are made redundant. The fear of losing a girlfriend or boyfriend. The fear of failing a driving test or an examination. The fear of not getting a pay rise or a promotion. Illusory fear is a 'what-will-happen-if' fear. It is fear of some-thing that has not yet started to happen, and in all probability might never happen. It is fear of the unknown. It is fear not of the thing or condition, but of a possible unknown outcome of that condition. It is illusory because it is fear of something that is not really there at all.

It is illusory fear that has to be overcome. That is the fear you have to defeat. But how? By not running away from it. By facing it with clarity of mind. By applying clarity of mind to every one of the examples I have given and many more like them, the fear itself would quickly vanish because the knowledge of how to cope with the situation would soon come to you.

12. *Manifestation*: MUSIC

Each directional Power finds expression for its essential quality in a particular human activity or group of activities. According to Medicine teachings, the essential nature of the South is manifested in music, singing, chanting and dancing – activities which can be entered into with youthful exuberance, free of inhibitions and psychological hang-ups. American Indians found much joy in such activities and regarded them as food for the soul and fuel for the spirit.

DIRECTIONAL QUEST:

Who Am I?

The answers to question like: Who am I? What am I? Why am I here? Where did I come from? Where am I going? What is the purpose of life? had eluded me through the corridors of Western philosophy and religions. Silver Bear explained that the answers to such questions cannot come through the logic of the intellect. The answers can only be obtained shamanically – and that means watching, listening and extending all the senses.

'Let the trees and animals and birds talk to you, for they will if only you will listen', he said. 'Even the wind speaks, though it may only be in a whisper.' Answers come, he said, in unexpected and surprising ways – sometimes in words implanted in the mind, sometimes in shapes, symbols and colours.

'Just be alert and at one with your surroundings', he advised, 'and take notice especially of the direction from which things come to you or go from you'. I pass on these words to you for I know them to be helpful.

It is advisable to find your own place of power in Nature for your Directional Quest, and since trees can be such powerful teachers, I would suggest you choose a place where there are trees and where you can sit undisturbed for, say, half an hour.

Sit with your back against a tree and for your first Directional Quest face South. Take with you a token of the 'kingdom' that is related to the South – the Plant kingdom. A few seeds, grains or coffee beans, perhaps. These provide another connecting link with the powers of the South. When you are comfortably seated, hold these in your left hand placed over your navel. Rest your right hand over your left hand. You have now established a focal point.

Now put the question: 'WHO AM I?'. It is a question which implies more than the identity of the personality self. It is concerned with your permanent self, your Spirit Self. Ask the question four times then relax and just watch and listen. An answer may not come right away. When it does come it is likely to be in an unexpected way. But anticipate an answer. Be patient. It will come.

Here is how an answer to a similar question came to me:

It was a fresh, crisp winter's day as I walked into a woodland near my home and found a secluded clearing among the trees. On this occasion I was seeking an answer to the question: 'What am I? – the 'I' being the One who thinks, observes and watches, the True Self I was seeking to come to know and to understand.

The Sun was shining quite brightly directly in front of me as I sat with my back to a tree facing South. Its rays shimmered through the trees and I allowed myself to become absorbed in the sheer beauty of the moment. I felt warm and protected and, strangely, loved as if held gently within the petals of some giant flower. What fantastic colours! The Sun was a golden orb and around it was a haze of orange merging into violet and then blue. It was like looking out on some idyllic place through specially-tinted spectacles. I moved my head up and down and then from side to side to make sure it was no optical illusion. No. I was immersed in a sea of pastel shades which was like a great aura around the Sun. And then the realisation hit me. '*I* am a sun surrounded by an aura.' The words bellowed through my mind. 'I am a sun looking at the Sun through my *own* aura.' It was an overwhelming experience and I felt tears welling up in my eyes.

I watched a cloud drift across the face of the Sun and majestically become a deep purple, hiding the Sun as if by a robe. 'I am a sun, centred within my own aura. A being of light locked within the dimension of Matter and hidden behind a cloak that obscures my true light.'

I had an answer to my question.

THE GIVE-AWAY

The Indian regarded needs as those things which, when denied, caused long-term pain. Needs are what we feel we must have, but can only be supplied by others. Satisfy the need and the pain vanishes – but only for a short time and then there is the need again, crying out to be satisfied. Needs continue, so only short-term pleasure is obtained by satisfying needs.

Desires were regarded as things that do not require outside help to satisfy. Desires were what you could obtain for yourself and always brought pleasure.

Since the South is related to the emotions, consider now what 'needs' of your emotional life you would like to have banished in order to attain emotional harmony. What emotional needs would you like to give-away? For instance, do you need acknowledgment and recognition for the acts you do? Do you feel emotionally hurt if your efforts do not receive the praise and reward they deserve. Then give away your need for recognition. Enjoy the *doing*. Determine to persevere whether you receive encouragement, support, praise, or none at all.

Associate the needs you are giving away with the seeds or beans you have been holding in your hand. Scoop up a little earth and bury the grains which now represent those needs. You are thus giving up that which has caused you pain. You are giving those needs to the Earth to be transformed. Such a symbolic act will impress itself on the subconscious mind which will then act on the 'instruction'.

Finally, consider what positive emotional attributes it would be desirable to give to others as an 'offering' to bring them pleasure. What has been a healing balm for you when you have suffered emotional hurt? The compassion and understanding of someone else, perhaps? Then determine to give your compassion and sympathetic understanding to whoever may seek your counsel, advice or help.

Before leaving your power spot, thank the Spirit of the South, the spirits of Nature all around you and the Great Spirit, for the help and understanding that has been imparted to you. As a gesture in 'earthing' your intention, take with you some cornmeal, dried sage, or mixed herbs, and sprinkle a little on the ground where you have been sitting. An Indian never took anything from Nature without also giving something in return and often carried such an offering in a pouch.

ADVENTURER TASK NO.2:

Erasing Personal History

Some people, possibly because of their background or upbringing, are reluctant to participate in ritual because it appears to have religious or supernatural overtones. Perhaps because of past conditioning, the idea of ritual raises fears of idolatry or the occult. There is nothing idolatrous or supernatural about the Rites described in these pages. They are psychological actions designed to convey intent and purpose, so before embarking upon this second Adventurer Task it is essential that you understand the meaning and purpose of ritual.

A properly constructed ritual is merely a way of converting thoughts and intentions into symbolic actions which are powerful enough to get through to the subconscious mind and make an impression. In this way, the subconscious 'gets the messge' and sets about grounding the intentions by bringing them 'down to earth' in physical form. Symbolism is a means of linking the person performing the ritual with their own 'centre' – the Spiritual Self – and with whatever the person's idea of the Source of Life may be.

Symbolism is the language of the subconscious, of the Spiritual Self, and of the inner planes of being, and a symbol is like putting together letters of the alphabet to form a word or words, except that – as you have already seen demonstrated – an effective symbol expresses far more than words alone could convey in a sentence or even several sentences, and a symbol can express concepts that words alone are too clumsy to communicate adequately.

When we speak or write words to others who know the language, the words convey our thoughts, ideas, feelings and intentions. But if the person hearing or reading the words does not understand our vocabulary, our thoughts will not get through to them. So it is with symbols. Symbols are the links between our objective and subjective existence, between one level of consciousness and another, between the conscious and the sub-conscious. So the symbols used must be in a 'language' that is understood at these different levels of existence. Put another way: symbols are a means of exchanging energy between different planes of existence.

The rites described in this book are powerful and very effective if carried out in accordance with the guidelines. The reason they work has nothing to do with the supernatural. They work because the intention behind them is made clear and precise in the mind of the person performing them, because they are conducted around an appropriate symbolic design – the Medicine Wheel, which is the encircled cross common to all ancient cultures – and because they have been proven in practice over many years. They are not literal versions of Amerindian rituals, but adaptations. They capture the spirit and intent of the ancient forms presented in a gentler manner that is more appropriate for the needs of modern times.

The first part of *Rite No. 2.* is performed indoors in your now familiar private 'space' and with your own personal Medicine Wheel. The only additional piece of equipment you will require is a white candle and a candle-holder. The rite may be performed at any convenient time when you can be undisturbed for 45 minutes to an hour.

Cover the surface in front of you with your covering cloth and set out your Medicine Wheel with the red marker stone nearest to you – that is, with you in the 'place' of the South facing North (or assumed North). Place the candle in its holder to the right of the green centre stone. Have your smudge mix, or stick, burner bowl, fan and matches handy, and a notebook and pen with you.

Now follow this sequence of activities:

RITE NO.2:

Erasing Personal History

1. Cleanse your aura and the area around you by smudging.

2. Be seated and relax the body and mind. Create your mind space where you are perfectly relaxed, perfectly at peace with yourself, and perfectly safe in your sealed and strengthened aura.

3. Meditate on the Medicine Wheel. It is a symbol of the universe and of the 'little universe' of your own personal reality. It represents, too, the physical plane of existence – its four directions indicating the Four Primary Powers, the invisible realities by which all material things are enabled to manifest – all contained and encircled within the embracing love of the Creator. Consider, too, the centre of the circle – the aperture through which the Infinite becomes Finite. Make a note of the thoughts that come into your mind.

4. Before lighting the candle, imagine that there is a flame within you, say around your heart area, which never goes out. Picture in your mind lighting the candle as if from this inner flame. Then light the candle.

Pause for a moment to consider what you have just done. The flame you have just kindled has been created by you for a specific purpose – the purpose of opening yourself to your own Source of creativity and power. The flame represents the inner light within you, the Spirit Self that never dies. It represents also the Sun which brings light and life to the material world around you, and it represents the spiritual Sun, the divine Source at the centre of Creation. Think on these things for a few moments with a realisation that the path to creative power and wisdom is thus illuminated and opening up before you. Make a note of your thoughts.

5. Now concentrate on the smoke from the flame. This smoke represents the element Air and the Breath of the Divine that keeps the flame alive. Think about this and note your thoughts.

Consider the circle in which the candle is burning and which is indicated by your stones. This represents the protective aura around you, the 'womb' that contains you.

Lighting a candle in this ritualistic way creates a communication centre which forms a link between your everyday self – your 'worldly', ordinary self – and your inner Self, your High Self, your Spiritual Self, your Source.

6. Read carefully the thoughts that follow and meditate on them. Savour each point. Take it slowly as you recall past experiences and bring them to mind as vividly as possible, then push them aside gently and move to the next point. Make a note of these memories.

Erasing Personal History means getting rid of the garbage of the past, of old beliefs and attitudes which you have been carrying around with you everywhere and which tie you still to a treadmill routine from which there appears to be no respite. Personal History can be defined as 'a strong attachment to a pattern of life'. It is a pattern so strong and you are tied to it so firmly that your thoughts and actions are conditioned to perpetuate it.

We all have strong attachments to our Personal History. Without such attachments life would appear to lack continuity and purpose, so why should we try to do away with them? Why attempt to wipe clear our personal history 'tapes' that programme our thoughts and actions?

Because Personal History is not as you might have supposed, a sort of curriculum vitae of your academic achievements, your qualifications and work experience, your marital state, and so on. It is what others know about you. It is what others think about you. Your Personal History is the picture other people have about you – about who and what you are – and which you endeavour to keep alive. Your parents, for instance, brought you into the world and raised you; they know who you are and what you are, or rather, they think they do! That is Personal History. And you may go through life reinforcing that personal history. Then there are friends, workmates, colleagues, the boss, neighbours.... All who know you – or think they do – and because of that knowledge, that Personal History, they expect you to behave in accordance with it. You continue to do what people expect of you, behaving the way they expect you to behave in accordance with that Personal History.

Personal History is fitting in with a package of other people's expectations. Personal History makes you feel obliged to explain and justify your actions and behaviour because of the way others expect you to act and behave. But, of course, if you have no Personal History, explanations are no longer necessary!

There are, then, people who know all about you and what makes you tick, but when you ask yourself questions like: Who am I? Where did I come from? What am I here for? Where am I going? – meaning the real you, the you who is thinking and perceiving, you're perplexed. By the real you I don't mean Joe Bloggs or Mary Jones. I mean the 'you' that is the 'Watcher within' — the real you, the Spirit You!

One reason why you have never been able to find answers to such profound questions before is that you have been trying to live like someone else. You have been trying to be what others expect you to be, and that is really not who you are at all, or what you want to be. So what everyone else knows about you is false. Does the need to erase Personal History begin to make sense to you now?

7. Think carefully now about those aspects of your Life that may have been conditioned by the positive or negative attachments which came from your parents, from teachers, from people who have been close to you in the past and have had a strong influence on your life at some stage. Perhaps in recalling such matters you find yourself telling yourself, 'Things would have been so different IF.....' And there you have it. The things that follow that IF are the very attachments you need to release.

So spend some time now going over in your mind the circumstances of your life and make a note of all the attachments you can identify. List them in your notebook. Only when you have completed this list should you move on to the next stage of this Rite.

8. Now you are going to let all those attachments go. They are going to be banished from your life. So meditate on the following:

Your physical parents conceived you and gave you the opportunity of incarnating at this time, and your mother bore you and delivered you into this physical world. Now, in your mind, thank them for that.

Yet your parents are not your real parents. They were but the physical vehicles of the Great Spirit through which your earthly experience came to be. Your true Mother is the Earth. Your true Father is the Sun. Think about that.

Your physical parents gave you physical nourishment. Thank them for that. Perhaps they brought you trials and troubles and failed to respond in the way you wanted, but they have given you their share of the Karma you needed and chose. Thank them for that. Perhaps they expected of you more than you were able to give, or loved you more than you were able to love them, but you were a mirror-image of them for in you they sought only to see success where they had failed, and see their hopes fulfilled in you. Thank them for that, and forgive them for that.

They did their best for you as they knew how. They may have failed in many ways but while they were your first teachers they were learning, too. Thank them for that and be grateful to them for what they have *not* given you as well as what they have given.

Your parents showed you their own imperfections. Thank them for that for your imperfections are many, too. Forgive them for anything you feel they did not do for you. And forgive them for whatever they did that has caused you pain. Now forgive yourself for whatever you thought or said or did not do that caused them pain. But above all, your parents gave you physical incarnation. So be grateful. Thank them and bless them for all they *have* done for you.

Now, as an adult, *let them go*. Let them be your *friends*.

On a piece of paper draw a simple representation of your mother and father. They need not be likenesses – simple stick figures will do. You are drawing only symbols. If one or both of your parents are dead, draw them just the same, for the attachments and dependencies exist and continue in most cases long after physical death.

Immediately after you close this session take this drawing with you into your garden, or find a small secluded space nearby where you can dig a little hole and bury the piece of paper as a symbol of releasing your dependencies on your parents. This is to be done in a spirit of gratitude and love, forgiveness and appreciation. Spend a few minutes now thinking about this.

9. Before extinguishing the candle flame, imagine as you snuff it out that it is merely being returned to the inner light inside you from which it came. Then snuff out the flame. Dismantle the circle and put your marker stones away.

10. Immediately go to the outside spot and there let your thoughts outlined in the 'letting go' passage flow gently through your mind. Then bury the symbols, and as you do so recognise that what you are burying is the false dependencies that have burdened and impeded you. You are now free from them. You have discharged the blockages that have prevented the love that is within your heart to flow out unconditionally as the natural love of a child wishes to do.

You have made your peace with the Past. You have begun a more meaningful relationship with the ones who made this incarnation of yours possible. Now they can be your friends.

Repeat this process for your teachers, enemies, ex-lovers – anyone who has conditioned you in the past to be what you are.

Finding the Centre

BEFORE MOVING TO A NEW DIRECTION, we are going to 'centre' ourselves by finding the neutral point of balance within, and to spend a quiet time considering and contemplating a single, essential topic. Have just your green centre-stone in front of you, then follow the procedure you did for Unit 1:

- Smudge yourself to cleanse your aura and the surrounding space.
- Relax, create your Mind space and seal and strengthen the aura.

The Centre is a place of stillness where power is not obvious because it is generated within. It is to the stillness within yourself that you must turn. The power to direct your own life comes not from an outside source but from inside you. What you need to acquire is the ability to listen to the silence.

Stillness is not inaction. It is not immobility. The Sun appears to be standing still but it is, in fact, moving at a tremendous speed. In stillness you have time to consider thought, which is quicker than the speed of light.

The Centre is where all motion is in perfect balance and where all directions are held in equilibrium. So the Centre is where we go to find greater perspective and to balance and harmonise what has been discovered 'without'. The Centre is the Source sometimes represented by the symbol of Wakan-Tanka, the Great Everything:

○Fig. 19

But it is also your source, your wholeness, your everything.

American Indian shamans looked upon the Centre as the 'eye' of Wakan-Tanka. In many philosophies the 'eye' was regarded as the window of the Soul through which the consciousness looked out onto what was manifested. The pupil of the eye was the 'Black Hole', the darkness out of which light comes and the entrance to the inner life of the Soul.

We all too often neglect or ignore the centre. Most of the time we are living on the rim of our own circle of awareness, oblivious of the fact that the power to overcome our problems and difficulties lies within, as in Nature the nucleus is to be found at the centre of the atom or the Sun at the centre of the solar system. As we go about our normal, everyday lives our attention is pulled in many different directions and our thoughts and energies scattered. In modern society there is so much activity going on competing for our attention and drawing on our energies. At our place of work our endeavours are towards meeting other people's expectations about ourselves. At home we are pulled out of ourselves to meet an entirely different set of expectations – as son or daughter, as a lover, as husband or wife, mother or father, or grandparent. Even in our leisure pursuits we try to emulate someone else. We can rarely, if ever, be ourselves.

To be 'centred' means to be in a state of calm receptivity. It is a condition that can be attained by focusing the attention on the centre of your being.

The centre of your physical being is at a 'point of balance' a couple of centimetres or so (about an inch) above the belly button. There the central control point is located. It is where your physical body was first knitted together after conception in your mother's womb.

To centre yourself you should focus your thoughts and feelings around this point of power where you were brought into physical existence. Indeed, energy can be drawn in from the cosmos and projected out into the world through this centre. But 'centring' is an act of equilibrium in which the intention is to harmonise and balance within yourself what is being absorbed. It is literally 'pulling yourself together' by releasing yourself from the demands of others and the masquerades that are enforced upon you, and concentrating your energies on being yourself. But who can you *be* unless you know *who* you are?

The South has stimulated you to examine your own identity and to get rid of some of the garbage you have been carrying around with you. At the Centre you can now contemplate who and what you are.

When you look in a mirror who is it that you see? You may say, 'It is me.' But the 'me' is not the 'I'. The image in the mirror is only a reflection of your physical body – the physical vehicle through which you are currently experiencing physical life. It is not You. It is only something that belongs to you.

Everything you see in physical life has been created or it could not be there for you to see. It has come into manifestation out of the unmanifest. And everything that is physical will one day return to the elements of which it is made. Your physical body will return to the Earth and release the substances and elements from which it is composed. So everything physical is temporal – it exists in manifestation in a particular form only for a period of time. The form is not permanent, not eternal. What is eternal cannot be seen.

You cannot see your Self. You can see everything but your Self. You cannot see your Self because your Self is spiritual and eternal and has no form on the physical plane. The Centre, then, is your invisibility, your true spirituality. Spirituality is Time-less and timelessness is eternal, too. Eternity couldn't be eternal if you could put a time on it. Timelessness is eternity, for eternity means there is no time. But that does not mean non-existence. Quite the contrary. It means an ever-present NOW, since past, present and future exist as one.

Where is eternity? *Eternity is where it is always Now.*

You are at the Centre now to discover the significance of the ever-present NOW. Meditate on that for a few minutes for when the realisation comes to you from within – from your own True Self – you will recognise the importance of doing the best you can at the given moment and realise also that no effort you make is ever lost.

Let us now pursue this concept of the eternal Self and the ever-present Now. The Indian observed the cyclic flow of the seasons, watched the wild flowers that pushed through the soil to new life in the Spring, blossomed in the Summer and then wilted and faded in the Autumn, seemingly died and vanished in Winter only to rise again in the Spring with the shoot of new life.

He observed the birth of a new baby in the tribe and compared childhood to Spring, the child blossoming into adulthood in the Summer of life, maturing and ripening into the wisdom of Autumn, then dying in the Winter of years and seemingly vanishing. But then came the Spring again and, he concluded, a new body to begin anew the cycle of Earth life.

This concept of reincarnation was understood through the seasonal cycles of Nature but was not, of course, confined to the Indian. Indeed, anthropological studies suggest that except possibly for the last 1,000 years it has been the generally-held view of the vast majority of mankind from the Indian tribes of North and South America through Japan, China, India, Egypt, Europe and Scandinavia. Today, even among those who profess allegiance to a religion that rejects the concept of reincarnation, many consider – if only instinctively – that it must be so.

Reincarnation presents man as being on a pilgrimage through many lifetimes and over a vast period of time, a spectator to great changes in the environment and the geography of whole continents, a witness to the rise and fall of nations and empires – even whole civilisations – perceiving from a constantly changing viewpoint and gathering experience as he travels on to the place from whence he came.

To the Indian, each lifetime was but a few moments in this great stretch of journeying, and though at the time the experiences of each life appeared to be so real and so permanent and enduring, they were in Reality but passing images, like those seen in a dream. Indeed, there is a song which is sung in tribal gatherings today which expresses this sentiment. In English it goes something like this:

> Row, row, row your boat
> Gently down the stream
> Merrily, merrily, merrily, merrily
> Life is but a dream.

The American Indian concept of reincarnation is that the True Self – the essential, conscious, individual essence – does not cease to exist when the body dies because it is ever-existing. It survives in a body that is best suited to its new environment, and in due course returns to the Earth in a new body, like putting on a new shirt or dress which, though they may change the appearance considerably, do not alter the individuality of the 'wearer' who remains the same individual.

This concept of the continuity of life *was not a question of belief*, but a question of cosmic and natural law. We each begin life as a baby and we grow and develop and become a child. The child becomes a youth, the youth becomes an adult and grows to maturity. Eventually there is ageing and the mature adult becomes an old person. Throughout this time the body undergoes many changes and goes through many cycles of constantly renewing itself, so that whatever age we are now, the body we have now is not the same body we had several years ago. The consciousness is the same individual entity it has always been but the body is not the same.

So when eventually the physical body is discarded at death, it is not so strange that the essential individual Self continues to be conscious, continues to be aware, continues to live on, albeit on a different plane of existence from the physical.

The physical body is the vehicle through which the individual entity experiences the physical plane. When it has served its purpose it is released and abandoned. While the soul occupies the physical body the body has value and is looked after, maintained and cared for, but when the soul leaves the body at death the body no longer has value and is cast aside to be buried or burned.

As the physical vehicle at death is cast aside, the Energy Body which is made up of fibres of energy in a web-like structure that links the physical with the more subtle planes, disintegrates. The Astral Body then becomes the focus of the consciousness and in this body the individual is in a condition of awareness not unlike that experienced in Astral travel or shamanic journeying.

After a period in this state, the Astral body breaks up and the individual progresses on through higher realms of awareness before the Circle turns and the individual begins the journey back to another lifetime, another birth, in a new physical body.

With each new birth the Individuality develops a personality through which to express itself and through which to perceive life. The personality is, therefore, transient too, being a by-product of a particular incarnation, and discarded along with the physical body at death. The Individuality, however, being immortal survives, to continue its existence and its awareness.

Among some American Indian tribes there was a system of personality profiling similar to astrology in which the time of birth was related to a position on the Medicine Wheel. Since each portion of the Medicine Wheel has certain characteristics and qualities and is identified with an animal totem which expresses those qualities, the human entity absorbs these traits into the personality at birth. In other words, you come into life with the broad characteristics of the part of the Circle where you enter physical life. I have called an adaptation of this system 'Earth Medicine'. Earth Medicine, therefore, played a part in self-knowledge because it provided vital clues to understanding why a person was as they were and also of comprehending the soul's purpose in this lifetime.

This system of self-analysis is described comprehensively in my book *Earth Medicine*.[1] However, unlike Sun Astrology, Earth Medicine is not a system of predicting the future but of identifying one's potentials and of understanding oneself and others. Equally important, it is a means of learning how to see things from the perspective of another individual, so it is quite a profound system of psychological understanding and human relationships.

Each life, then, was seen as a means of gaining knowledge and experience on a never-ending journey of self-awareness. Death was observed as not an *end* but a *part* of life – a vital element in the cycle of life, as night is to day and winter to summer – as the Moon is to the Sun. Death was a return to another plane of existence where the lessons learned from the lifetime just lived could be absorbed and understood and where the Individuality, after a period of rest, assessment and renewal, determined what was necessary for its continued development in the next lifetime.

Whilst the one certainty of life may be said to be death, so the one certainty of death is a new life. To the Indian this was not an article of faith but a matter of fact. The whole of Nature demonstrated its reality. Only organised, man-inspired religion said otherwise.

This concept of the Individuality's continuity of life after death, and of a return to Earth again in a number of bodies — some male, some female — and in a number of personality guises, was not confined to a particular tribe or tribes, but was widespread among all Indian tribes.

The Indian's attitude to reincarnation was demonstrated in a number of ceremonies in which respect was shown to 'the ancestors'. It was not until I was privileged to participate in a Medicine Wheel outdoor ceremony in which some 30 men and women took part that I began to understand the connection the 'ancestors' had with the Amerindian concept of reincarnation.

Quite by chance — or so it seemed — I found myself occupying the Southeast point on the Medicine Wheel and this, I was told, was 'the Place of the Ancestors'. At first I surmised that as I was perhaps the oldest of those taking part in the ceremony, this 'chance' positioning seemed symbolically appropriate. But as the ceremony unfolded it revealed to me that 'knowing the ancestors' implied rather more than a respect for tribal predecessors or past members of one's family tree whose identity may be lost in the mists of time.

What was being communicated to me was that the ancestors I was being drawn to 'know' were me! The ancestors were the past lives I had lived. The ancestors of each and every one of us taking part were our own past lives which we were recognising had culminated in bringing us to the life we were now living, to be among the ones we now love and with whom we had shared some aspect of our past lives though not necessarily the same relationship, to be among the friends we now have, and even the very situation in which we find ourselves at this time. As I 'marked' the Place of the Ancestors I realised that I was more than a representative figure or a stand-in for those who had lived their lives on Earth in past times. I was my own ancestors — my own grandfathers.

Silver Bear afterwards explained it to me simply: 'You are the product of what you have been. The blood that runs in your veins is the blood of your ancestors.' Our past lives have shaped our present destiny and brought us to the place in Time where we are now. Our present life, our present attitudes, will shape what we are yet to become.

I was told of an Indian saying that eternal life is through one's children. The Indian honoured a Sacred Law that says: 'Nothing shall be done to harm the children'. Protecting the children was seen as a way of protecting the future and the possibility that one might choose to return in the body of one's own descendants. Silver Bear put a conundrum to me: 'You are your own grandfather, and are you not also a child of your own grand-children?'

But what is the purpose of it all? Part of the answer was given to me in two simple words: 'To enjoy'. To enjoy? But haven't we been given to believe that life was intended to be a struggle to endure, to control and subjugate?. That is a false concept. A purpose of life is to enjoy aliveness. To enjoy pleasure. Not in the sense of self-indulgence, but in the know-ledge that joy, excitement and fulfilment from exploring, discovering and creating are what life was given to us for. Self-development comes through experiencing the conditions and circumstances we create for ourselves as a result of our own creativeness. Silver Bear explained: 'You are constantly creating yourself with every moment. You change your Fate, your direc-tion, your circumstances, your environment, by changing your thoughts. Never forget – the power is in the Now. Power always lies in the Present.'

Attributes of the West

THE WEST IS OFTEN REFERRED TO IN American Indian cosmology as the 'Look Within Place' because it is the direction of inward-looking — of introspection. So we make our journey to the West to examine our inner self with a view to determining what we need to change in order to make progress. For the emphasis of the West is on change and transition. It is also where we have to face the truth about Death, and the recognition that every change is the death of what has gone before. Death is a transition to that which is a new beginning.

The West is also the Place of Dreams and Visions about the future. American Indians talked of 'dancing a dream awake', meaning the turning of dreams into physical realities by being practical and realistic.

The West can be likened to Autumn which is the season of consolidation when growth stops and the preparation for renewal begins. So we have come from the 'fast growing' place of the South to the West where we can prepare for renewal. The West can also be likened to twilight and dusk — the period of the day which was once regarded as the time to turn the mind from physical to spiritual things. It indicates the power which comes from knowing oneself.

The components of the West are:

1. *Quality*: Change and transition.
2. *Totem*: Grizzly bear.
3. *Element*: Earth.
4. *Colour*: Black.
5. *Kingdom*: Mineral.
6. *Heavenly Body*: Grandmother Earth.
7. *Human Aspect*: Physical body.
8. *Time Period*: Present.
9. *Season*: Autumn.
10. *Numbers*: Two (..) and twelve.
11. *Enemy*: Powerlessness.
12. *Manifestation*: Magik.

- So, set up your Circle.
- Smudge your aura and working area.
- Assume the West position (black marker in front of you).
- Relax and create your Mind space. Then proceed as with Unit 1.

1. *Quality of the West*: CHANGE AND TRANSITION

Life is enveloped in uncertainty and the unexpected. Some cynics might say that you cannot really be sure about anything. Change is inevitable, and one thing is certain — one thing that became an unalterable fact from the moment of your birth — you are going to die. The journey of Life leads to Death! That's some trip! No wonder we don't like actually talking about it. That's why we prefer to turn a blind eye to it and pretend that Death isn't there.

Just imagine. If before you entered this world as a helpless baby, even before you were nurtured in your mother's womb, before you were conceived. … Just imagine. Long ago you had conscious existence, just as you do now, except perhaps in a different form. That conscious awareness of be-ing — of being *You*. A unique individual, independent of all others, with your own identity, and duplicated nowhere, faced with a decision — a rather awesome, frightening decision. The decision of whether to become a physically incarnate human being! You would realise that once the decision was made you would be embarking on a truly great adventure — a journey into the material world — a physical dimension of existence where you would die. No ifs. No buts. No possibilities or probabilities. Not even a maybe. Your death absolutely guaranteed. Make the trip to mortality and death is an absolute certainty.

Oh yes, there would be an assurance that though your body would get buried in a hole in the ground or be incinerated in a crematorium, the provision would be there to get the Essence of You back to where it came. Sure, you'd be beamed back in some way. But do you think now you'd rush to *volunteer* for such a trip? You'd be hardly likely to get hurt in any rush of volunteers, would you?

Perhaps it wasn't quite like that. Perhaps the 'volunteers' — who included you — were chosen, as if under military rule: 'Okay, we need volunteers. You, you, you and YOU!' 'Me? Not me, surely? You cannot be serious!'

Or was it that you were just petrified into making the trip, sucked into it by some irresistible force? An attraction like the moth to candle flame. A pull so powerful that you were carried along in its magnetic power like some small piece of metal caught in the field of a huge magnet.

Speculation? Perhaps. But an important area of thought, surely? Because, before we can determine where we're going and what we're changing to, we need to have an idea of where we're from, and what we are changing from.

The shaman knew of a Sacred Law which was also a natural law because he observed its action all around him.

Life leads to death.

But he also knew the reverse side of that Law:

Death leads to life.

He knew and understood it, because Life and Death are just turns of the Circle.

Everyone fears Death. But is death the most traumatic experience you are ever likely to face? Consider this: Can death be more traumatic than was your coming into Life? That was some trip. The Essence of You was to be contained within a vehicle of flesh and blood, bone and sinew, which would be knitted together and assembled inside the abdomen of a woman. Then, in due course, you would be pushed through a tiny, suffocating tunnel and into the light. That was going to be a claustrophobic experience.

And when you'd made it through that narrow, confining tunnel, your life support system would be cut. You'd be completely helpless for many many months, at the mercy of some inexperienced human being who claimed to be your mother. Even when you were able to take full control of the vehicle you'd been supplied with, you'd be faced with all the traumas, dramas, hazards and uncertainties of living. Worse still. … Worse? Surely there can't be anything worse? Worse — you'd lose all memory of who you are, what you are, where you're from and why you'd made the trip in the first place. If that is Life, surely Death can't be all that bad after all?

Of course, the concept we have been brainwashed with is that death is the end of life. But the *reality*, as Nature tries to show us, is that death is a *part* of life. Death is part of the process of rebirth. And you have an example to prove it to you every day. You don't *fear* going to bed to sleep. At the end of the day your body is tired and your mind seeks refreshment too. Indeed, you even look forward to a good night's sleep, and you wake up next day refreshed, revitalised and recharged with 'new' energy, ready to start another new day.

You haven't stopped being You while you were asleep. The 'I' doesn't stop being the 'I'. You wake up next morning being precisely the same conscious individual you were the night before. Death, like sleep, is not an ending either, but part of a creative process in which the Soul is returned to a place of rest, renewal and refreshment.

In the process of dying there is a sensation of being in a tunnel, of being surrounded by a sound that is unusual but pleasant, and of travelling forwards and upwards towards a distant point of light. The process of birth is similar but more traumatic. One is aware of a sensation of being carried on a wave of sound along a tunnel – which is the mother's uterus and birth canal. With birth there is a sensation of confinement, of being gripped by a pressure that is bearing down and is engulfing, whereas with death there is a sensation of release of pressure like a burden being lifted.

If, therefore, you survive after the body dies, then you also have existed before the body was born – just as it is the same 'you' that wakes up after sleep.

Death is thus a part of life and it is in this whole context of the continuity of life that another cosmic law – the Law of Karma – operates. There are many theories about karma. One is that it is simply cause and effect – what is sown is ultimately reaped. Adverse circumstances, trials and tribulations, handicaps and burdens, are regarded by this school of thought as karmic burdens to compensate for some misdemeanours of the past, even of a past life. The Indian shaman understood it differently and in a more positive light.

Karma is a teacher indicating where aspects of one's life are out of balance and need to be corrected. Karmic experiences are repetitive patterns in life – the same old problem or problems recurring again and again, perhaps in different guises and under different conditions. In other words, karma comprises the life lessons that are part of one's destiny. They are predetermined learning experiences to be encountered to help us grow, develop and evolve spiritually in order for us to fulfil the true purpose of our life which is the education and development of the Soul and Spirit.

2. *Totem of the West*: GRIZZLY BEAR

The grizzly bear is renowned for its great strength. We might liken that strength not so much to physical might, but to inner power – like that which comes to the Earth in the Autumn, which is the season of the West.

The Indian observed that the Bear seemed to be introspective about its decision-making, and this quality served as an example that the human being should be inward-looking too, before making important decisions. We too should look within ourselves to determine our own strengths and weaknesses and we should look within our own heart to examine our true intentions if we are to learn the lessons we must, and make wise decisions.

The Bear knew the Earth so well that it was aware of what was needed to aid healing in sickness or injury. We can learn from Bear by turning our attention towards the more natural foods to sustain the body rather than manufactured and processed foodstuffs, and to natural remedies to maintain physical health – ones that have no harmful side-effects. Just as Bear prepares itself for the renewal time of hibernation to come, by strengthening its body, so we must first attend to the physical and mundane and put our everyday affairs in order before spiritual renewal can be effected.

3. *Element of the West*: EARTH

The characteristics of Elemental Earth are solidity, inertia and stability. It is *motion at rest*. Elemental Earth is elemental 'substance' coming into form and shape and becoming tangible and recognisable – coming 'down to earth'. Matter is that which appears to be. It is important to bear in mind that matter is an *appearance*, and it is this that makes Elemental Earth perhaps the least understood of the elemental substances.

On a practical level, we spend much of our time being concerned with the acquisition of physical, tangible things, but at the same time we dislike the restrictions and limitations that the material puts on us. The West is the place of the material, of appearances, of the world of form, of physical manifestation and of learning to cope with it.

You cannot develop your spiritual awareness by *rejecting* the material or turning your back on it. The physical and material is all part of Creation, not a secretion to be got rid of in some mistaken quest for 'spirituality', not something to be flushed away as something 'not nice'. Don't allow yourself to be misled by a sense of false spirituality. You are here in the material world of form. You live in the material world of form, and part of the reason for your being here is to learn how to control the material through the use of natural laws and cosmic forces and principles. Spiritual work is of little value unless it can be 'earthed'.

Do you not think that it gave *pleasure* to the Cosmic Intelligence to bring the physical world of form into manifestation? Go out into the countryside or into a park or woodland and look around you at the beauty of the natural Earth. Even though man has shaped most of it by farming, does it not give you a thrill of pleasure to absorb its magnificence? We are not intended to reject the material in preference for some nebulous spiritual alternative, but to appreciate the physical and at the same time to look for the reality behind it. Both in equal partnership.

Physical objects only look and feel solid because their atoms are spinning at fantastic speeds. As in a movie, people and vehicles appear to move but what we are seeing is a succession of static pictures being projected at such a speed that there appears to be movement, but the appearance is, in fact, an illusion. An atom is mostly space. If it were possible to expand a single atom to the size of a sports stadium like Wembley in West London, England, or the Giants stadium in New Jersey, USA, its centre or nucleus would be the size of a pea in a referee's whistle. If this were placed in the centre spot, the electrons would be whirling around it at the top of the grandstands.

All matter is as roomy as the universe appears to be, and atom particles are like the stars and planets moving about in a continual pattern. If we could travel far enough away in outer space and look back at the universe, it too would appear solid.

Earth is often represented by its most durable form — a stone. A stone suggests not only solidity but resilience and security — qualities of people strongly influenced by Elemental Earth. Earth is yin — passive, receptive, nurturing.

4. *Colour of the West*: BLACK

Light comes out of darkness, and Black is the colour of the formlessness from which everything comes. Black absorbs, stores away and is protective. It is the colour of mystery, of hidden depths and secret longings. Black is concerned with the Unconscious and with germination.

Without blackness there could be no light, for darkness is light's opposite and contrasts its specific qualities. Black absorbs all colours within itself and is the receptive polarity of the colour spectrum. It is the 'colour' of the 'Look Within' Place, of introspection and withdrawal. It is concerned with dispersal and with transformation.

Black is related to the feminine aspect of our nature — whether we are male or female — to receptiveness and sensitivity and to deeper feelings.

5. *Kingdom of the West*: MINERAL KINGDOM

When the Earth itself was in its embryonic stage, the primitive rocks developed like the human skeleton and can be regarded as the Earth's 'bones', while the land surface may be likened to skin, the trees and vegetation to hair, and so on. The Indian regarded quartz crystals, for instance, as the brain cells of Grandmother Earth.

Shamans knew that although rocks and stones do not have eyes like animals and humans, they do have a sense of 'sight', and though they do not have ears, there are stones that 'hear'. To the shaman there was a connection between the sense organs of the human being and certain stones that had healing powers for the particular organ with which it was related. Beryl and aquamarine were related to the eyesight, onyx to hearing, carnelian to touch, topaz to taste, jaspar to smell, ruby to the intuition and opal to the intellect.

The Mineral Kingdom is seen as the *holders* and *controllers* of energy, and is the most ancient of kingdoms for the rocks and stones were here on Earth before there were plants, animals or humans. The quartz crystal was particularly highly regarded. It has very special properties, not only as a storer and transformer of energy, but because it has the same chemical composition (S_1O_2) as silica, which is a natural mineral within the body.

In some esoteric circles, crystals are believed to have been strategically produced by Nature within the Earth's crust to maintain the balance of the electro-magnetic fields which surround the Earth. The pattern of energies which flow around the Earth is like an intricate grid of millions and millions of intersecting lines and the tension within this energy grid is maintained by the crystal clusters. The human body is similar. It, too, has an energy field – the Aura – with its network of interpenetrating lines – meridians of electro-magnetic energies. The balance of these energies in the human Aura is maintained by silica.

The human body is dependent on essential inorganic minerals. Indeed, disorders of the human body can often be traced to deficiencies in one or more of these inorganic minerals which, as energy storers, need to be renewed or replaced. A deficiency of calcium, for instance, can cause bone problems, especially of the joints, and a lack of sodium can bring about digestive troubles and even rheumatism.

Any huge boulder you can lean against or any small piece of rock or stone you can hold in your hand is of very great age. Hold a piece of quartz crystal in your palm and you are in touch with something that existed long before the first human beings appeared on this planet. I have in my possession a pair of solid onyx bookends that were carved out of a single piece of solid onyx by Mexican Indians, and both my wife and I receive impressions of its great antiquity whenever we hold them. They are part of what the Indian called Grandfather Rock who has been around since the early days of the planet – through all the great transformations, through the arrival and development of different life forms and through the rise and fall of many civilisations.

Grandfather Rock has survived all the great cataclysms in which many forms of life perished and became extinct, and during which the whole face of the Earth was changed. Grandfather Rock has been through it all and knows of it all. No wonder the Indian revered Grandfather Rock.

6. *Heavenly Body of the West*: GRANDMOTHER EARTH

American Indians treated the Earth as a living being who was truly their 'mother' — the one who provided their physical body, whose substance was their substance and the one who made it possible for them as spirit entities to incarnate and so experience the physical realm. The Earth Mother was to be loved and taken care of with the same kind of feeling and emotion one should have for a human being to whom one is devoted.

The West, then, is an appropriate place for us to ask ourselves: 'Should we not love the Mother power of the Earth as the Indians loved the Earth and all things of the Earth?' For if we lack true respect for the Earth and for any living creature, do we not risk losing respect for the sacredness of life itself? History, sadly, indicates that we do. It is only by coming close to the Earth Mother as a child seeks to be close to its mother, that we can become sensitive to the powers of the Earth.

Here is a little outdoor Experiment which should help you to quickly relate to the Earth. Go out as soon as convenient when the weather is fine and find a secluded spot in a park, your garden, or in the countryside, and there you are going to feel good about the Earth. It will be a feeling that will go a little deeper than just a sense of well-being. It will be the kind of feeling that comes from the sense of security one enjoys from being loved and protected. Take with you a little cornmeal or a few dried herbs in a small bag or pouch.

EXERCISE NO.5:

Relating to Mother Earth

When you have found your secluded spot, look around and spend a little time absorbing its loveliness. Appreciate the natural beauty that is around you.

Sprinkle a little cornmeal or dried herbs on the ground around you as a token of gratitude. Then thank the place for being so beautiful. That's right. Express your appreciation vocally. You don't have to make a speech. You have only to say something quite simple, like: 'Thank you Earth for being so beautiful.'

Have you never thanked the trees and shrubs and flowers for their loveliness and fragrance? Well, thank them now.
Have you never praised the birds for the joyfulness of their singing? Thank them now.

Have you never thanked the Earth Mother for her bountiful beauty and for sustaining and protecting you? Thank her now.

Don't concern yourself about what other people might think about such expressions of appreciation. Other people aren't with you now. Other people have enough concerns of their own. Do your own thing your own way. Your expression of love and respect will not go unheeded as you will soon discover and experience for yourself. It won't matter then what other people might *think*. You will *know*.

Sadly, the Earth Mother is becoming sore and sick in so many places through the abuses of mankind who regard the Earth not as a living being who supports all the life forms, but merely as a lifeless stockpile to be used and exploited.

The Amerindian has witnessed the continuing rape of the Earth Mother as well as the virtual destruction of his own race, but he knows that the Earth Mother will not always be submissive. There is a time to come when the Earth Mother will cleanse herself from the despoiling. In Hopi Indian prophecies it is known as the time of the Great Cleansing when Nature will seek to redress the imbalance inflicted on Earth in an attempt to restore equilibrium. Mankind will dismiss such upheavals as 'Acts of God' rather than the results of humanity's baser qualities of greed, lust and vanity. The Earth Mother, however, responds lovingly to those whose attitude is sincere, respectful and caring.

Should you not sense an immediate response, perform the Experiment again at another time. Be patient. The response will come.

7. *Human Aspect of the West*: THE PHYSICAL BODY

The physical body is a vehicle or garment for the indwelling Spirit and Soul.

When the forces which operate in the physical body are in harmony and balance, the body is in good health. If there is disharmony or imbalance they materialise as sickness or disease. The maintenance of good health is a matter of keeping the forces within the body in proper harmony. The restoration of good health is achieved through bringing those forces into balance.

The positive side of the elements operating within the body perform the processes of building, sustaining and repairing, while the negative aspects are concerned with dissolving and breaking down. The neutral 'point of balance' is concerned with preserving.

Our physical body is a complex and sophisticated piece of equipment, the most wonderful vehicle that has ever been devised. Yet in spite of the progress of medical science and research, man is still ignorant about why some parts of the body function as they do and what actually causes them to malfunction. Modern medical science still persists in treating the symptom rather than the person.

In other words, there is still much about the human body which the most knowledgeable of physicians are still uncertain or even ignorant about. The ancients were aware of internal resources of the human body, sense organs and energy systems which modern medical science has yet to discover.

8. *Time Period of the West*: THE PRESENT

The Past has gone. You cannot change the Past, only learn from it. The Present is happening now. The Future is not yet in existence but can be influenced by our Present thinking. That is why the Present is so important, for it is only in the Present that we can work Change.

You create much of your Future in accordance with your beliefs. If you want a better Future than the Past, you need to change your belief system − your pattern of belief.

The beliefs, values, standards, ideals − patterns that were 'programmed' into you by your parents, teachers, religious leaders, social customs and the society in which you have lived − have conditioned and moulded the Present. You have been programmed for the kind of life you are now living. If you are dissatisfied with any aspect of your life as it is now, you have to change the programme. Your future happiness lies largely in your hands. Change the beliefs and attitudes and you change the programme. Change the programme and you change the future. That was one of the secrets of the ancients.

9. *Season of the West*: AUTUMN

Just as Autumn is one of the most beautiful times of the year, when the foliage is a riot of mellow and gentle colours, so in the West direction we can undergo some of our most beautiful spiritual experiences.

Autumn is Nature's time of inward turning. It is the time when the Life essence begins to withdraw into the seed. By withdrawing ourselves for a time from the busy-ness of external activities, we can look within and discover truths about ourselves which can ultimately blossom forth into a newness of life.

10. *Number of the West*: TWO (..)

Two is the number assigned to the West in the Twenty Count. Two has gentle and receptive qualities − those of the feminine principle and of introspection. It is the number of duality. The whole material Creation which is being emphasised in the West, is an expression of this dualism.

Duality is the most evident thing in existence. It is night and day, summer and winter, inhalation and exhalation, hot and cold, Sun and Moon. Even Truth itself is dual in nature for it is exoteric and esoteric — there is the truth of what appears to be and the truth of what is. Medicine Way teachings, too, have a duality of meaning.

Two suggests bonding, and generating force being nurtured into form.

On the inner planes, twelve is the number of organisational stability on a spiritual level. It is also concerned with the spirit of the planets.

11. *Enemy of the West*: POWERLESSNESS

The enemy of the West is Powerlessness. We need power to achieve and attain. Indeed, as we purify ourselves and seek to exchange the garbage of the past for wisdom, we come into the Present and awaken our power. We need power as a friend and ally. The lack of power is thus an enemy.

Look around and observe how people are using the power they have. More often than not, power is being used to control the lives of others, to use others for entirely selfish purposes and to satisfy lust and greed. This is because the victims suffer from powerlessness.

Power can be used for good or evil — just like electricity or nuclear power. The abuse of power is all too common and that is why the ancient wisdom was guarded and the secrets of the Medicine Wheel teachings hidden within the oral traditions of the shamans. When power is abused or misused it is self-destructive — it can turn back on the one who abused or misapplied it. When power is used constructively and for the good of all, then it is our friend.

Develop optimistic self-confidence. Be positive. If what you wish to do hurts no-one, including yourself, do it. Exercise your power. Do not be powerless. Resist abuse of power and oppression.

12. *Manifestation of the West*: MAGIK*

Magik is a component of the West because Magik is about *changing* things. Magik is not entertaining trickery, nor is it the supernatural hocus-pocus supposed by some religionists and projected by cult movies. True Magik is

---

*Magik** This is a deliberate spelling to indicate the difference between the magik of bringing into being desired changes, the magic of illusion and trickery and superstition, and the magick of the ceremonial occultist.

the art of bringing about desired changes. The West is also about the *physical*, as we have been finding out, and before you can perform Magik you must first learn to control the physical.

Magik is the weaving and shaping of unseen forces and energies into form. So Magik might be described as the craft of shaping things the way we want them to be. The shaman, with the wisdom and knowledge to shape Magik, was thus a 'Wise Shaper'.

Magik is the art of bringing into your life, or the lives of those who seek your help, the changes that are wanted, whether in the form of physical objects or in conditions and circumstances. It is the wilful direction of energies in order to bring those changes into existence.

As we have already discussed, physical matter is alive with energy. Indeed, every single material manifestation is but a complex pattern of energy. It is not the physical object which determines what that energy pattern is, but rather the energy-pattern determines what the physical form is. Magik is achieved by bringing into physical existence the required energy-pattern for the elemental substances to arrange themselves. The energy-pattern is established through the power of thought.

Again, contrary to popular superstitious belief, Magik is not in the tools, implements or paraphernalia used. These are merely aids to represent an idea, to act as a symbolic representation on the physical plane of that which exists on another plane, or which serve as links or connectors for the energy to channel through.

The real Magik is within the mind of the maker of Magik – the Mage. For Magik is made by the imagination and the Will, and that is why creative imagination is stressed so strongly in these pages, and why it is necessary to exercise and control the imagination for creative work. It is the image seen in the mind's eye becoming manifest as a physical reality that is the Magik.

The Mage is like a magnet – a mage-net – who sets up a thoughtform in the energy field of unformed substance and draws into it the primary elements required to build the image into material reality so that it can be seen outwardly as well as imagined inwardly. The imagined object, condition or circumstances often comes about in unexpected, but perfectly 'natural' ways.

Magik is about accepting responsibility as a 'creator' – and in truth that is what each of us is. Knowingly or unknowingly, wilfully or 'accidentally' we are bringing into our own lives the circumstances, conditions and things which we ourselves have been creating with our belief systems through the operation of natural and cosmic laws.

When you wilfully 'work' Magik, you accept responsibility for your own life. No longer can you blame others, circumstances, fate, God, Satan, or whatever or whoever, for you then recognise that it is you yourself that has brought it about.

Where Did I Come From?

Go again to a place among trees where you can sit quietly for up to half an hour and, with your back against a tree trunk, face West. Take with you a token of the 'kingdom' of the West – the mineral kingdom. A small quartz crystal or a gemstone. Hold this in your left hand resting on your navel and with your right hand on top. This will focus your efforts. Ask the question: 'Where did I come from?' four times. Again, the question of your Quest is not concerned with your temporary, personality self, but with the Real You, your High Self or Spirit Self. Repeat the question a few times then wait expectantly for an answer – being relaxed and at ease but alert, watching and listening.

This is how an answer came to me. I had come out of the hurly-burly of normal, daytime town activity to a quiet spot among some trees. I took up a position with my back to a tree, facing West, and put the question: 'Where did I come from? What is my source?' I was immediately aware of how peaceful it was. Not a soul in sight. No sound of civilisation. Not even a murmur of traffic from a distant motorway. A strange silence, but I allowed myself to be absorbed in it.

Suddenly I was aware of the singing. Birds singing. Many varieties of bird for there were different songs. Their singing seemed to get louder and louder as more and more birds joined in until I seemed to be immersed in the sound.

I looked up. It was all around me, but where was it coming from? Where does the birds' song come from? Then I realised I was echoing my original question.

A bird clearly sings from the heart. I could almost touch the joy that was in the singing. Then I found myself asking another question. Do I not come from a Place where song comes from the heart? Perhaps a Place of musical sound? A Place of happy sound? And then the following thoughts flooded into my mind:

'I came into this dimension of Matter from a Joyful Place. A musical place. A Place where, as with the birds, it is the heart, not the voice, that sings. I was carried into physical life on a song. On the sound of my own Note!'

When I later related the incident to my wife she reminded me of a near-death experience she underwent some years before when our son was born. It was a difficult breach birth and before I was allowed into the maternity ward to see my wife, a hospital doctor had taken me aside and warned me that my wife's life was still at risk. During that night my wife had an experience which she wrote down immediately afterwards, in the form of a letter to me. She wrote the letter because she felt that if she lay down and closed her eyes again she would be dying.

She described an experience of being sucked into a dark tunnel at the end of which was a pinpoint of light. She felt herself being drawn through the tunnel on a wave of sound. It was an unusual sound, but strangely comforting. A pulsating sound which comprised several notes. She thought it must be the sound of Life. Each of us, she was inspired to write, has a unique sound – or, perhaps, is a sound. The sound carries us into the physical realm at birth and the first cries of a newborn babe are an expression of the soul's sound. A mother recognises the cry of her own baby from all others in a maternity ward. A baby's cry, however, modifies after a few hours. It is as if each human being has their own unique vibration or combination of notes, and this is expressed in the cry of the newborn as the soul makes the change from one dimension of existence to another, though it is retained for only a short while.

My wife wrote that if she lived we would have time together later in life to discover the relevance of the sound. That incident happened more than 30 years ago. The sound of the birds had recalled it to memory.

Some time after my Quest incident, my wife rediscovered the sound she had heard in that near-death experience. It happened during an altered state of consciousness while undergoing training in shamanic counselling in Sweden. She 'sang' the sound she was hearing and it was recorded. Later, back in England, she incorporated the sound into the music of a song she wrote which she entitled, 'Listen to the Silence'. At the same time I was to make a discovery too – that a shaman's own unique 'power song' is the recall of that individual's soul sound.

THE GIVE-AWAY

The West is the Place of 'earthy' things and of the physical, so in determining the 'Give-Away' it is a matter of identifying what physical actions, habits and idiosyncrasies are causing you pain, discomfort or embarrassment, which you would like to get rid of. Or, perhaps, in reviewing your physical 'needs' you may wish to give away your dependency on physical things. This does not mean the denial of physical things, merely the dependence on them to attain satisfaction. What such a 'Give-

Away' sets out to achieve is that whether you have a physical object or not will make no difference to the way you are.

If your Give-Away is a negative physical condition, consider its polar opposite which you would like to replace it with.

Associate those things you want to banish from your life with the gemstone in your hand. Now bury the gemstone beneath the surface of the soil near where you are sitting. Give them to Mother Earth to transform into positive qualities.

Consider now what you can give away of yourself to bring benefit to others. Physical effort, perhaps? In other words, determine to become a 'doer'. Walk your talk.

Before you leave the site, thank the Spirit of the West, the spirits of Nature, the Great Spirit for what has been revealed to you, and Mother Earth for her transforming power. Sprinkle a little cornmeal or herbs around the area where you have been sitting, as an offering.

ADVENTURER TASK NO 3:

Death as an Adviser

Leo Rutherford, an Englishman with an American Degree in Holistic Psychology, who devotes much of his working life to running workshops in esoteric subjects including American Indian teachings, told me a story of an Inca shaman whom he studied under in Peru.

'You cannot seek enlightenment until you have faced your own death' the Inca shaman, Don Eduardo Calderon, told him. Eduardo, who is known in his part of the world as 'the Wizard of the Four Winds', went on to make this point: 'The white man on the spiritual path only *glances* at death, for he comes from a culture that takes a great deal of trouble to keep death hidden from him.'

And that is true. Our meat comes from supermarkets and shops where it is packaged and displayed in such a way that it has little connection with a dead animal and the slaughter-factory. Old people are put into homes for the elderly or tucked out of sight in geriatric wards. Funerals are conducted discreetly and quietly, almost apologetically, so that only those directly concerned will notice that they're happening at all. And when someone close to us dies, we feel almost embarrassed about raising such a 'delicate' matter in conversation.

How do you face your own death? By looking at death not as an enemy but as an adviser. Look death in the face and it will tell you what you have to change, for death *is* change – a transition from one state to another.

Every change in life is a 'little' death. Every change we make is the death of what has gone before and a birth of what it has changed to.

How do we look Death in the face? By thinking about it and writing it down.

When this proposition was made to me by Leo I was asked to write on a piece of paper my own death as I would choose it to be – as one who had lived a full life and one connected to the Great Spirit. On another piece of paper I was asked to write my own death as it is 'programmed' for me by the culture in which I have lived.

This is the death I chose to die:

'This is a good day to die. I'm 98 and I've lived a full and active life, right up to this very day, and I have all my faculties working still. But my body is tired and I know it is moving to its end, so I am going to lie down and rest and invite my Spirit to leave.

'It has been an enjoyable adventure. I have loved and I have been loved. I have given what I could of myself and of my time – which is my life – and I have received much in return.

'It has been a life of journeying – of moves to many different places to find what I thought I did not have. It has been a life of discovery – of looking for what I could not find because it was too close for me to see. So the greatest discovery was finding my own Self and my connection with the Great Spirit who was not to be found 'out there' or 'up there' because He was 'in' here, closer than my heartbeat, nearer than the breath I breathe.

'I have done what I came to do.

'Since the days of that great discovery, I have tried my best to serve the Great Spirit and the planet and to be in harmony with my 'relatives' in the Four Kingdoms.

'I have said my farewells, and now I consciously move into familiar territory for as a Spirit Traveller I have journeyed into the Astral realm many times before. This time I am leaving this physical body for good.

'So now I move to the next adventure with joy in my heart and thankfulness to the Earth Mother for her teachings and to the Great Spirit for giving me the opportunity of life on Earth as a creator.

'And now I say, farewell Earth ...'

On another piece of paper I wrote my death as it might be programmed by the culture and lifestyle I had lived to that point. It read something like this:

'I have just had a heart attack and I've been brought to this hospital. I am only 58. I say *only* because that doesn't seem old at all – no different from when I was 48 or 38 or 28 or even 18. Whatever age, I am still the same 'me', yet I know now that I am going to die.

'I didn't expect to die so soon and I feel so frightened and helpless. My chest and my arms are hurting as if I'm in a huge metal clamp.

'My wife and family are on their way to see me but I feel terribly alone. I'm not really prepared for this. What's going to happen? Where will I go? Or will I just not exist any more?

'I'm afraid to let go … I'm afraid … I'm afraid …'

I was told that I was to burn this second piece of paper containing my death as culturally programmed, in a fire ritual together with a list of all the things that hinder me and which I want to change by their 'death'. In this way I would be leaving behind the Past that keeps creating my destiny and then I would be free to take charge of my own Future.

I now invite you to do the same. Write down your own death in two ways – the death you fear but which is a likely outcome of the way you have been living and of the society in which you live, and the death you would like it to be.

When this task is completed, spend some time considering what parts of your past are holding you back from being what in your heart you want to be and prevent you from doing what it is you want to do. List these things on a separate piece of paper.

Finally, compile a third list. This one is a list of conditions and circumstances you are in and would like to have changed. Perhaps you are unhappy at work. Perhaps you are limited by restrictions and circumstances. Perhaps you are deeply in debt. Lonely? Frustrated? Neglected? List them all down.

I am now going to outline a *Fire Ritual* which will enable you to let go of all of these things. They will 'die' in the flame along with your own 'pro-grammed' death, to be transmuted so that you are no longer weighted down and imprisoned by them. Free then to 'travel' to the East – the Place of Enlightenment – where you can begin to take charge of your own Future.

Ritual Preliminaries:

As a sole adventurer it may not be practical for you to have an actual fire for this ritual, so a candle flame will serve the same purpose and carries the same meaning. The entire ritual can be performed in your own home in the place you have set aside for your Medicine Way workings. In addition to a white central candle and your smudging gear the only equipment you will need is a small tray or bin to drop burnt paper into, and four small candles

— one red, one white, one yellow and one black. Blue can be used if black is difficult to obtain. Before you settle down to perform this Rite, make sure you won't be disturbed for at least half an hour.

Set up your Medicine Wheel as before and sit in the West, or 'assumed' West, with the black marker in front of you. The four small candles will represent the cardinal points. The white candle is for North and the element of Air so place it to the left of the central candle. The yellow candle represents East and elemental Fire and should be placed behind the central candle. Red represents South and elemental Water and should be placed on the right of the central candle, and the black (or blue) candle for the West and elemental Earth should be put in front of the central candle. Your smudge mix or stick and smudge bowl and fan should be placed conveniently on your left and the container for the burnt paper to your right.

Set out your working surface with each small candle about 10cm (four inches) from the central candle. Make sure each candle has a holder:

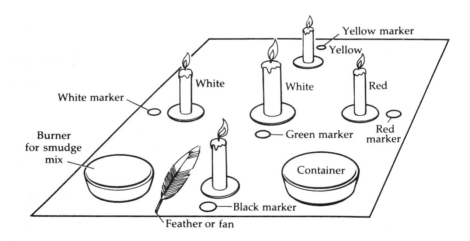

∘*Fig. 20*

RITE NO.3:

Freeing Attachments

    1. Seat yourself comfortably and check that everything is to hand.

2. Light the central candle as if from your own Inner Light, and remember that it also represents your Divine Source.

3. Using a taper, from the central candle light all four other candles, acknowledging that their light comes from the Source at the Centre, and that each represents the energy of the Elemental Powers.

4. Light the smudge mix and smudge yourself and the area around you to disperse any negative vibrations and unwanted influences.

5. Read through the three notes you have written:
   i) the account of your 'programmed' death.
   ii) the circumstances of the Past which affect you now and which are holding you back.
   iii) Present circumstances you would like to have changed.

Let your mind dwell for a time on each. Turn them over in your mind. Then – LET THEM GO. Release them. Imagine them being taken away, lifted from you like a great burden off your sholders. *Feel* the relief as the burden you have been carrying is no longer weighing you down.

Let go of the Past. You cannot change what has happened. It is done. But you can break the chains of the past that are enshackling your Present. Imagine those chains being cut. Throw the chains down. You are FREE.

See the death that 'would have been' being taken away. It no longer has a hold on you for in facing it and confronting it, you have vanquished any power it had over you. You no longer fear Death because you have already confronted Death and transformed it from an enemy to an Adviser. You have taken your Power and are no longer powerless in face of Death.

6. *Ask* the fire of the central candle flame to consume all those aspects of your past that have been limiting your life and leading you to that 'programmed' death.

Ask to be released from the thoughts and concepts that have been shackling your mind and your Spirit through false beliefs and customs.

Ask that you no longer be a victim of circumstances or of the mind conditioning of other people.

Ask that you now learn to choose the rest of your life consciously and become what You desire to be, and to choose your own death.

7. Now, take each piece of paper in turn, fold it into a loose taper so that it will burn easily, and hold it to the central candle flame. Watch it burn. Consider the thoughts the paper contains as the fire consumes it. Drop the remnants of each piece of paper into the tin or container.

   The paper containing the account of your 'programmed' death should be burned last of all. As you watch it being consumed in the flame, see your death as it would have been. Death no longer holds any fear for you. You have faced it and as the flame consumed the paper you have watched it vanish before you. Yet you are still the same, conscious You. Death has been swallowed up in victory.

8. Now, pass your hands gently through the flame of each candle in turn, then place both hands across the forehead.

   Pass your hands through the flame of each candle and place both hands on your Heart.

   Finally, pass your hands through the flames again and place them over your Solar Plexus.

   You have now symbolised the bringing of the Divine Flame to your Mind, your Heart (Spirit) and your Body.

   The divine gift of Freedom has been given and accepted.

9. Now think on this:
   You have given to the Fire – the Divine Spirit – all that has hindered you, and it has been received and taken from you. You have watched it being transmuted so that transformation can take place.

10. Extinguish the four small candles.

11. Before extinguishing the central candle, imagine that as you snuff out the flame it is being transferred to the Inner Light within you.

12. The Rite is now completed. Write down your experiences.

You are now ready to continue your journey of the Medicine Way. You must return to the Centre to balance and harmonise within you what the West has taught you.

The Human Space Capsule

AFTER TIME ON THE PATH OF THE WEST, we go back to the centre to seek balanced understanding and to contemplate another topic — this time on how we are equipped to experience our conscious awareness. As this is a Centre working you will just need the green marker stone in front of you.

- Smudge yourself and the area around you.
- Relax, create your own Mind space as before, and then concentrate

for a few minutes on the Centre and on its significance to your understanding so far. Then read on slowly and thoughtfully making a note of any related thoughts that come to mind.

The ancient wisdom embraced a knowledge that man was immersed in an infinite cosmic reservoir of energy which the American Indian described as the Great Spirit. In it he lived, moved and had his being, and through it and because of it he was not isolated and separated but linked to all things through an awesome and intricate web of inter-penetrating, omnipotent and omnipresent energy.

Man has now 'forgotten' that he, too, is in essence a being of light and that he himself comprises a number of high frequency energy systems which extend beyond the form of the physical body and its seemingly mechanistic functioning. Indeed, in addition to a physical anatomy, man has a subtle 'unseen' anatomy upon which the physical form is actually dependent and through which the physical body is connected to formative forces that permeate the human being and every living form — and, indeed, the entire universe.

According to this ancient wisdom, the individual human entity is more than just a physical body equipped with a bio-computer called a brain. The human is a most complex and sophisticated being — a conscious intelligence operating within a cocoon of interpenetrating energy fields called an Aura. The word 'aura' is derived from a Greek word which means 'breeze', for the aura is a force field of radiant energy which, like a breeze, is constantly in motion though normally unseen.

The aura itself is composed of a complex network of fine energy threads, or lines of light, which are structured like the fibres of a feather. It is because of the similarity of structure in the way the fibres lie in relation to one another, that the Indian shaman used feathers as a tool for harmonising and healing the aura.

Sickness was looked upon as disharmony or malfunction within the aura and may have resulted from or been the cause of a misalignment of the auric energy field. Healing took place through manipulating the energy threads back into alignment. The saying, 'having your feathers ruffled' (meaning that one feels aggrieved or irritated) is more than a colourful colloquialism. It is describing a literal fact. One's auric fibres – one's 'feathers' of energies – have been disturbed adversely. Similarly, the expression of being 'torn apart' is a vivid description of auric fibres being literally torn asunder – pulled open – and as would be the case with a bird's feather, unable to properly support the body.

The aura is egg-shaped and, like a balloon, extends in front of and behind the physical body, above the head and beneath the feet. So, imagine yourself – the individual, independent intelligence that is within you – as an astronaut contained within an egg-shaped space capsule. Through this space capsule you are able to observe the reality that is happening all around you, and experience it through the use of various facilities and vehicles at your disposal. We will call these vehicles 'bodies' which are actually like sheaths for the consciousness to experience different 'realities'.

The shaman was not only aware of these different 'bodies' but actually worked with them and through them. In performing healings, for instance, a skilled shaman could discern in which body the cause of the sickness originated and thereby was able to deal with it at source rather than merely treat the effect. The more deep-seated the source, the 'higher' or 'finer' was the body in which it was located.

Let us examine briefly the different bodies or vehicles that comprise the human entity:

The vehicle you are most familiar with – and most people operate as if it were the only vehicle they have – is the *Physical Body* which we have been considering as a component of the West. The physical body is one you travel about the material world in – the realm of solids, liquids and gases. Through its use you are able to manipulate the material substances and make use of physical things. Through the scanning equipment of the physical body – the sensing devices called sight, hearing, touch, taste and smell – you are able to experience physical reality for yourself.

But you have other vehicles – other bodies – to enable you to be aware of existence beyond the range of the sensory equipment of your physical body. These other bodies are also contained within the cocoon. Each interpenetrates its coarser neighbour and together they occupy the same three-dimensional space, although there is a wide difference between each body because they radiate or vibrate on different wavelengths or frequencies. 'Tuning in' our consciousness to any one of these vehicles is like going up the frequency scale when tuning in to a radio station.

The *second* of our bodies is, therefore, composed of a finer and more subtle substance than the physical body and is vibrating at a frequency that is out of the range of our normal eyesight. It has been called the etheric body but I prefer the description that was given to me – the *Energy Body*. The energy body extends perhaps a couple of centimetres or more (an inch or so) beyond the surface of the skin and to those people who can see the aura it appears to glow with a whitish/bluish radiance. It completely interpenetrates the physical body and vitalises every cell in it.

The energy body deals with finer energies than those released by the metabolism of the food we eat, which sustains the coarser and more solid physical body. The energy body supports and energises the physical body by supplying the gas, liquid and solid structures with the subtle energies they need. It in turn is sustained by energies released by food, by breath energy which also vitalises higher bodies, and by light which energises the higher and highest bodies. The energy body integrates the individual into the energy field of the Earth. It is also the link to other, more subtle, bodies.

The 'organs' of the energy body around which it is built and sustained are circular whorls of spiralling energy which are generally called 'chakras'. 'Chakra' is a Sanskrit word meaning 'wheel' or 'vortex'. The American Indian shaman saw them as swirling discs of energy spinning at different rates and in different directions.

Just as the heart, liver, kidneys, lungs and other vital organs fulfil specific functions in maintaining the efficiency of the physical body, so the chakras perform essential functions in keeping the energy body and other subtle bodies working effectively. There are ten (not seven) major chakras and they are situated in a line from just beneath the feet to above the head at points where strands of energy radiate out, crossing and recrossing one another as ley lines do on Earth. Eight of the chakras are situated vertically along the line of the spinal column and in positions which roughly correspond with certain physical organs or nerve centres from which they take their name – the heart, the brow, throat, solar plexus, and so on.

Extending beyond the physical and energy bodies is a *third* vehicle – an emotional unit called the *Emotional Body*. It is with this vehicle that we are able to experience emotion and desire, love and joy, and feelings of elation as well as adverse sensations of discomfort and doom.

The emotional body is a vehicle which is more mobile than the physical or energy bodies, and is able to sense vibrations which the physical and energy bodies are unable to deal with because they are simply not equipped to do so. The emotional body is able to convert thought to feelings and vice versa. It works through glands and the nervous systems, that is, through chemical and electrical functioning.

The *fourth* vehicle is the *Astral Body*. The astral body is a 'double' or 'twin' of the physical body but is constructed of a very fine substance which interpenetrates physical matter. The astral body is designed to enable you to function on the astral plane – which is another dimension of existence. In 'out-of-body' experiences, sometimes called astral projection, the consciousness is transferred from the physical body where it resides most of the time, to the Astral Body which relates to the astral plane just as the physical body relates to the physical plane.

You are familiar with the astral plane because it is the place you visit in your dreams. When you are asleep and the physical body is being renewed and refreshed, like putting a battery on charge overnight, you are active on the astral plane in your astral body and have recollections in what many people call 'dream'.

On the astral plane things are similar to those we are familiar with on the physical plane except that the forms we see within it are less stable. Things are more fluid and change shape and this is because astral 'substance' is capable of taking any form that is impressed upon it. Another difference is that time and space are not the limiting factors they are on the physical plane. As a consequence time can be 'stretched out' or contracted. Apparent great distances can be travelled in an instant and long portions of time concentrated into moments. When we awake from a dream our astral body slips back into alignment with the physical and energy bodies.

The astral body is connected to the physical body by a silver umbilical cord not unlike that which attaches an astronaut to his space capsule when he ventures out of his craft. This silver cord is severed at death as the umbilical cord which joins the new-born baby to its mother is severed at birth.

The *fifth* vehicle is a mental unit – a *Mind Body*. It is through the mind body that you are able to experience mental and intellectual communication with other humans and with non-human intelligences. The mental body is concerned with the realm of thought which is the very substance of creation. Thought is at the very essence of everything that exists for before anything can manifest it exists first as Thought.

Mind is different from brain. The brain, as we discussed earlier, is a physical 'organ' – a functional, computer-like piece of equipment which relies on the mind for its instructions just as a computer relies on an operator to set it into motion. Unlike the brain, the mind is not tied to physical form, nor to one plane of existence. It is multi-dimensional and able to perform on all levels.

The sixth 'vehicle' — the *Soul* — is the life expression system. It enables the Spirit — the individuated essence and identity within — to express itself at conscious, subconscious, unconscious and superconscious levels. It is where the High Self is located. It stores the experience gained from this and other lives. The soul can suffer damage or fragmentation as a result of traumatic Earth plane experiences — an accident, a severe emotional upset, shock, bereavement, divorce, abortion, rape, incest, and so on. Sometimes individuals who have suffered a trauma feel they have 'lost' something of themselves as a result of the experience — that they are no longer the person they were. Somehow, they feel, some part of themselves 'left' them. Shamans were well aware that much illness was due to soul 'loss' and among their healing techniques was a method that enabled them to retrieve the 'missing' or fragmented part and restore it to the individual thus making the person 'whole' again.

The soul contains the High Self which survives after every vehicle has been jettisoned, one by one, after physical death. This High Self might be described as the personal *permanent* Self as compared with the *temporary* personality self which is the one whose birthday you keep and whose likes and dislikes, loves and hates, moods and whims, you are so familiar with. This temporary personality self exists for the space of a single lifetime and is being continually modified by life-conditioning and through the environment, work, personal relationships, disabilities, wealth/poverty, and so on. The personality self is constrained within a physical body with which it is identified. The permanent Self has no such constraints for it is contained within a soul body that can be projected into space, launched from one dimension of existence into another, and can take up 'residence' time after time in a human body to experience the realm of matter and thereby further its development or evolution.

The person you are — or, think you are — the temporary self is your terrestial self. I have called it the personal self because it has certain personality characteristics and qualities, likes and dislikes, and so on. The word 'personal' is an apt one to identify this 'self' since it is derived from the Latin word 'persona', which means 'mask'. The temporary personal self is, indeed, a 'mask' that is put on, it is transient and can be taken off in due course, by the High Self. However, the experiences which produced it would be absorbed first so that the experience is not wasted. The High Self is using the personality mask, is experiencing life and expressing itself through that 'mask' and that temporary personality. The temporary self is the human self and is the way the High Self gets experience by projection of itself into lower — or rather, slower — rates of vibration.

The temporary personality starts out on its life mission with clean memory tapes. The memory of what has happened before, of where it came from, has been withdrawn to the Soul. The memory tapes about previous lives and of experiences before birth are stored in the Soul.

Why should the temporary personality start out with clear memory tapes? So you can experience free will. We don't bring those tapes with us so we cannot immediately play back past life memories, or even know who we are, what we are, and why we are. We have to find out for ourselves sooner or later, and 'how' means having access to those tapes.

Each lifetime, each incarnation, has a purpose — let's call it the Soul's purpose — and reasons for being here now, at this point in history, and in the place where we are. What you were sent here to experience, what you had to find out about yourself is what it's all about. Enlightenment is the discovery of what the Soul's purpose is. Illumination is the experiencing of the High Self — of what some have called 'cosmic consciousness'. It is an awareness that brings not loss of individuality, but rather an expansion of individuality, so that you become more than you were. It is the awareness of one's own perfection and therefore of what is possible.

All the bodies I have described here interpenetrate one another and, to an extent, occupy the same space. This is because the various planes and dimensions of existence also interpenetrate and occupy the same space.

It is like filling a big jar with very small pebbles until it is full and you cannot get any more into it. But if you have another container holding very fine sand and you carefully pour the sand into the jar of pebbles, gently shaking it as you do so, you will find that quite a lot of the sand will go into the jar which hitherto appeared to be so full. The sand has occupied some of the space between the pebbles. Now the jar is full of both pebbles and sand. But if you have a cup of water and pour that into the jar, you will find there is room for quite a lot of the water, too, and that has occupied the same space — the inside of the jar. There is nothing more that can go into the jar without pebbles, sand and water spilling over.

But if you consider that pebbles, sand, and water are each made up of individual atoms, and those separate atoms are electrons whirling around a nucleus like planets around the Sun, and that each atom — like the solar system — is largely 'empty space', what looks like a jar solid with substance is, in fact, largely empty space. The fullness is an illusion.

The 'solidity' of matter is like that as we have discovered in our short 'walk' along the Path of the West.

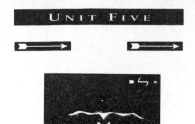

Attributes of the East

WE HAVE FACED DEATH IN THE WEST and come to terms with it, and since we have confronted our own death we fear it no longer – as a consequence we no longer fear life either. That's been one of our big hang-ups. We've been frightened of *life*. Frightened to live. Guilty about enjoying ourselves. The evidence in people's lives all around us testifies that it is not just death that terrifies people. It is *life*. Most of the psychological and spiritual problems we suffer are caused by being afraid to face up to life's realities – or, what we *believe* to be realities.

When the Adventurer comes to the EAST a realisation begins to dawn – the realisation that living is meant to be *enjoyed*, not suffered and endured. Life is intended to be *pleasurable*. The purpose of life is not to learn to put up with pain. It is to gain pleasure and knowledge in balance and harmony.

That does not imply a life of riotous living and the free expression of lust, greed and vanity. Those qualities have been in evidence in great abundance even in the most repressive times of religious rule and puritanical influence. Nor does it mean, of course, that you will not suffer pain and discomfort at times. After all, there is no change without pain. All is part of the process of living on Earth. The key is 'balance and harmony' and moderation in all things.

The East is the Direction of fresh, vibrant energy – the kind that can seemingly work 'miracles'. It is the place for undergoing self-renewal and where the Inner Light can shine forth and reveal your own intended Path. Another attribute of the East is beauty. And the seeker for knowledge in the quest for enlightenment should, in the language of the Indian, 'touch the world with Beauty'. Beauty might be defined as a combination of qualities that brings delight.

So if you come into balance and harmony and life becomes a pleasurable and exciting adventure as you seek knowledge, then you *will* touch the world with your beauty. For then you will be firmly on the Path that *is* the Beauty Way, a beautiful way, and you will have come to know true enlightenment, for the special qualities the East has to impart are Illumination and Enlightenment.

The components of the East are:

1. *Quality*: Illumination and Enlightenment.
2. *Totem*: Eagle.
3. *Element*: Fire.
4. *Colour*: Yellow.
5. *Kingdom*: Human.
6. *Heavenly Body*: The Sun.
7. *Human Aspect*: The Spirit.
8. *Time Period*: Momentary.
9. *Season*: Spring.
10. *Number*: One (.) and eleven.
11. *Enemy*: Death and Old Age.
12. *Manifestation*: Art and Writing.

So let us work the East:

- Set up your Circle.
- Smudge the Aura and the area around you.
- Assume the East position with the yellow marker in front of you.
- Relax and create your Mind space.

1. *Quality of the East*: ILLUMINATION AND ENLIGHTENMENT

The EAST is the Place where you can see where you are! The American Indian called it 'the Far-sighted Place' because it was where an over-view of life could be obtained.

The Power of the East is the power of Light, of mental and spiritual enlightenment, and of the inner vision that comes from an awareness of the unity of all living things. When we are 'in the dark' we are afraid to venture far beyond what we already know or have experienced — that which is familiar. But once there is access to light to illuminate the way, we can have the courage to venture into unfamiliar and even unknown realms, as we are doing on this journey of the Medicine Way. So the East provides us with en-*light*-enment to have the courage to be *adventurous*. After all, an adventure is intended to be not only thrilling, but enjoyable, exciting and stimulating. Your whole life can become enjoyable, exciting and thrilling from now on if you will let it.

The East is the place for extending the vision, of seeing things from afar, of being able to stand back and see the broader picture and so understand where everything 'fits together'. It is like seeing a picture of a jigsaw puzzle rather than just the collection of individual pieces. The picture shows us what the 'whole' looks like, so we are better able to determine where each separate piece fits. So the East is where we can learn to put things into perspective.

It was explained by my mentors that the East is the place of the Seer and when I expressed this thought to one enquirer he asked: 'If the East is the Place of the See-er, shall I be able to see God?' He argued that unless you could actually see God, how could you know that God existed? The East is the Direction to put such questions and to wait for answers. An answer I obtained was that the Great Spirit is revealed only in His work. The Great Spirit is reflected in all the work of the Creation and appears in every stone and rock, tree and plant, bird and beast, and in humans, too. That is how the Great Spirit is omnipotent, because It is present in all things, not separate from them, and that is why it is so important to have a *loving* relationship with Nature. Then you will *know* and not merely believe. That is enlightenment. Ignorance is the concept that only after one dies can one look on the face of God. The face of the Great Spirit is everywhere around us and in everything we see if only we can learn to look.

2. *Totem of the East*: EAGLE

The Eagle flies higher than any other bird and sees far and wide. To the Indian, the Eagle flies 'closest to the Sky' and since in Indian cosmology the sky is likened to Spirit, the Eagle represents that which is closest to Spirit.

The Eagle can fly directly into the Sun, and this ability symbolised to the Indian the receiving of a direct flow of inspiration from the power of Light, which is the Great Spirit.

The Eagle teaches balance, for even the moulting of a single feather from an Eagle's wing is balanced by the shedding of a feather from the other wing.

3. *Element of the East*: FIRE

Fire is the radiant energy of the Universe, the spark of life. At the human level it is expressed in enthusiasm, ambition and enterprise. Fire is a very powerful element. Its results manifest quickly since its characteristic is expansion, and like physical fire it can spread very quickly. It is the quality of combustion for elemental Fire energises. It is what powers the engines of motor cars, and aeroplanes. It is what generates electricity in power stations. It is what powers our factories. It powers our physical bodies, too, for it is the elemental Fire activity of our digestive system that makes possible the availability of substances that provide heat and energy for our bodies.

Those of us fortunate enough to have been brought up in houses with open fires can, perhaps, better understand the friendliness and comfort that fire can bring with its warmth. Sitting in front of a fire and watching the flames brings a feeling of contentment and well-being and one often gets inspiration from the 'pictures' one sees in the flames. People brought up in modern houses and flats that lack fireplaces may find it less easy to relate to the Fire element.

Fire energises and purifies, but can also be all-consuming and penetrating. According to ancient wisdom, the entire universe is Fire in the process of transformation. Everything in physical existence was regarded as condensed Fire — as 'solidified' light.

4. *Colour of the East*: YELLOW

Yellow is the colour of sunlight and as such is a cheerful and happy colour. Yellow expresses the need for constant stimulation and activity. It is an inspiring and expressive colour which expands the mind and the capacity to understand. Yellow is associated with the mentally adventurous. It is the colour of the solar plexus chakra.

5. *Kingdom of the East*: THE HUMAN KINGDOM

To the shaman trained in esoteric wisdom a human being was far more than an intelligent animal, or even a creative animal. A human being was a divine mortal. The real Self or Soul Self within was a spiritual entity that manifested through a physical body to experience the physical plane of existence. Man was thus a dual being existing in two realms — Matter and Spirit — one temporal, the other eternal.

According to the oral traditions of travelling shamans, human life came to the Earth some 250,000 years ago. The human being is a duality — a mortal, physical being who is a child of the Earth, composed of the substances of the Earth, and an immortal spirit, a child of the stars to which it is ultimately to return.

According to the Indian, man was 'related' to all living things not just because mankind, animals, plants and minerals all originated from the same Source, but because a human being was *part* of the mineral, plant and animal kingdoms since the human body was composed of elements from these three kingdoms. The Indian recognised that All is One.

Day and Night were not opposites, but aspects of the same thing. So were ice and water. Similarly, the Indian shaman did not consider the physical to be the opposite of spirit, nor man the opposite of God, the Great Spirit. God and mankind were aspects of the same thing. Man was the physical aspect of

Spirit, and God the invisible aspect of Spirit. Creation was but the transition of the invisible to the visible.

Therefore, visible things are only the reflections. Reflections of what? Reflections of invisible things. The visible could not appear if the invisible did not exist, any more than you could see your reflection in a mirror if the physical did not exist. So mankind was created in the likeness of the Universe. What is found in the universe is found in man, who is the universe in miniature.

6. *Heavenly Body of the East:* THE SUN

The East is the direction of the sunrise and of the miracle of new birth. It is the Sun which causes all creatures to awaken from their slumber to start a new day with freshness.

Grandfather Sun is the masculine, penetrating force at the very hub of the universe – the force which brought light out of darkness, order out of chaos, and the One of whom the physical Sun is but a symbol – an outward, physical representation. As everything in our solar system revolves around the physical Sun, which is the prime energy source of everything, so does everything in existence revolve around the Spiritual Sun – Grandfather Sun – who is the Source of Everything and upon Whom all life depends. The physical Sun is so powerful that it lifts great masses of vapour into the skies from all the great oceans of the Earth. The Spiritual Sun is so powerful that the whole Universe is lifted up and suspended likewise in Nothing.

The Indian and the ancients no more worshipped the physical sun than a solider worships the flag of his country. Is it an act of worship to stand in silence as the national emblem is raised or lowered on certain ceremonial occasions? By so doing you are paying tribute and respect to the country which gave you birth and in which your roots are, and you honour the culture and traditions of the country which protects you.

You can pay tribute and respect to the physical sun, too, particularly at times like its rising and setting which are when it is at its most magnificent.

Whilst you could live without your country's flag, you would not exist a single day without the Sun and its light. But even the physical sun whose light you cannot live without, is but an emblem of Grandfather Sun, the Spiritual Sun without whom you would not be.

The Sun, too, is a symbol of the Inner Light in every person – the divine 'Sun' within us all. Each and every one of us is a Sun, which is a star, and we are offspring of the Sun. In truth, we are Sun-men, Solar-men – beings of Light, children of the stars.

7. *Human Aspect of the East*: THE SPIRIT

A dictionary definition of spirit is 'a vitalising life force or vital principle that is unseen and intangible'. Spirit may be described as the driving force behind the living form, be it human, animal, plant, human or celestial. One difference between spirit and energy is that spirit has inherent intelligence. It required more than power to create a universe. It required intelligence. Blind, undirected energy requires intelligence to direct it and spirit to determine its direction.

The Amerindian shaman made clear distinctions between soul, spirit and ego. The soul was regarded as the expression for the individuated spirit which was itself considered to be a 'spark' or 'globule' or 'cell' of the Great Spirit. The 'I' of the spirit was of the permanent Self — the eternal Self — whereas the ego belonged to the physical Self, the temporary personality which came into existence at birth.

A person's spiritual life is thus the most important aspect of his or her humanity. That is why we should *determine* with the spirit — let our spirit make the decisions. To be 'in balance' we need to receive knowledge into our mind, but it is the spirit that should be the determining factor in how we apply that knowledge in living our lives. The distinction can be made clear this way:

> Mind *creates*.
> Spirit *directs*.
> Force or energy *performs*.
> Matter *appears*.

8. *Time period of the East*: MOMENTARY

This time period stresses the importance of the moment. A moment is not only a point of time; it is also a power or force that causes rotation and movement. To most of us, a moment may be regarded as just a fleeting second that is quickly gone. But life is made up of moments in an ever-moving stream. The power of a moment lies in the quality of the thought that is contained within it. Bear in mind that a flash of inspiration comes not over a long period of time but in a moment.

9. *Season of the East*: SPRING

Spring is the season when new life that has been hidden in the womb of the Earth is awakened and bursts forth in splendour. The East, then, is the direction of Awakening and of becoming aware both 'within' and 'without'.

It is the Place of coming forth into newness of life. It is where we can find the answers to our needs in Nature and in the spirit.

10. *Number of the East*: ONE (.)

The number One represents the individuality. One is the monad, the first, the commencement, the individuation that comes out of nothing. It is the principal number – indivisible and immutable. It signifies existence and identity. The upright figure One is a phallic symbol which stresses One's masculine nature, the conceptual quality that is the seed of all other numbers. One has the thrustfulness of the masculine principle in Nature. It is the symbol of the Will acting through the Spirit.

One, in the East, is the power of clear vision and of perceiving the main target or goal. It stresses independent action and self-organisation. In other words, One stresses the need to get your own act together!

Eleven is its counterpart for inner plane communication and to link in with the Collective Unconscious to make possible access to ancient knowledge.

11. *Enemy of the East*: DEATH AND OLD AGE

Death is an enemy until it can be converted into an adviser which we learned about in the West (and remember that death does not apply only to the transition at the end of physical life, but refers to every change we make – every change being the 'death' of what went before. We make death an adviser by learning the lessons of those changes, whether enforced or willed).

Old age, on the other hand, is an enemy the spiritual Adventurer will never be able to defeat completely. The best we can do is to fend it off. How? By remaining active and creative and open to new ideas – by not abandoning ourselves to the ravages of Time. The secret is in acquiring *youthful* old age.

In the context of the East, the realisation comes to us that if we lose our physical body through the ravages of old age or by physical death before enlightenment comes, then we are in need of a 'refit' and will return to Earth again in another physical body to go through the same process of seeking, learning, experiencing and of trying to reach – ENLIGHTENMENT!

12. *Manifestation of the East*: ART AND WRITING

Since the East is symbolic of light rising out of the darkness, creativity is the coming to light of that which was 'hidden' in the Self and then expressed in art and writing. This is why art and writing give pleasure to the person performing them. Each is an expression of the Self coming to light.

DIRECTIONAL QUEST:

Where Am I Going?

> Return to your place among the trees and this time sit so you are facing East. Take with you a token of the 'kingdom' associated with the East – the human kingdom. A lock of your hair, or nail clippings would do. Wrap them in a small piece of tissue and hold them in your left hand at your navel. Rest your right hand on top of your left. This again serves as a focal point. Then put your question for a vision of the future: 'Where am I going? What is my intended Path?' Wait patiently but expectantly for a response.

Let me share an experience of mine. I had closed my eyes and as I contemplated the question I became aware of the bite of the cold East wind on my face. What gives the wind its direction? I found myself asking. Does it determine where it blows?

I opened my eyes in anticipation that something would catch my attention, to trigger, perhaps, a response to my question, but as I looked around I was aware only of the entanglement of undergrowth and bracken surounding me. From where I was sitting I could not even establish the whereabouts of the forest footpath which had led me to this spot. But then life is like that. We have to get through the entanglements of attachments to reach the path that will take us forward. Often in life we are so closed in by our attachments that we cannot see the way ahead. We need a sense of direction so we can free ourselves from the entanglement of 'belongings' and find a clear path beneath our feet. But where does the path lead? What way should I go?

The wind slapped my face, and brought my attention back to the original question: Where am I going? Well, wind, where are *you* going? The wind is going nowhere but where it is. Likewise, I am going nowhere but where I am. I am always where I am now. It is only the surroundings that change and the way I perceive them. I am going to where my True Self will predominate. Then I shall be enlightened.

Then I was aware of voices – human voices – through the trees and I caught a brief glimpse of a couple walking along the woodland footpath which was hidden from my view. They were moving from my left to my right – from the North to the South. The South is the direction of the red race of humans and I took this to indicate that this was the path I must stay and explore. I had an answer to my question.

Shortly afterwards I was privileged to participate in a number of ancient Amerindian ceremonies during which time I was 'commissioned' to write this book.

Listen to the whisper of the wind.

THE GIVE-AWAY

The East is associated with the Spirit so ask yourself what spiritual matter may be impeding your progress to enlightenment and spiritual freedom. Could it be your 'need' for freedom – your 'need' to do exactly as you like? Are you hurt by constraints and frustrations? Then the path to freedom may lie in giving away your need of it in order to attain contentment. Think about that. When you have determined what it is you want to banish from your life, associate it with the token in your left hand. Then bury that token in the ground. Consider what positive spiritual qualities should replace it and seek the transforming power to enable them to be brought about.

Then consider what positive attributes you can give to bring a blessing to others. What of your Spirit can you 'give away'? Is it your time? Time is a great gift to 'give' to others for time is a measurement of life and you can give no greater gift than your life. Consider how you can devote some of your *time* to bring pleasure to others.

ADVENTURER TASK NO.4:

The Link with Sun and Earth

The South Adventurer Task was to erase our personal history, to free ourselves from the attachments that were hindering our development towards enlightenment and self-realisation. In the West our Task was to face our own death, to show willingness to accept change and to leave behind those burdens of the Past that were obscuring the Present.

Now having journeyed to the East to seek enlightenment and truth, we need to activate our intentions by endeavouring to re-establish our links with our 'true' parents – the Earth, who is our Mother, and the Spiritual Sun who is our true Father. These also represent the female and male energies of Creation.

The following Rite will open up your perceptions and expand your awareness in many, many ways if you will act it out naturally and with feeling. Having performed this ritual, you will experience for yourself in the days, weeks and months that follow, a closer relationship with the natural world around you, a closer affinity with Nature, an atunement with rocks and stones, trees and plants, animals and birds, that you have never known before. New understanding will come into your mind through quite ordinary, everyday activities, and life will begin to take on a new meaning and purpose.

You might even find yourself 'inspired' to express yourself in some creative way.

Preliminaries:

The Rite *must* be performed out of doors and in a secluded spot where you will not be disturbed for at least half an hour or so. Perhaps a small clearing in woodland, or a place near a quiet river or stream, or on a hilltop or tor.

You will need to take with you:
  i)   A compass to enable you to establish the cardinal directions.
  ii) Your five coloured marker stones.
  iii) A pouch or package containing cornmeal, sage or mixed herbs.
  iv) A notebook and pen to record your experiences immediately afterwards.

Any other items required will be found on the site you have chosen.

RITE NO. 4:

Linking with Sun and Earth

On arrival at the site, take off your shoes and socks or tights. It is best that this ritual is performed barefoot so that you actually *feel* the Earth under your feet.

Choose your centre point on the site and place your green marker on the ground there. Then, using your compass, find the South direction. Take two or three paces from your centre marker to the South and mark the spot by placing your red marker stone on the ground there.

Return to the centre and with your compass find the North. Take two or three paces from the centre to the North and place your white marker on the ground there.

Back to the centre, and find the East. Take two or three paces East and mark the spot with your yellow stone.

Return to the centre and find the West. Take two or three paces West and place the black stone on the ground there. Then return to the centre and face *West*.

Remember, West is the direction for dealing with the Earth and with earthly things, with physical matters and material needs. In this Rite, the desire and intention must remain clear in your mind – it is to make connection with Mother Earth and to establish an affinity with the Soul of the Earth.

Take one step forward, kneel on the ground and with your hands held with palms upwards and little fingers touching as in a gesture of offering say aloud:

> MOTHER EARTH, FROM WHOSE BODY HAS COME MY BODY
> OPEN MY HEART AND MIND TO YOUR LOVE
> AND TO YOUR BLESSINGS.

Bend forward and kiss the earth. Stay in this kneeling position for a few minutes and visualise your picture of Mother Nature. Don't 'force' anything. Don't 'try'. Just allow a picture to come into your mind. It may be an impression of a woman. It may be a blue and white globe suspended in space. Whatever picture comes into your mind, allow yourself to gently dwell on it for a few moments. Then when you are ready stand up and return to the centre.

Now turn and face the *South* marker. Remember, the South is the direction of elemental Water and of the emotions.

> Take one pace forward, kneel, and, cupping your hands into a bowl shape, say:
> SPIRIT OF THE FLOWING WATERS
> POUR FORTH YOUR BLESSINGS UPON ME.

Now imagine for a few minutes that moonlight is shining on a calm sea or upon the still waters of a wide river. You might even see in your mind's eye a figure of a woman on the water walking towards you. Just fix the moonlight over the water and let the picture in your mind dwell on that or develop from that. When you are ready, stand up and step back to the centre.

Now turn to the *East* marker. Take a pace forward, stretch your arms out wide with your hands just above the level of your shoulders, look up towards the Sun and say:

> GRANDFATHER SUN, GIVER AND GUARDIAN OF LIFE AND
> LIGHT SEND ME ENLIGHTENMENT.

Again, pause for a few minutes. Let a picture come into your mind. Reach out with all your senses. Then, take a step backwards to the centre.

Now turn to the North marker. The North, you will remember, is the direction of elemental Air, of Mind, Knowledge and Wisdom. Take a pace forward and stand with your thumbs linked and hands spread out like wings, and say:

> GRANDFATHER SKY, GIVER OF THE BREATH OF LIFE
> GRANT ME KNOWLEDGE AND WISDOM.

Again pause for a few minutes. Let a picture come into your mind, and again reach out with all your senses.

Step back to the centre, turn to face the East and with your arms outstretched with palms upturned and cupped to receive a blessing, say:

> GREAT ONES, SEND ME YOUR POWER AND LIFE FORCE
> TO AID, INSPIRE, AND UPLIFT ME
> ON THE PATH OF BEAUTY AND TRUTH
> NOW AND THROUGHOUT ALL TIME.

Keep your arms upstretched for a few moments to receive the blessing you have asked for.

Then kneel or sit for a few minutes. Open your senses to receive any link that may be made. When you feel that the ritual is completed, say 'Thank You' and then write down immediately what thoughts or impressions came into your mind at each direction and any experience you may have had.

Then stand up and walk around the circle indicated by the marker stones sprinkling the cornmeal or herbs as an offering to Mother Earth. This is your 'give away' since to receive you must give and in giving you will also receive. The cornmeal or herbs is merely a token of your 'givingness'.

Stamp your foot on the ground firmly four times and take a deep breath. This is to gently remove the delicate barrier that has cut your circle off from the mundane world and to ground you back to the here-and-now plane of everyday existence.

You have worked anti-clockwise for this Rite because the Earth itself turns this way and the idea was to take you from the mundane plane of existence to a higher plane of reality.

Pick up your marker stones in the reverse order that they were laid down: black first, then yellow, white, red and finally green.

Look around the site carefully before you leave. Should you notice any object or objects that you were not aware of when you arrived at the site, take them home with you. It may be a flower, a stone, a feather, pinecones, whatever. The significance will become clear to you in due course.

The Human Power Centres

WE AGAIN RETURN TO THE CENTRE, this time to consider a 'hidden' part of the human anatomy – the power centres. So:

- Place the green centre-stone in front of you.
- Smudge yourself and the area around you.
- Relax and create your own Mind space, and centre yourself. Make notes of any relevant throughts that come to mind as you contemplate the following:

The shaman picked a flower and by looking at it confirmed the ancient wisdom – as you can, too – that the whole of Creation works like a flower, developing from the unseen to the seed, from seed to growth, from growth to bud, from bud to bloom, from bloom to seed, and from seed to unseen again. From invisible cause to visible effect. From unity to diversity. From centre to circumference, and back again. He was aware that there was a vital cosmic energy that was in constant motion and which was absorbed by the breath. This life energy was taken in with the breath and was vital for the functioning not only of the physical body but of the other subtle bodies of which the human being was composed.

Some Amerindian tribes called this vital force 'mana'. Western mystics, who are aware of this same cosmic energy, have usually referred to it by the Sanskrit word 'prana', and in the East it was known by the Chinese as 'chi', by the Japanese as 'ki'.

The principal vehicle for this 'mana' or 'prana' is not the physical body, however, but the energy body which vitalises the physical body and the nervous and endocrine systems. The vital force is drawn in from the cosmic reservoir with the breath, much as a fish extracts oxygen from the water in which it is immersed, is absorbed into the energy body and 'refined' through the chakras before being distributed to the physical and subtle bodies.

The essence of all life is in what the Amerindian shaman regarded as the Divine Breath, and sometimes referred to as the 'breath of the Invisible'. Breath is air so air, it was concluded, contains this vitality of life. The 'breath of life' is thus an aeriform substance which contains within it the

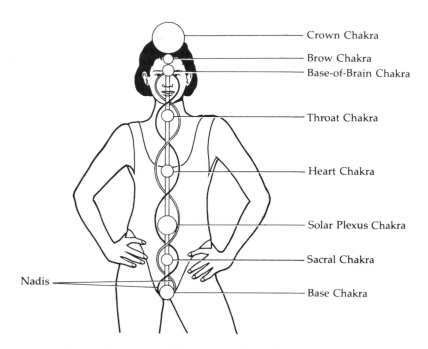

Crown Chakra
Brow Chakra
Base-of-Brain Chakra
Throat Chakra
Heart Chakra
Solar Plexus Chakra
Sacral Chakra
Nadis
Base Chakra

Fig. 21. The nadis – vertical tubes or channels which convey currents of energy to the chakras

fiery, vital force which encapsulates the very essence from which all matter is ultimately formed and from which arises the building blocks of physical manifestation.

With each inhalation of breath it is taken into the energy body through vertical tubular channels. In Western esoteric circles these are usually referred to as 'nadis', a word 'borrowed' from Hatha Yoga of the East. There are three major 'nadis' located in the energy body in a line that corresponds to the spinal column of the physical body. One extends from the chakra near the base of the spine to one positioned at the crown of the head. The two others are entwined around this central nadi and weave in and out between the chakras.

The nadi starting at the right side carries the 'positive' current and the nadi starting on the left side carries the 'negative' current. They weave from side to side of the central nadi which is neutral. The positive and negative nadis are linked with the nostrils and extract Aetheric substance from the physical air. The two currents of energy cross at points between the revolving chakras where the energies are absorbed and distributed.

Seven of these power centres are located vertically and roughly in line with the spinal column – the base of the spine chakra, the sacral, solar plexus, heart, throat, brow, and crown chakras. There are three other major chakras – one located beneath the feet (the root chakra), one between the ankles (the feet chakra), and one at the base of the brain. The root and crown chakras fulfil purposes concerning the polarity and flow of auric energies surrounding the physical body. The other eight are arranged in an octave in accordance with the universal Law of Harmonics – the structure of cycles of eight. This law is at the foundation of the Medicine Wheel teachings and those of the eight-spoked circle of Western and Eastern esoteric traditions. This arrangement also indicates that the root and crown chakras are in different dimensions from the eight other major chakras.

Each chakra is sometimes represented as having a number of 'petals' like a flower. The one with the fewest petals is the Root chakra beneath the feet which has only one. The greatest number of petals is at the Crown chakra at the top of the head which has 972. The number of petals indicates the frequency of the energy at that point. The greater the number of petals, the higher the frequency range and the finer the energy flow. The lower the frequency range, the denser is the energy flow.

The knowledge of the entwining nadis and of their function was encapsulated by the ancients in the symbol of the Caduceus – two snakes, one black and one white, twisting their bodies around a winged staff or wand. (Fig. 22, p 156). The Caduceus symbolised the flow of energies within the human entity. It is not without significance that the Caduceus later became the emblem associated with healing and the medical profession.

According to the ancient teaching, this flow through the nadis and into and out of the chakras alternated between both the vertical and horizontal polarities. In other words, it acted like the flow of energy in a quadripolar magnet. Indeed, the human system is three-dimensional, not two-dimensional, with a vertical axis which can be represented by 'above' to 'below' and a horizontal axis by the symbol of an equal-armed cross. If you stand, from above to below can be represented by a vertical line   and right to left and front to back by an equal-armed cross X . The binding of these simple representations together result in the symbol,   ⚕ which expresses the whole concept.

So the vertical poles of the human system are like a magnet with the chakras acting like rotors. Furthermore, each chakra – each rotor – is quadripolar with energy flowing into it and out of it. Outgoing energy is experienced by the human being through *action*, and incoming energy is experienced through *sensing*.

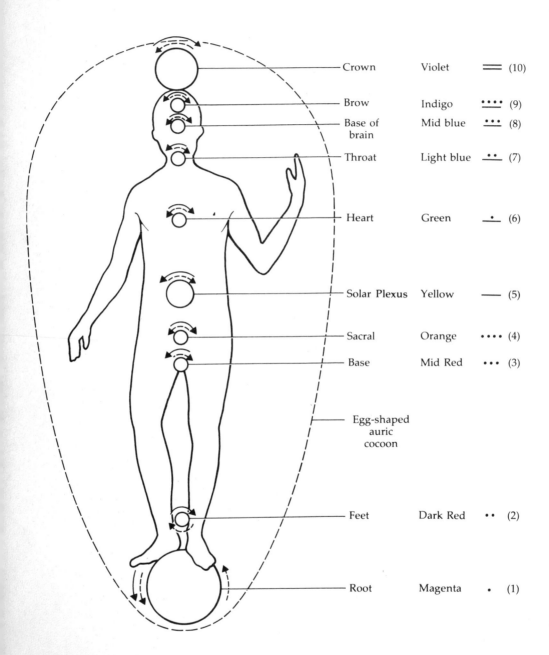

Crown	Violet	═══ (10)
Brow	Indigo	⋅⋅⋅⋅ (9)
Base of brain	Mid blue	⋅⋅⋅ (8)
Throat	Light blue	⋅⋅ (7)
Heart	Green	⋅ (6)
Solar Plexus	Yellow	─── (5)
Sacral	Orange	⋅⋅⋅⋅ (4)
Base	Mid Red	⋅⋅⋅ (3)
Egg-shaped auric cocoon		
Feet	Dark Red	⋅⋅ (2)
Root	Magenta	⋅ (1)

○*Fig. 22. The approximate position of the ten major chakras and the directional flow in man and woman*

Fig. 23. The Caduceus. The ancient symbol which revealed the secret of the entwined nadis twisting around the chakra power centres and the input of Prana with the air represented by the wings located at the Base-of-the-Brain chakra. In this symbol, the central rod also represented cosmic Fire, the entwined snake on the left – Life, and the snake on the right – Consciousness. It also symbolised the Four Elements – the rod representing Earth, the Wings Air, the snakes Fire and Water (indicated by the wave movement)

The chakras are located along the line of the spinal column where strands of fine light energy – of which the aura is composed – cross and re-cross each other many times. The currents of energy alternate in a way similar to that of electricity generation. In a simple generator, for instance, the rotor rotates between the poles of a fixed magnet, cutting the lines of force first in one direction and then in the other. In the human being the energy currents alternate between the 'north' and 'south' polarities and the 'east' and 'west' polarities, being a complex vector sum of these at any instant, since the human 'magnet' is not fixed. And this is all linked with the incoming and outgoing breath.

The pranic or manic force, with its elemental energies charged by the Sun, comes into the energy body through the breath, is drawn into the nadis and chakras, and vitalises the organs and centres of the physical body through the blood, the parasympathetic nervous system and the endocrine glands. The parasympathetic nervous system may be considered to be an extension of the nadis, and the endocrine system as an extension of the chakras.

The parasympathetic nervous system is a highly complex and sophisti-cated communications network through which impulses of 'electrical' energy and chemical carriers travel and operate the 'motor' functions of the body in opposition to or in combination with the sympathetic nervous system which reacts to the stimuli received from the senses. We react, therefore, to inputs at both the higher and lower energy levels.

The endocrine glands are groups of special cells which secrete hormones into the bloodstream. Hormones are chemical 'messengers' which control many of the functions of other cells and tissues. For instance, the suprarenal or adrenal bodies which cap each kidney produce a number of hormones which control such functions as body fluids, the breakdown of protein, the amount of blood glucose, total body fat, the production of anti-bodies to deal with infection and inflammation, and the secretion of adrenalin. The thyroid gland produces the hormones which control the general metabolic rate, the heartbeat, the blood pressure, mental activity, fertility and growth.

The pranic–manic life force is thus channelled to the physical body and its organs via the nadis and the chakras in a way not unlike the extraction of oxygen from air which is drawn into the lungs and distributed to each individual cell through the bloodstream.

A chakra may be a tiny, saucer-like disc which is inert and lacking in lustre and intensity – as would be the case with a seriously ill person or with someone motivated by selfishness and greed – or quite large and radiantly active in the case of a healthy and spiritually 'alive' person. Indeed, in a spiritually-developed individual, the chakras are like blazing spheres, functioning in perfect unison with one another and creating an effect of great beauty.

So the degree of chakra activity depends on a combination of the emotional, mental and spiritual development of the individual as well as on physical good health. In other words, they reflect the *quality* of the individual's life as a holistic entity.

Chakras, like physical organs, can be impaired and even damaged. For instance, a sudden shock through an unfortunate accident or experience, a traumatic emotional upset or a sudden bereavement, are among the most common causes of chakra malfunctioning. Fear, anxiety and stress, can take their toll by disturbing the dynamic energy balance of the chakras. Psychological problems may cause 'blockages', obstructing the flow of energy into or out of the chakras. An obstruction is effectively an area where energy has ceased to flow, caused by energies opposing natural ones and produced by traumas, anxieties and so on. Such obstruction anywhere in the energy flow can result in an erratic endocrine gland functioning and a consequent imbalance of the hormone activity.

Each chakra has a particular function, but in general terms those below the diaphragm deal with the energies of the more mundane activities of physical existence – with what might be called 'survival' functions – while the energies of the chakras above the diaphragm are related to creative and expressive activities.

Within the vertical polarity, the slowing down of the vibratory rate of the power centres in descending order, indicates the changes of motivation of activity, from the 'highest' and 'spiritual' centre to the 'lowest' and densest 'physical' centre. The chakras can thus reflect the individual's attitude to life – whether the emphasis is directed largely towards materialistic things and 'earthy' activities or whether there is an involvement with the reality of spiritual things. Ideally, they should all be fully developed and be in complete dynamic balance.

As a person's interest and involvement in other than materialistic pursuits develops and more use is made of the latent 'psychic' and spiritual functions, so the higher chakras awaken and become more active. As this happens, an expansion of consciousness takes place providing the individual with insight into other realms of existence and within themselves.

The level of chakra activity is reflected in the aura – in its colours, tones and hues – for when a person sets out on the path of enlightenment, the chakras are consciously or unconsciously affected and begin to operate at a higher level of their potential.

Let us now examine in a little more detail each of the ten major chakras so that we can have a fuller understanding of its functions.

The root and crown chakras

The one beneath the feet at the bottom of the auric cocoon (the root chakra) and the one above the crown of the head in the auric dome are concerned with the control of the auric energy-system and with its blending in with the Earth's auric field. The root chakra, as its name implies, is like the roots of a tree. The crown chakra receives the Sun's rays. So we as individuals are thus polarised between Sun and Earth. The crown is the chakra which has a Sun within it and this we can experience as that centre of consciousness known as the High Self or Higher Self which draws its energy from the Sun. The root chakra is associated with the colour magenta, and the crown chakra with violet.

The feet chakra

Of the remaining eight power centres, there is one between the ankles called the feet chakra whose function is related to movement and balance. Its colour is dark red.

The base chakra

The next major chakra above it is the base chakra at the bottom of the spine. This not only supports the other chakras above it but serves also to energise the physical body. It is concerned with our physical well-being. When our basic security is threatened in any way, it triggers the adrenal glands with which it is linked and these release quantities of adrenalin into the bloodstream.

The base chakra thus guards and protects the physical form and reacts to any stress by preparing the body to 'fight' or to 'flee' when threatened. The base chakra also has a connection with the cellular substance of the physical body and governs the kidneys and the spinal column. The base chakra has four petals — in other words, a frequency multiple of four. It responds primarily to the colour mid-red and its functional significance is elimination.

The sacral chakra

The fourth is located below the navel and is generally referred to as the *sacral chakra*. It externalizes as the gonads which govern the reproductive system and influence the sex life. It has to do with *motivation*, with what 'turns us on' emotionally, and how we feel about others. It responds primarily to the colour *orange* and its functional significance is *reproduction*. It has a frequency multiple of six.

The solar plexus chakra

The fifth is the *solar plexus chakra* whose focus is located 2–3 cm (about an inch) above the navel. 'Solar' means Sun, 'plexus' means 'network' and the solar plexus chakra is concerned with absorbing energy from the Sun's light and distributing it through a fine and complex network throughout the body. It is linked with the digestive system and the pancreas which is the organ that controls the balance of blood sugar, and the conversion of food that is being digested, into nutrients which the body can use. The pancreas secretes insulin which is a vital chemical in the control of the body's metabolism.

The solar plexus chakra's functional significance is *growth* and *balance*. From this centre, fibres connect us to all other living things. It has a frequency multiple of ten. It responds primarily to the colour *yellow*.

The heart chakra

The sixth power centre is in the central chest area and is generally known as the *heart chakra*. It is the 'desire' centre and is related to love, devotion and compassionate action. It is linked with the heart, the blood and circulation and with the thymus gland.

The heart chakra is the distribution centre for the magnetic energies of life, just as the heart is the physical distribution centre for the blood of life. Its functional significance is *love* and emotional energies. It responds primarily to the colour *green*. The heart chakra has a frequency multiple of twelve.

The throat chakra

The seventh is the *throat chakra* which is located at the base of the neck. It is linked with the thyroid and parathyroid glands which regulate growth and tune the nervous system. It is also linked with the lungs and with the vocal apparatus. The throat chakra is concerned with *communication* through the spoken word. It is also linked with our 'inner voices' and with clairaudience and telepathy. Its functional significance is the spoken word. The Soul's energies are expressed through the throat chakra. It responds primarily to the colour *blue* and its frequency multiple is sixteen.

The base-of-the-brain chakra

The eighth is the *base-of-the-brain chakra*. Its functional significance is action and it responds primarily to *mid-blue*. It has a frequency multiple of thirty-six.

The brow chakra

The ninth is the *brow chakra* which is located behind the forehead above the bridge of the nose. It is concerned with how we perceive reality, and might be described as the psychic command post. Its functional significance is mental power and the ability to see the reality behind appearances. It responds primarily to the colour indigo (blue-black) and its frequency multiple is 96.

The crown chakra

The tenth is the *crown chakra* in and above the top of the head. It connects with the pituitary gland which governs all other glands, and is concerned with knowing. Its functional significance is wisdom and intuition – which is knowing without being taught. It has 972 petals and is sometimes referred to as 'the thousand-petalled lotus'. It responds primarily to the colour violet.

There are, within the auric cocoon, three key *control centres*. One is located in the right chest area near the heart, the second centre is a moving one and the third is situated near the navel. When we were born these three control centres were all located in the navel because at that stage we were in harmony and alignment with the universe and with the Source from whence we came.

During the first three years of life, one centre moves from the navel, up the central chakra line and across to the right chest area where it rests. The precise position is determined by the High Self before birth to enable the individual to perceive reality in the way best suited for the kind of growth and experiences needed from that particular lifetime. This control centre is a small focal point of energy which flashes on and off. Although this control centre usually remains in position it can shift. The more spiritually developed a person becomes, the more this point will move towards the central chakra line and then downwards towards the navel again. When it is positioned in the right chest area the perception is narrow and confined. The nearer it is to the central chakra line the more the person's spiritual awareness is developed. A shift of only two or three centimetres is enough to bring about a considerable expansion of conscious awareness and spiritual discernment. As the control centre moves to the central chakra line and downwards, so the perception continues to expand and spiritual development continues.

Shifts of this control centre can be brought about through meditation, through ritual, through Medicine Way workings, through shamanic chanting and dancing and through the deliberate use of crystals. It is *not* possible for intellectual knowledge alone toeaffect a shift, any more than book knowledge without practical application and experience is sufficient to acquire technical competence.

The second centre is a moving one and deals with Earth energy. Earth energy flows up through the auric fibres or meridians and establishes cyclic ebbs and flows called *biorhythms*. Biorhythms affect all aspects of our being — the physical, emotional, mental, spiritual and sexual. They set up our daily, monthly and yearly energy cycles. By recognizing and becoming aware of these cycles and arranging our lives in harmony with their natural flows, we can increase our overall energy level, come to know the best times for certain endeavours and thus bring our lives more into harmony with all that is.

The *third* control centre remains in the navel area throughout life. It is the point from which your 'I' assembled you as a human being. It is the transmission point between the human being and the Source of Everything. It is from this centre that luminous fibres connect us *outwards* into the cosmos and into contact with all that is within the Great Everything.

The ten major chakras and the three control centres are connected to the sensory equipment of the eyes and ears. The left eye is connected with the base chakra at the bottom of the spine and the right eye to the sacral chakra. But the shaman knew of eight other eyes in the human being whose presence was recognised by the ancients but have yet to be 'discovered' by modern medical science. There is an eye usually referred to as the 'third eye' located behind the brow and between the eyebrows. Its presence is known to many so-called 'psychic' people and by clairvoyants, for when it is opened and exercised it 'sees' into the astral realm where unmanifested 'substance' is taking shape before taking form. A *fourth eye* is located in the bridge of the nose and is connected to the heart chakra. It 'sees' any danger before it is actually observed or sensed by the physical senses. It also 'sees' the truth. For instance, when someone says, 'I see that', implying that they comprehend the meaning of what is being said, they are 'seeing' it with their fourth eye. A *fifth eye* is located on the crown of the head. It is this eye that 'sees' dreams – also back in time to scenes stored in the memory. The fifth eye is connected to the throat chakra. A *sixth eye* is in the palm of the left hand and sees the spirit or essence of what is touched. It is because of this sixth eye that psychometry works. Impressions of an object held in the left hand are transmitted to the brain to provide a mental picture. Sometimes it is possible to describe something of the history of the object and of its owner or owners. The sixth eye is connected to the brow chakra, which is why the mental pictures appear in the brow region. The *seventh eye* is in the palm of the right hand and is capable of seeing how the object the palm touches was used. The seventh eye is connected with the feet chakra. The *eighth eye* is in the sole region of the left foot and is sometimes referred to as the karma eye because it is capable of reading past life experiences. It is connected to the chakra at the base of the brain. The *ninth eye* is located in the sole of the right foot and sees the way the auric system is designed. It can perceive any imbalance. It is connected to the root chakra beneath the feet. Finally, there is the *tenth eye* which is located in the solar plexus region and is connected to the crown chakra. It sees the interconnection of all things.

Now to the ears. Our own physical ears pick up sound vibrations which produce movements of Air just as our physical eyes pick up light vibrations which are produced by Fire. The left ear is linked with the base chakra and the right ear with the sacral chakra. There is a *third ear* located in the brain area of the skull. It is the ear that hears the inner dialogue when we talk silently to ourselves. When we 'hear' our own thoughts we are, in fact, hearing with this third ear. It is the third ear that picks up the dialogue between our personality self and our High Self. It is linked with the base-of-the-brain chakra. The *fourth ear* is connected with the heart chakra and

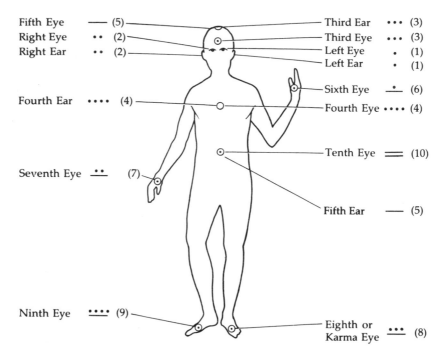

Fifth Eye	—— (5)			Third Ear	••• (3)
Right Eye	•• (2)			Third Eye	••• (3)
Right Ear	•• (2)			Left Eye	• (1)
				Left Ear	• (1)
				Sixth Eye	•_ (6)
Fourth Ear	•••• (4)			Fourth Eye	•••• (4)
				Tenth Eye	= (10)
Seventh Eye	•• (7)				
				Fifth Ear	—— (5)
Ninth Eye	•••• (9)			Eighth or Karma Eye	••• (8)

○*Fig. 24. The location of the ten eyes and five ears of the human being*

hears the unspoken language of truth and untruth. The *fifth ear* is connected with the control centre at the solar plexus. It hears the interconnection of all things within the Great Everything.

With a medicine bundle that contains items that link in with all aspects of his or her personality and psyche, the shaman is able, by holding it to the control centre at the navel with the left hand (the sixth eye) and right hand (the seventh eye) over the fifth ear, to interconnect with other levels and thereby 'see' and 'hear' things which normally could not be comprehended. The whole level of awareness is thus extended.

In this Unit I have attempted to explain how the human being is an amazing complexity of functions and processes with each part, each organ, each cell dependent on another, and each aimed at integrating the diversity of structures into a harmonious and smoothly-functioning whole – all to support the intelligence, the being, the Spirit, within it.

The human entity is equipped to extend its consciousness beyond the range of its energy field and to experience higher frequencies of activity. Indeed, part of the purpose for your being on Earth and experiencing life on the material plane is to learn to make use of all the equipment with which your own personal spaceship – your auric cocoon – has been provided.

Attributes of the North

WE NOW TRAVEL TO THE *NORTH* to seek wisdom and understanding and to 'stop the world'. What is meant by 'stopping the world'? It means to stop seeing the world as people have been telling us it is. It means putting a stop to the conditioning that has prevented us from relating to the Creation all around us, leaving us isolated from it.

In the sixteenth century when European mariners 'discovered' the Americas, the so-called 'civilised' world believed that the Earth was flat. Indeed, in some countries you could get yourself thrown into prison for heresy for disputing the then dogmatic Christian belief that we lived on a flat Earth. Today we are conditioned very much by media manipulators and by the way not only commercial products but political policies and ideas are packaged and projected, and people and countries are presented not as they are but as others want us to see them.

In the North we 'stop the world', we silence the chatter and confusion of the air waves all around us and come into harmony with the Creation from which we have been isolated.

When you 'stop the world' and learn to 'see' and to 'hear', then animals and trees and all living things are able to communicate with you. In the realm of 'ordinary' people that, of course, cannot happen because they are conditioned to believe that it cannot happen. Trees, animals and insects cannot talk! They don't have the vocal cords to enable that to happen. That is a scientific fact, they will tell you. But in the realm of the shaman where you can become one with all living things, they can communicate with you, and you can know they can because you experience that communication for yourself.

'Stopping the world' means changing one's perception from the 'ordinary' realm of the 'not possible' to the 'non-ordinary' realm of the possible, as we shall discover.

It is to the North that you can look for ideas that can be turned into action to bring about the kind of changes you want to happen in your life.

It is also the Place of Purification and Renewal in preparation for new beginnings – for 'rebirth'. An ancient American Indian tradition which was a rite of purification and renewal was the Sweat Lodge. A sweat lodge is a temporary circular beehive-like structure constructed from branches of trees to form its framework and covered with blankets, rugs or skins. Participants sit naked around a fire pit in which the shaman places white-hot stones which have been baked in a bonfire, and pours cold water over them to produce steam and heat. Its nearest modern equivalent is a sauna, although a sauna is a poor comparison. More hot stones are carried in to the shaman and more cold water is poured over them and in a ceremony which may continue for an hour or more the participants are not merely cleansed physically but purified emotionally, mentally and spiritually. As I discovered for myself, through a sweat lodge experience, one can seek to cleanse away the dross that has gathered in one's life and focus the mind on the pure intention behind one's actions. Purity of intent is just one of a sweat lodge's many benefits.

The components of the North are:

1. *Quality*: Knowledge and Wisdom.
2. *Totem*: Buffalo.
3. *Element*: Air.
4. *Colour*: White.
5. *Kingdom*: Animal.
6. *Heavenly Body*: The Stars.
7. *Human Aspect*: The Mind.
8. *Time Period*: The Future.
9. *Season*: Winter.
10. *Number*: Four (....) and Fourteen.
11. *Enemy*: Certainty.
12. *Manifestation*: Philosophy, Religion and Science.

So let us work the North Direction:

- Set up your Circle.
- Smudge the Aura and the area around you.
- Assume the North position with the white marker in front of you.
- Relax and create your own Mind space.

1. *Quality of the North*: KNOWLEDGE AND WISDOM

Knowledge is that which is *known*. It is the process of knowing. To know is to have an understanding through personal experience of what is known. Knowledge goes *beyond* belief. Belief is a trust in the word or opinion of another. Belief is a *not* knowing. When what is believed becomes known it is no longer belief but knowledge.

To the ancients, knowledge embraced philosophy, religion and science which were not separate disciplines but integrated into the one knowledge. However, the acquisition of knowledge alone was not of itself considered sufficient. Knowledge had to be extended into wisdom.

Knowledge answers such questions as What? How? When? Where? and Who? Knowledge becomes wisdom when it provides answers to the question Why?

Wisdom also is knowledge *applied*. True wisdom is knowledge applied with Love. Wisdom manifests when knowledge that embraces philosophy, religion and science is applied with Love. That is the lesson that the quality of the North has to teach us.

2. *Totem of the North*: BUFFALO

The buffalo was the most important animal to the American Indian because it provided everything that was needed to sustain life. Its flesh was food, its skin and hide provided material for clothing and for the tipi home. Sinews were used as thread, and the bones were made into needles, knives and other implements.

The buffalo was thus an animal that gave of its entirety, in order that man could live. The buffalo symbolised the Spirit that gives totally of Itself and of Its essence in the process of life. It was also a symbol of man's dependence on Nature for his very life.

3. *Element of the North:* AIR

The characteristic of Elemental Air is movement, motion, locomotion, constant change, often sudden and sometimes unexpected. It is lightness, freshness, freedom and exhilaration. Air brings the 'breath of life' and is transforming. It is the quality we refer to when we talk of something entering our lives 'like a breath of fresh air', transforming the whole atmosphere.

Air has the characteristic of being a carrier. Our thoughts, dreams and aspirations are carried as if by air. Thoughts seem to come 'out of the blue' – out of the air. So Air represents the characteristics of Mind which has the ability to move freely and quickly.

Learn to listen to the wind for it brushes the soul of all living things and carries on its travels a particle of everything it touches. When you learn to ride with the wind, you are no longer locked within your vehicle of flesh, but free to soar and wander like a bird. Then you come to realise that you, the birds, the animals and the trees are all one, breathing in the one Great Wind and being breathed by It.

You cannot see the wind but it is there, and if you will only pause from all your hustle and stay still for a while you will feel its presence and, just as certainly, the presence of the Great Spirit. The wind bends mighty trees and sways them with a whisper, yet you cannot see it – only be aware of its presence and its mightiness. It comes and it goes, yet it is always 'there'.

Likewise, you cannot see the Great Spirit except, perhaps, in the majesty of each new dawn and in the rhythm and flow of Nature all around you if you will get out into the countryside and look. If you listen you will hear His voice in the wind and in the song of the flowers as they lift their heads in acknowledgement. If you listen you will hear His poetry in the trees, hills and valleys. You will hear if you will listen and you will see if you will look.

4. *Colour of the North*: WHITE

White is the colour of purity, of balance, and of life renewing itself. White is the sum of all the colours of the rainbow and thus represents perfection or completion. White symbolises the highest aspirations. White indicates purity of intent.

5. *Kingdom of the North*: THE ANIMAL KINGDOM

Civilised mankind, living in big cities and engulfed in push-button techno-logy, has lost touch with Nature so is wholly confused about the Animal kingdom. On the one hand love is expressed to domestic animals but often in an unbalanced way so that dogs, cats, birds, fish and sometimes even reptiles, are treated like spoilt and pampered humans. On the other hand animals can be treated as unfeeling objects and of value only to the extent to which they can be used to satisfy man's requirements.

Part of the reason for the disregard of the intrinsic value of animal life is the belief that animals do not have souls and are merely here on Earth to be used as mankind sees fit. Until modern times there was an almost identical belief about women and theologians argued for centuries about whether women even had souls!

But the Indian knew that just as man has a spirit which enables him to have conscious awareness of his environment and of the reality that is now, so do animals. An animal spirit experiences the physical environment just as much as humans and just as intensely, but in a more restricted and disciplined way, for it is not gifted with free will in its expression as is the human spirit, and it is motivated by instinct. However, from a spiritual point of view an animal spirit may be further developed along its evolutionary path than the spirit of many humans with which it may come into contact. If you have kept a domestic animal, particularly a cat or a dog, you will have experienced how an animal can show love and loyalty and bring comfort and understanding. So the Red Indian did not regard animals as *inferior* creatures, but as expressions of the Great Spirit operating in a different way.

Just because an animal cannot speak a human language, are we right to assume that it is 'dumb' and lacking in any sensitive psychological awareness? The Indian recognised that animals had a *different* way of knowing. He observed how closely in touch with the spirit of trees and plants they were. He observed how animals appeared to move away from an area of impending danger, often long before such danger became apparent. He noted by their behaviour how they prepared for weather changes even before an impending change in the weather pattern appeared in the skies. By recognising all these things and by developing an understanding of animals, the Indian acquired something of the animals' ability and by so doing extended his own range of awareness. We can do the same.

The Indian learned most of what he knew about foods and medicine from animals because he observed that animals appeared to be guided to the right plants to cure their own sickness or wounds. Bears, for instance, covered their wounds with hemlock. Some animals nibbled snakeroot leaves to protect it from the venom of snakebites. Various small animals and birds relished the fruit of the bearberry honeysuckle which Indians found of particular value as a laxative.

In 1787, Dr Johann David Schopf, a German physician, published a list of 335 vegetable remedies indigenous to the eastern United States, many of which were said to have been learned from Indians. The pharmaceutical historian, Herbert W. Youngken, listed 450 plant remedies used by Indians and this was published in the *American Journal of Pharmacy* (No. 96 July 1924, No. 97 March 1925 and No. 98 April 1925).

Animals, birds, insects, reptiles and fish are all part of the animal kingdom which the Indian categorised as four-leggeds and two-leggeds, winged ones, crawlers and swimmers, and they can all communicate with the human by sending an impression which is seen in the mind. And because each creature is itself an expression of the Great Spirit, it can thus communicate to the human mind 'messages' from the Great Spirit. So the

animals which are depicted as 'receivers' of energy in Amerindian cosmology can transmit that energy to the human mind and thus be the great
helpers of mankind.

6. Heavenly Body of the North: THE STARS

It is estimated by astronomers that there are about 5,000 stars that are
visible to the naked eye and more than 200,000 that can be seen through
binoculars with a 50mm lens. The galaxy, it is estimated, contains at least
several hundred million stars!

Even though the Indian was limited to what could be seen with the
naked eye on a clear night, the stars were profuse enough and awesome
enough to serve as a symbol for universality and divine protection. Stars
figured in prayers to Grandfather Sun 'and all the stars that are Suns for
other planets' for such stars were the great life-bringers, like our own Sun.

Although to us stars appear as just intensely radiant points of light, each
tiny pin-prick of light is a whirling sun. Some, by comparison, dwarf our
own Sun being thousands of times larger.

Our own Sun is said to be 863,370 miles in diameter, yet light from it
takes about eight minutes to reach us, travelling at a speed of 186,450
miles a second, or 670 million miles an hour. Yet light from the stars takes
many *years* to reach us, and in some cases even thousands of light years.

Our own solar system is said to be near the rim of the mighty Milky
Way galaxy which itself is a disc-shaped system which turns in space like a
gigantic Catherine Wheel. It contains within it several hundred million
stars. It is said that light travelling at 670 million miles an hour takes
100,000 years to travel from one end of the galaxy to the other. Such is the
vastness of the Cosmos. On such an awesome scale the Earth can be
likened to a single grain of sand on a beach.

Is it logical to assume that one insignificant grain is the only place that
supports intelligent beings able to organise themselves into civilised societies?

In spite of all the scientific advances of the twentieth century, mankind
still has little conception of the realities of the Cosmos. Is it possible that
the ancients had a greater knowledge of the Cosmos than modern man and
that this knowledge was lost or destroyed?

There are legends among the Cherokees that their ancestors back in the
mists of time were the 'children of Star People'. The Mayan Indians claimed
to be 'the children of the Pleiades' which is a cluster of stars some 400 light
years away in the constellation of Taurus. There are more than 250 stars in
the Pleiades cluster, but it is the seven brightest that figure prominently in

the myths, legends and scriptures of different cultures throughout the world.

Is it possible that this cluster of stars contains planets with advanced civilisations that are historically and anthropologically linked with Earth? The Pleiades is so deeply embedded in ancient cultures as to suggest a link far greater than the mere pinpricks of light which reach us from the seven stars.

They are mentioned in Chinese annals which go back as far as 2537 BC and in the legends of the ancient Greeks. The ancient Egyptians are believed to have dedicated the seven chambers of the Great Pyramid to them. The twelfth century poet and philosopher Omar Khayyam refers to them as 'the Begetters' and 'the beginners of all things'. South American Indian tribes refer to them as 'Grandfather' and hold festivals in their honour. Australian aborigine tribes have a dance in honour of the Seven Stars. So there is here a race memory of some significance.

The symbol of the cosmic Bull of Heaven − the sign of the Taurus constellation which contains the Pleiades − is on countless ancient artefacts and statues unearthed by archaeologists all around the world, indicating that the bull was deified by ancient peoples. But the bull was worshipped not because of any glorification of an animal, but because it was symbolic of the cosmic Bull of the universe − the constellation of Taurus which is the 'home' of the Pleiades.

It is not without significance that the Star symbol is a symbol which inspires mankind towards perfection.

7. *Human Aspect of the North*: MIND

The brain is the grey matter inside the skull. It is physical, material, confined within the thick protective shell of the skull. The brain keeps us alive. The mind is not physical and material. It is invisible and unconfined. It can go anywhere, and directs our aliveness. The brain has energy that can be measured with an instrument known as an electroencephalograph. The brain is said to have some 18 billion neurons or nerve centres which activate energy force every time we think, however random a thought might be.

The mind has energy which cannot be measured, only partially experienced as consciousness. The energy of the mind goes where the consciousness goes. It is this mind energy which is the source of power that is beyond the scope of physical science to measure. The brain is the tool of the mind and of your consciousness. Although you are not conscious of your brain it obeys your consciousness and contributes to it. Unless a sensation reaches the brain we are usually unaware of it.

We have already established that you are not your body. Your body is just a vehicle you need to explore and experience the physical, material dimension. You are your consciousness. That's as near as we can get to describe the essence of your existence in words. So if you accept yourself as your consciousness and that consciousness is like energy that can never be destroyed but only change its form, you are near to understanding the truth of your own being.

The Great Spirit — or whatever name we choose to give to the great Creative Source — can perhaps be likened to a Greater Consciousness, a Cosmic Consciousness, perhaps, of which your Superconsciousness is a part. If we liken the Mind to a sphere, your sphere of the Mind is like a globule surrounded by other globules, other mind spheres, and the super-consciousness of each is in touch with all others. It might be likened to globules of spray from the sea splashing on your face on a beach. Each globule is part of the ocean. Each globule is also the sea. So your individual consciousness is part of the universal Cosmic Consciousness in which you live and move and have your being. This Cosmic Consciousness has the freedom to individuate Itself like those globules of sea water and still retain Its essence — the water is still the sea. But it individualises Itself not in one way but in a vast variety of ways and forms, each of which is unique in itself.

The mind is non-material. It is what is used to think with, to convey thought, and with which to express the Will. It is part of the Soul.

8. *Time Period of the North*: THE FUTURE

To a large extent we create our own future out of the deeds and actions of the past and through the choices being made in the present. According to ancient teaching there is a random or 'chance' factor which some call 'Fate' which cannot be controlled. This random factor entered in at the instant the Cosmos was separated from Chaos. The ancient teachings claim that some Chaos was trapped within the cocoon of the Universe and consti-tutes about 20 per cent of all energy within that cocoon. It is this factor which accounts for what religionists call 'God's Will' and for accidents and catastrophes labelled 'Acts of God'. These are neither willed nor caused by the Great Spirit, but brought about by the chaos factor and allowed to happen by the Free Will of the Great Spirit. Indirectly they serve to advance our own spiritual development and evolution. However, our destiny is largely created by ourselves, by our own individual and collective decision and actions.

So the Future is largely in our own hands. But the future is not distanced from us, from our present reality, but is part of it, as it is also part of our past which influences our future. What the North Direction has to teach us is that the Future is contained within the Present. So if, like most people, you seek a better future, you must take hold of the Present. The seeds of your Future are contained within your thoughts and actions now. Improve the quality of your thoughts now and your future will be better than the Present.

9. *Season of the North*: WINTER

The characteristic of the North is that of Renewal. Winter is the time when the Earth is dormant and apparently asleep. But that dormancy is only external, for in the period of apparent rest, the deepest energies of the Earth are going into preparation for the rapid growth that is soon to come. It is paradoxical. Rapid growth is cloaked in rest, just as life is hidden in death. Another lesson here, that things are not what they appear.

10. *Number of the North*: FOUR (....)

Four is 2 × 2 — that is, Form (2) squared — Form reinforced and made 'solid'. It is duality paired and in balance. It is the power of balance, alignment and harmony. Four thus gives a state of 'permanence' to what is being brought into existence and 'holds on to it' by putting a boundary around it as in a square. Four is thus concerned with the reality of appearances.

Four is a sacred number among American Indians. There are *four* Great Powers, *four* Elements, *four* Directions, *four* Winds, *four* Seasons, *four* Races (white, red, yellow and black), *four* Ages of human development (childhood, youth, adulthood and maturity), *four* Lessons to be learned (self-knowledge, self-understanding, self-control and self-realisation). Four in the North is regarded as the power of endurance and persistence.

Fourteen gives access on the inner planes to the spirit of animals and to the masculine aspect of the Earth.

11. *Enemy of the North*: CERTAINTY

Certainty can be defined as that state of mind when you think you know all there is to know about a subject, or when you are set in your ways or in your thinking through past beliefs and attitudes. Should such thoughts as 'I *know* all that!' or 'I *know* what *I* believe' or 'I've *read* about that sort of thing before' come into your mind, you are in danger of being overcome by certainty.

Certainty tries to block the realisation of new truth and it is at its greatest threat after one has experienced illumination and the truth of something becomes clear at last. Such knowledge can 'go to your head', hence the need for wisdom to accompany knowledge. The true teacher imparts knowledge with humility. Indeed one cannot obtain esoteric knowledge without humility. Certainty is the enemy of clarity of mind and purpose.

12. *Manifestation of the North*: PHILOSOPHY, RELIGION, SCIENCE

Dictionary definitions may help us to understand the affinity and the difference between philosophy, religion and science:

Philosophy is defined as 'the pursuit of knowledge and wisdom and of the Ultimate Reality and deals with the principles of things. *Religion* is the recognition of a personal all-knowing creative and controlling power that is entitled to worship. *Science* is defined as a systematic and formulated study of the phenomena of the material universe and its physical laws.

The American Indian, like all ancient peoples, did not separate philosophy, religion and science into separate 'disciplines' but regarded them as aspects of the same thing. The Spirit of the North helps us to understand them holistically, too.

Let us look at *science*. To the Ancients, science was the knowledge of the natural and fundamental forces of the universe and of the Cosmic laws with which the physical world was brought into being and sustained. Such knowledge enabled a person to manipulate these hidden forces and thereby influence their own environment. This was such real power that tests of character were imposed upon those who sought instruction in the so-called 'mysteries' to ensure that it would be in the hands of those with moral responsibility who would use it wisely and for the benefit of all. The 'mysteries' were kept hidden from general view and obscured from those who might use the knowledge for entirely selfish or even destructive ends.

Astrology was part of that ancient science, but it bore little resemblance to the modern-day counterpart of horoscopes which attempt to predict the future and which is included in the media as a piece of light-hearted fun. Ancient astrology was a serious tool for self-analysis and for discovering the purpose of one's present incarnation. It indicated the potentials and possibilities waiting to manifest within the individual and the times in life when they could be most effectively brought into manifestation.

The ancients did not subscribe to the superstition that the Sun, Moon and planets had some kind of power or influence over human affairs and determined and controlled our destiny. To the Ancients, the Sun, Moon and planets were the physical indicators of unseen and subtle energy patterns. What came into manifestation at any particular time, whether it was a human being, a country, an enterprise or even an idea, contained within it a mirror image 'below' of energy patterns 'above'. Each human being was a unique individual and the components of the inner qualities reflected the way the subtle energies were put together and arranged. This is discussed thoroughly in my book *Earth Medicine*.[2]

The Ancients also had a sophisticated science of numbers which, when linked with astrology, saw the Cosmos as developing within changing cycles of time. The Mayan Indians, way back before the time of the ancient Egyptians used the Twenty Count and based their calendars on it. The Mayan year comprised a cycle of eighteen 20-day 'months' to which were added five days which were regarded as outside the calendar, to form a complete year of 365 days. Indeed, the 'Stone Age' Mayans fixed the true passage of the Earth around the Sun as 365.2420 days — only two ten-thousands of a day shorter than the most up-to-date computer calculations of present-day astronomers which is 365.2422 days. Their calendar was more than just a way of telling the day or the time of year. Each day was one of 20 steps to enlightenment, and thus a reminder of the purpose of one's life.

The great cycles of change were seen as Ages — long periods of time sometimes referred to as a Solar Month. Each Solar Month was part of the Solar Year or Great Year. A Solar Year was an astrological period of 25,868 years divided into 12 ages or 'months' lasting 2,165 years as the Earth itself passed through each of the constellations which lay behind the Sun at the vernal equinox.

Modern astronomy confirms that the Earth wobbles on its polar axis as it orbits the Sun, and this polar axis describes a circle which takes nearly 26,000 years to complete. The constellation which lies behind the Sun at the vernal equinox changes very gradually over the centuries until it is replaced by the constellation next to it in 2,165 years!

For the last 2,000 years the constellation behind the Sun at the vernal equinox has been Pisces, but the Earth is now on the cusp between Pisces and Aquarius. When the Earth 'changes' from one Age to another there are traumatic and often violent changes in the affairs of mankind. The turbulent, restless and dangerous times in which we live, the rapid alteration in social, political, moral, and sexual behaviour are all indications of moving out of the influence of the Age of Pisces and into the Age of Aquarius.

According to Mayan cosmology, the Age of Pisces ended on August 16/17 1987 and the Age of Aquarius then began. But for some years the Earth will still be moving through the cusp where the two Ages overlap.

The *religion* of the Ancients was far removed from the belief systems which we call religion today. It rested not on 'belief' or 'faith' but on personal experience, and following the sacred laws. The religion of the Ancients was a directing inward, not outward, for the 'God' was to be found within.

Philosophy might be defined as a study of the fundamental source of all that exists and of the principles by which things operate. Philosophy might be described as a love of wisdom.

DIRECTIONAL QUEST:

Why Am I Here?

Go to your power spot among the trees and this time take with you a token of the Animal kingdom with which the North is specially related. If you have studied Earth Medicine take something that connects you with your animal totem. Otherwise, a feather or a small piece of fur. Hold this in your left hand over your navel as you sit with your back to a tree facing North.

The question to be asked on this Quest is: 'Why am I here? What is my soul's purpose in this life?' Again, stay alert, watch and listen.

Here is how one answer came to me. I had been sitting for some time immersed in the stillness and enjoying the tranquillity, but no answer had come. I had almost decided to abandon my vigil and continue the quest another day, when just in front of my face a tiny 'money' spider descended on the slenderest of threads and landed on the back of my hand.

Before my first promptings of shamanic understanding, my immediate reaction would have been to brush it aside or even crush it with my other hand. Instead I found myself welcoming my little visitor.

'Hello, little spider', I found myself saying. 'Have you come to visit me?'

Then I realised it had come from the direction 'above', to land where my hands were connecting me to the animal kingdom and the power of the North. So it was a 'teacher' and had come to impart knowledge and wisdom which are attributes of the North.

'What is it you have come to teach me, little spider?'

I watched closely as it moved across my hand. It was so delicate that it seemed hardly possible that it had a life and an awareness of its own, a purpose in its being, just as I have. Then I realised there was another similarity. I was like the spider – suspended in the dimension of Matter for a time, held here by a slender thread which was somehow anchored 'above' in a higher realm by my High Self.

'But why am I here?' I echoed the question that was the purpose for my being seated beneath this tree.

'The North is the direction of knowledge and wisdom. So I am here to know. To experience. To use my senses. To hear means to listen. How rarely have I truly listened! To see means to comprehend and gain understanding. To taste means to distinguish. To touch means to feel and experience. To smell means to nose out and discern.

'My temporal self is like a spider which descended here to be aware, to gain understanding, to discern and experience. I am here not just to be *aware* of physical existence and *experience* it but to have pleasure in that awareness. But what is my purpose?

The spider lifted itself up off my hand and ascended slowly, pulling itself up to the branch from which it had come. Then the sudden realisation: 'I am here to climb, too – to reach beyond that which I presently see with my limited vision – and to acquire wisdom by so doing. Like the spider, wisdom is delicate. It can be easily brushed aside through ignorance of its true value, or even crushed when it appears in some unexpected guise. So wisdom needs to be approached gently and with respect before its treasures become revealed.'

Thank you, spider, for so precious a lesson.

THE GIVE-AWAY

Since the North is associated with things of the Mind, ask yourself what you need to give away of your mental life in order to find truth and wisdom.

On one occasion the realisation that came to me was that I must give away my thoughts! What areas of your thinking do you wish to banish from your life? The negativities? The despondencies? The hateful and destructive? The lustful? The greedy needy? The revengeful? Determine what it is you want to get rid of and what its polar opposite is with which it should be replaced and associate this with the feather or fur in your hand. Then bury the token as a sign of banishment, and of its being transformed.

What must I give away to bring blessings to others? My thoughts. How? By sharing inner thoughts and mental discoveries with others. Why?

Because truth and wisdom cannot be locked away as in a vault. It must flow or it will stagnate, wither or die. New understanding is received to the extent that what has been learned is passed on so that others may benefit.

This book is a tangible example of a Give-Away of the North.

ADVENTURER TASK NO. 5:

Crystal Power

Through your journey round the Medicine Wheel you have come to recognise your oneness with the universe and its powers, and your relationship with all who share the Earth environment with you. You have come to realise also that at the centre of it all dwells Wakan-Tanka and that the centre is everywhere, within you and within everyone and everything.

You have come to know the Spirits of the Four Directions. First, the Spirit of the South symbolised by the totem, Mouse, which has empowered you to begin to see what is right in front of your eyes and to touch the world with an attitude of childlike wonder. Then the Spirit of the West whose totem is Grizzly Bear, who has taught you to listen to your inner voice and to trust your inner self. The Spirit of the East has revealed to you that the Eagle is a symbol of your High Self who can empower you with the enlightenment that can bring the vision of your High Self into your everyday life. Finally, the Spirit of the North, whose Buffalo is a symbol of the Great Provider, has empowered you with the knowledge and wisdom of sharing and caring. And you have come to know the powers of Light and Life of the Sky 'Father' above, and the powers of Love and Law of the Earth 'Mother' beneath.

You have also come to know of the unique 'holding' power of crystals and of their great value to mankind and the planet as mirrors of energy. In this Adventurer Task, before you move to the Centre, you are going to charge a crystal to become a powerful means of channelling harmonising and healing energies into your own energy system and into the world.

Crystals are precise energy patterns structured in geometric forms and in perfect balance. So, if energy is put into a crystal it will hold it under control and give out an equal amount of energy like a mirror or reflector. A thought can be instilled into a crystal which will hold that thought-energy in perfect balance and reflect it without deviation or distortion.

Choose a quartz crystal that fits comfortably in the palm of your hand. It is one that you are going to carry with you at all times — a constant companion — so in looking for it have that thought firmly in mind. In selecting your crystal, hold it first in the left hand, then in the right. Let your intuition be your guide. It must 'feel' right in either hand. When you have made your selection, cleanse it by holding it under a running cold water tap for a few moments and leave it on a window sill where it will catch the sunlight and moonlight for a day or two. Then take it to your quiet room and smudge it with smoke from your smudge mix or smudge stick.

Then hold it in your left hand and rest it on your navel. As you have learned, this is the centre of your being which some call the shamanic centre. Now perform the four-fold breath, and every time you breathe in 'feel' the power of the Directions being drawn into the crystal. Concentrate on each in turn — South, West, East, North, then Sky and Earth.

Now hold the crystal in front of your eyes and project into it feelings of love and beauty.

Transfer the crystal into your right hand and hold it to your navel. Consider this: the crystal now holds within it power from the universe — from the Sun and Moon and from the six Directions. It also contains the greatest power of all — love — and all is encapsulated in beauty.

Close your eyes and perform the four-fold breath for a few minutes, imagining energy being drawn into you through the crystal as you breathe in and radiating out from you into the world around you as you breathe out.

The more frequently you perform this the more powerful will the crystal become as a helper and ally. For the crystal will become a companion to help you draw vitality from the universe into your own centre and to radiate love and acceptance out into the world as you go about your daily life. So carry your crystal with you wherever you go.

Breath of the Invisible

HAVING JOURNEYED TO THE North on the Path of Knowledge and Wisdom we can now pause to contemplate the American Indian's most treasured possession – the Sacred Pipe. The Sacred Pipe is at the core of Medicine teachings and ceremonies. It is a summation of the American Indian's wisdom and outlook on life, for the Pipe is more than a spiritual tool, more than a ceremonial implement. It is even more than a symbolic representation of all that exists and shares a common source and a common breath, for it contains an 'aliveness' that can unlock some of life's deepest mysteries. But before we examine that 'aliveness', let us look at the structure of the pipe and how it is made.

The Sacred Pipe is made in two sections – the bowl and the detachable stem. When not in use, the bowl and the stem are separated and carefully wrapped individually and carried in a hand-made pipe bag.

Pipes that are sold as souvenirs or for show in museums and exhibitions are generally made with the stem attached to the bowl. This is because the pipe with a detachable stem is considered a sacred object and venerated by the Indian, in the same way as for example, as a crucifix or holy relic may be venerated by a Christian.

The bowl, as its shape suggests, symbolises the female aspect of divinity, and the stem symbolises the male aspect of divinity. The joining together of the stem and the bowl is thus symbolic of a sacred act of union.

The most favoured material from which the bowl is carved or sculptured is a hard, rock-like substance called catlinite, but more popularly known as pipestone. Pipestone comes mainly from Minnesota or Wisconsin. There is a pipestone quarry in Southwestern Minnesota on land which once belonged to the eastern Sioux and which is now venerated by all tribes. The right to quarry pipestone there for the making of pipes was given to all tribes when the Pipestone National Monument was set up by the United States Congress in 1937.

There are many legends surrounding the Sacred Pipe and some are about pipestone itself. Some suggest that thousands of years ago there was a great natural disaster which overtook the Earth and all but a comparatively few people perished. The multitude of peoples who occupied land in that region of what is now known as the United States, were crushed under the tumbling earth as it was engulfed in great tidal waves and by a great flood which covered the land. The blood of these ancestors, say the legends, solidified under the great pressure and became the petrified blood-red rock now known as pipestone.

Whether one believes in a literal or allegorical interpretation of such legends is of little real importance. The significant truth is that the bowl is made from the substance of the Earth and that the Earth itself contains the substance of our ancestors whose bodies, like our own, were derived from the Earth and in due course are returned again to it.

The stem of the pipe is made from wood, sometimes cedar or ash or from a wood that has a soft, pithy centre so that a channel for the smoke can more easily be made.

The carving of the bowl from the red pipestone is very much an art form. Some bowls are carved along clean, simple lines, with a straight, chimney like this:

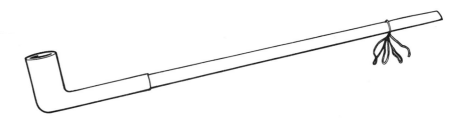

○*Fig. 25*

A Pipe shaped like this is generally held by a young, unmarried man whereas a pipe shaped like an upturned letter 'T' indicates that its holder is a married man who has already started a family (see Fig. 26 opposite).
Others can be very ornate and may be carved into effigies of animals or birds, or even humans.

When it is assembled, the Pipe represents the four kingdoms. The bowl, being made from Earth, represents the *Mineral* kingdom; the stem, made from wood, represents all that grows – the *Plant* kingdom. The feathers and fur that are hung from the stem when it is united with the bowl represents the birds and animals – the *Animal* kingdom. The *Human* kingdom is represented by the person who made the Pipe and by the one who puts it together and smokes it.

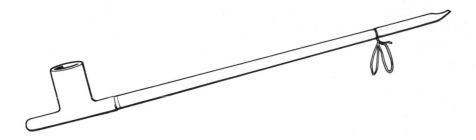

○*Fig. 26*

All the elements are also represented. *Earth* by the tobacco and herbs that are smoked. *Fire* by the fire when it is alight. *Air* that is sucked in to keep the smoking mixture alight, and *Water* by the spittle. *Aether* is represented by the smoke.

The bowl also represents the *Earth Mother* and the stem represents the *Sky Father*. So the Pipe becomes a bridge between the unmanifested, invisible, unchanging Spirit personified in the Sky Father, and the manifested, ever-changing Spirit visible in Nature as personified by the Earth Mother. In other words the duality of the Creator Source – the two aspects of the Great Spirit – and of that which can be seen and is tangible, changing and temporal, and that which cannot be seen but is infinite, eternal and permanent, is impressed within the symbology of the sacred pipe.

The Creator Source – Wakan-Tanka – is seen as both male and female as well as the common Source of all that exists. It is the common 'breath' of animals and plants, rocks and human beings.

The Sacred Pipe is thus a symbol of the Great Everything, of the 'big universe', as well as the 'little everything' within the individual human being's 'universe'.

How, then, did the Pipe originate? Again, one must look to the legends which say that the Sacred Pipe was brought to the Indian people thousands of years ago by a beautiful young woman dressed in white buckskin which was so exquisitely decorated that no human hand could have made it! In the legends of other cultures, such a figure would have been described as a Goddess.

Her hair, the legends say, hung loose on the right but the left side was tied with buffalo hair. She is described as 'the White Buffalo Woman' because she was seen on the horizon by two young warriors who went out hunting and mistook her white figure in the distance for the rare and sacred white buffalo.

When the White Buffalo Woman was taken to appear before the whole tribe she was carrying the bowl of a pipe in her left hand and the stem in her right hand – and that is the way the pipe is held to this day. She then instructed the people into its use with these words:

> With this holy Pipe you will walk a living prayer, your feet resting upon Grandmother Earth, the stem reaching all the way up into the sky to the Grandfather, your body linking the Sacred Beneath with the Sacred Above.
>
> Wakan-Tanka smiles on us because now we are as one – Earth, Sky, all living things, and the *ikce wicasa*, the human beings. Now we are one big family. The pipe binds us all together.

This sentiment is expressed at the end of every important American Indian ceremony with words that in English mean 'for all my relatives'. The 'relatives' are all plants, rocks, animals and humans, for all are seen as one big universal family and we are related one to another, connected with each of them.

The legendary White Buffalo Woman told the women of the tribe that it was the work of their hands and the fruit of their wombs that kept the tribe alive, so their task was as great as that given to the warrior and the hunter. The Sacred Pipe thus bound both men and women in a circle of love.

The little children were told that what grown-up men and women did was for them, the children, for they represented the coming generation and the continuing life of the people, the circle without end.

'Remember this and grow up and then teach your children', the White Buffalo Woman said to them.

As she departed, the White Buffalo Woman sang a song which in English proclaimed: 'with visible breath I am walking', meaning that breath is not just life, it is life while remaining *oneself* and of breathing from the breath that embraces all life. The visible breath she was breathing was like the visible breath of the buffalo on a cold day, and this expression served to remind them that the pipe, man, the buffalo – which supplied all their needs – and Wakan-Tanka were all One.

The legends say that as the people watched the White Buffalo Woman walk away into the distance she turned into a White Buffalo and then disappeared on the horizon.

Any attempt to literalise the legends might lose their essential point and certainly their charm. But to the American Indian the essential message was clear – that the Sacred Pipe came to them from a non-human Source. We may consider that Source as an Avatar, just as Christ, the Buddha and

Krishna were Avatars. Indeed, the Aquarian Age Avatar will also be female.

The essence of the teachings concerning the Sacred Pipe were given to me in these words as the Sacred Pipe was demonstrated to me by Silver Bear:

THE SACRED PIPE

Behold, the Sacred Pipe
Which is a holy altar
A place of communion for the individual
And for the people.
For the bowl is Goddess, Mother, and Grandmother
The receptive Circle with a centre
The point within the circle
The Womb and Source of all.
The bowl is also the zodiac
The circle of the Medicine Wheel
The centre of the universe
And also the heart of man.
So let this bowl transform you
Let it take you from the outside in
From space to spacelessness
From time to Timelessness
From form to Spirit.

Then consider the stem.
It is the God, Father, and Grandfather
The rod, the lance, the conceptual force
And creative seed of us all.
Let your mind be as straight and as true
As the way of the tiny hole
That leads along the stem
To the heart of the bowl
And the centre of all that is
The connecting link
Between the Heavens Above
And the Earth Beneath
Joining that which is Above
With that which is Beneath.

By putting this Pipe together
You join more than stem to bowl
Sky to Earth.
You are joining all things to yourself
So that when you smoke
All things send their voices to the Great Spirit

Along with yours
In this Pipe all the Elements are involved
Earth, in the red stone of the bowl
Fire, which will be contained in it
Water, by the spittle from your mouth
And Air and Breath by the smoke which will come forth
To the Great Spirit
From which all things have their origin.
So when you pray with this Pipe
You pray not to Wakan-Tanka
But with Wakan-Tanka
And with Grandmother Earth and all the Planets
And with Grandfather Sun and all the Stars
And with everything that is
Everything the Great Spirit has created
Everything the Great Spirit is in.

Behold the Sacred Pipe
The smoke from which
Will touch the Earth with fragrance
And reach even beyond the heavens
That you, too, may touch the Earth with beauty
And that your thoughts may be elevated
Above the stars.
With this Pipe you shall walk a living prayer
Your feet resting on Grandmother Earth
The Pipe stem reaching into the sky
To the Grandfather
Your body linking the Sacred Beneath
With the Sacred Above.
From above, Wakan-Tanka has given you
This Sacred Pipe
So that you may have a companion
As you walk the Earth
To bind you to all your relatives
That through it you may have knowledge
And through knowledge, understanding
And through understanding, wisdom.
So through it, every dawn as it comes
And every day from this time forth
Becomes holy.
For so great a treasure
Be grateful
And Walk in Beauty
Throughout all Time.

I was taught that before any attempt is made to prepare the pipe for
smoking, permission must always be sought and that I would know

inwardly when such permission was given. And if it was refused? 'Perhaps a sensation like a tap on the back', said Silver Bear, 'you will know'.

The smoking mixture of tobacco and herbs represents all things and offering the Pipe to all six directions before it is smoked indicates that all space is included. The bowl is filled a pinch at a time and with each pinch a prayer or petition is said. In filling the Pipe in this way, the Pipe holder identifies with it and with the whole universe. In reaching out to all six directions — East, South, West, North, Above and Below — the Self is being expanded, ceasing to be a part of a fragment of the Whole like a single grain of tobacco but actually becoming Whole — becoming (w)holy.

The Pipe is smoked for various purposes or intentions, and the number of fillings and the method will vary according to that intention. Smoking the Pipe is a very personal and profound experience. It is an act of communion which reaches out and embraces all things in manifestation, each puff of smoke represents the breath of the Invisible made manifest and returning to invisibility.

Once you have shared in a Pipe ceremony the experience has only to be recalled to mind in moments of difficulty or danger to release an abundance of love and power to augment your own. For wherever you are and whenever the time, its blessing is always with you.

Attributes of the Centre

YOU HAVE TRAVELLED TO THE *South*, adopted an attitude of trust and innocence and rid yourself of the garbage of the past and the impediments that have held you back. In the *West* you learned to look inward and there faced your own death – by so doing you accepted change as a transformational process that leads to a new beginning and to progress. In the *East* you have experienced enlightenment about yourself. In the *North* you sought knowledge of the 'how' and the wisdom of the 'why'. Now you are going to the *Centre*, not this time just to contemplate on what has been learned, but to actually take charge of your own power so that you can accept responsibility for your life from now on, no longer a victim of circumstance, but enabled to 'Walk Your Talk' – do as you say – and touch the Earth with beauty wherever you go.

So set up your Medicine Wheel:

- Smudge yourself and the working area.
- Assume the Centre. Use only the centre green stone.
- Relax, and create your own Mind space.

The Centre is the centre of your own being, so before we examine the different attributes of the Centre, let us consider what is the centre of your being. On the Medicine Way we have established that the centre of your being cannot be the brain because the brain is but a bio-computer and a holographic storage system – a piece of equipment you carry around in your physical body. You have established that it cannot be the mind because the mind is a faculty you *use* in order to think. The mind is not you, the user. Is it the Spirit then? But we have discovered that the Spirit is the individuated, organised Life Force which requires *intelligence* to direct it.

Intelligence requires *consciousness* in order to be aware of events and that consciousness needs to be educated to know the required action to be taken. So what is it that is still 'there' at the centre of being when all these coverings have been stripped away? What is it at the centre of being that is still identifiable?

It is conscious awareness. Awareness of being. Knowing that you are. The realisation that 'I' AM.

What is consciousness? Consciousness is not your thoughts because thoughts are a response to the stimuli received through consciousness. Consciousness does not think. It is just an awareness that you *are*. You think with the mind expressed through the brain. Consciousness is a state of awareness which emanates from within the self. It is the 'I' being aware that 'I' *am*. This is 'self' consciousness. It extends to others and to matter when it gains awareness of things outside itself.

Where does this consciousness – this 'I' that has self-awareness – come from? And how did it come into existence? Materialists have supposed that consciousness arises out of matter. They have theorised that somehow matter appeared in an evolutionary process and at some stage in its development that evolutionary process produced conscious life. But you have discovered in your quest for knowledge and wisdom something that has eluded some of the world's most learned men and theologians:

Self consciousness is a primal cause and not an effect.

That's right. *Self-consciousness emanates from the 'I', or Individuality, itself.* Consciousness does not *think*. Consciousness just *is*. The 'I' seeks expression and understanding of itself and all life. Consciousness is not life itself, therefore, as we have been led to suppose. Self-consciousness is the 'I am' which enables us to be aware that we are alive. It is an awareness of ourselves, of our individual separateness and identity, and of what is happening around us. It exists not just on one level or in one plane of existence, but on *all* levels of being. Everything – even a humble stone – has an 'I', an individuality!

Going to your Centre – let us call this activity 'centring' – is what to do to come into touch with your essential Self. It is where your consciousness may be expanded and extended into other levels. It is where to contact your own High Self, the Universal Mind, and what has been called the Collective Unconscious. It is where to touch the Mind of the Great Everything – Wakan-Tanka. In other words, it is where to contact the divinity within you.

It is the place of Harmonious Being.

In the Centre you come to love your Self because of a recognition of what the Real Self *is*. Through that realisation you come to love others too because of what they are. For love is generated by love. Love comes from love just as life comes from life. Those who despise themselves despise others also. Respect yourself and you will have respect for others. Value your Self and you will have regard for the values of others.

How do you get to know your Self? In the same way as you get to know others. By spending time with yourself – time to be alone, time on your own. Examine your behaviour. Why did you do or think or say or forget that? Why did you think that about someone, or say what you did, or even forgot to say? Analyse your actions to get to know yourself. When you get to know your Self, you can begin to *be* yourself and no longer need to 'conform'. It is not necessary to be 'like everyone else'. You have a right to be different. You have a right to be you. To be as you are. You. At the Centre you can get to know You. And there come to love You.

The Centre is your Place of Harmonious Being. Imagine a circle centred on your body, parallel with the floor and with its centre at your central point just above the navel. Then imagine a vertical shaft, like a spindle, rising from this centre and up through the top of your head and continuing above you. Visualise it going down from your centre through your legs and continuing down beneath your feet.

At the centre of You burns your eternal flame. Visualise this for within it is the very Source of your being.

You cannot explore any of the four directions around you without shifting your position from the centre. You can, however, move up or down the spindle and examine the 'above' and 'below' and still remain 'centred' in that central shaft. This what a shaman does in shamanic 'journeying'. He or she goes to the centre of their own being and from there has the spiritual technology to explore the 'above' and 'below' while retaining full conscious awareness and under full control of the Will.

For the purpose of visualisation you can imagine a sphere sliced into three horizontal portions. The middle portion represents your world of 'ordinary' consciousness, your everyday, objective reality, the lower portion is the under-world, the realm of your subconscious reality, and the upper portion the 'higher' realm of your superconscious reality.

You may have recognised that I have not referred to the 'lower' and 'higher' realms as supernatural. The reason is that they are not. The supernatural, along with superstitions and other fantasies, belongs to belief systems. Like the Middle World of the Here and Now with which you are familiar, they are perfectly *natural* and like the realm with which you are familiar through your physical senses and operate in accordance with natural, cosmic and sacred laws.

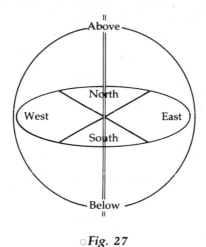

○*Fig. 27*

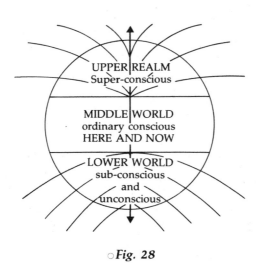

○*Fig. 28*

The spindle through the imagined globe can be regarded as the Tree of Yggdrasil of the ancient Northern traditions – the evergreen ash whose roots joined the underworld, whose branches reached into the heavenly realm and whose trunk was the Middle World of ordinary reality in the Here and Now.

The Centre, then, is the Place of Harmonious Being and the Place of Harmonic Energy, so before exploring the specific qualities of the Centre, here is a simple exercise you can perform that will help you to harmonise your energy-system:

EXERCISE NO. 6:

Centring Your Energies

Place the palm of your left hand on your navel, centred two or three centimetres (about an inch) above your belly button. This is the centre point of your physical body and the centre also of your entire system, for it is where your Central Control Centre is located. This Control Centre is where your individuality assembles the 'world' as you see and experience it. It is where all the energies you attract, produce, hold, use and channel, are focused. It is the lens of your being. Now put the palm of your right hand on top of your left hand. Breathe in from the abdomen as if you are taking in air through this central area. *Breathe in* to a count of four, *hold* the breath to a count of four but do not strain in any way, *exhale* to a count of four, and then *pause* for a count of four before repeating the sequence. Keep up this pattern for a few minutes.

By this four-fold rhythmic breathing while centring on the central point in your body you are actually modifying and harmonising your vibrational pattern and bringing it closer to the rhythmic pulse of the universe. What you are doing is to move your energy system into a condition of 'centred' space — that is, of equilibrium — coming into harmony with the centre of your being and with the universe. After a few minutes you should feel completely calm and relaxed but alert and vibrant.

Now, say aloud the following words. Speak with meaning and authority:

I CALL BACK INTO MYSELF
ANY PART OF ME
THAT I HAVE INADVERTENTLY
OR WILLINGLY GIVEN AWAY
OR HAVE HAD TAKEN FROM ME
AT ANY TIME AND IN ANY PLACE.
I CALL IT BACK INTO MYSELF *NOW*
THAT I MAY BE WHOLE,
FULLY *RESTORED*,
FULLY *HARMONISED*,
FULLY *EMPOWERED*.

Continue the rhythmic breathing for a few more minutes and feel yourself taking full control of yourself in a condition of self-mastery. You have restored your own energy-system to a state of wholeness and you have assumed responsibility and power over your own life. You now know that you are at the cause of your own happenings rather than being at the effect of others. Realise that now you are in a position to awaken and actualise your dreams, and that you are empowered so to do.

Feel the glow of confidence embracing your whole being. Revel in it. *Experience* it. Your whole energy-system is now *vibrant* and *alive*. Take a long, slow, deep breath, then exhale gently. Get up and have a good stretch.

You can peform this exercise any time you feel 'out of sorts' or when you are about to face a particular difficulty or stressful situation.

The components of the Centre are:

1. *Quality*: Life-Law; Light-Love.
2. *Totem*: Smoke-Breath.
3. *Element*: Aether-Void.
4. *Colour*: Blue-Green; Magenta-Violet.
5. *Kingdom*: Celestial-Soul.
6. *Heavenly Body*: The Cosmos.
7. *Human Aspect*: Sexuality.
8. *Time Period*: Timelessness.
9. *Season*: The Year.
10. *Number*: Five (___).
11. *Enemy*: Inertia.
12. *Manifestation*: Spirituality.

1. *Quality of the Centre*: LIFE-LAW; LIGHT-LOVE

Imagine a field which represents a Void. The soil of that imaginary field has seed – which is LIFE – planted in it. The seed receives LIGHT and water and LOVING nurturing. The size to which the crop grows and the manner of growth will depend on the LAW of its being. That Law was determined by the One that formed the seed (Life) in the first place. LIFE and LAW come directly from the Source, from the Great Spirit which is all things yet no-thing.

The Great Spirit also expresses Itself as the Great Grandfather and the Great Grandmother. Great Grandfather may be considered by us as our *Sun* Source of LIGHT and Great Grandmother as our *Earth* Source of LOVE. Thus LIGHT and LOVE became participants in Creation of the Cosmos with LIFE and LAW. These Four Great Primary Forces brought all that is into being and sustain it.

Love is the binding, unifying, nurturing Force – the power that holds all things together. It is the power that gives entirely of itself for it is a force that seeks not to control and overpower, but to merge, unify and harmonise. Without Love, life cannot be sustained. Without Love there is a falling apart. Without Love there is barrenness. Love enlightens and Love is also lightening. Love is uplifting. Love puts purpose into any action and lightens any burden. Love is the power that sustains the Universe and binds it together.

Light is the power that gives movement to the Universe and provides it with its energy.

Life is conscious awareness of being – it is evolution, trial and error, learning and developing. All life is the expression of a thought in the Mind of the Great Spirit 'in this form, in this place, and at this time.' Life is the act of *being* and its essential essence.

Law is the geometry of relationships, linking all things. It is the force-form, harmonic balance, the plan, the structured behaviour system, universal throughout the Cosmos. Know the Law and you can approach some understanding of the Mind of the Great Spirit.

2. *Totem of the Centre*: SMOKE-BREATH

The totem of the Centre is not an animal or bird, plant or tree, or even a mineral, but something as elusive as smoke and breath. To the Indian, both had great power. Indeed, the words 'smoke-breath' themselves are 'words of power'. Each has connections with the Sacred Pipe.

Smoke is visible breath, and breath is the life force. Everything breathes. Humans, animals, trees and plants, and even rocks breathe. So everything in manifestation depends upon the breath of life. Breath is invisible like life itself. It cannot be seen. We can only be aware of its existence. The Great Breath is the Great Spirit. Smoke, then, is the breath of life made visible.

When an Indian smoked the Sacred Pipe he saw his words, his thoughts, his prayers, being carried to the Great Spirit. The bowl of the pipe is female and represents Great Grandmother (*Love*); the stem is male and represents Great Grandfather (*Light*). Tobacco, the living plant, represents *Life*. The ritual way in which it is smoked represents *Law*. So by using it the Four Great Primary Forces are invoked and harmonised with.

Smoke from the pipe is produced by fire (spiritual illumination) consuming the tobacco and herbs (material manifestation) which is aetherialised and liberated from form by fire so that their spirits are freed to go to their highest vibrational realm. Smoking the Pipe was regarded as a sharing of the breath (the life and spirit) of the Four Great Powers of the Universe.

Inhaling and exhaling the smoke from the Sacred Pipe represented the ebb and flow of life – from invisibility to visibility and back to invisibility again. Inhaling brought the smoke into the body and was a reminder of what was being accepted and nourished through all the activities of physical being. Puffs of smoke in the exhaling represented what was being released and what must be transcended. Inhaling was of the Sky above. Exhaling was of the Earth beneath. Together it was the marriage of Sky and Earth.

The European explorers of the sixteenth century discovered smoking from the American Indians and found it soothing and relaxing, an aid to social intercourse. However, the Indian never smoked the Pipe for personal pleasure or as an act of self-indulgence and certainly not out of addiction. Smoking the Pipe was a sacred act which had symbolic meaning and specific intention – a power for good. As with so many things, 'civilised' man took hold of that power without understanding it, abused it and directed it harmfully, and it has turned on him. Indeed, substance abuse is a major sickness of Western society and springs directly from lack of understanding and lack of respect for plant and rock beings. The sacred act of smoking has thus been transformed into a scourge.

3. *Element of the Centre*: AETHER-VOID

Aether is the Source Element – the undifferentiated formless substance which contains the Four Elements – Air, Fire, Water and Earth. It is that which is *not* formed and from which the world we are aware of is created and derived, that which is acted upon by the Four Great Primary Forces.

The Void is the space in which is Aether, the undifferentiated energy which is not in characterised existence. The Void is at the centre of being, and our Spirit is the organiser and mover. Aether/Void is thus the quintessence of all there is, all that has been, and all that ever will be – in a very real sense, all that is a thought in the Mind of Creator. Nothing ever happened that was not preceded by Thought. Therefore, all is created by thought and all *is* thought.

The Void cannot be represented by anything, only by no-thing, for it is the most intangible of intangibles – incomprehensible, yet the most powerful.

When the Great Spirit characterised the Aether within the Void, all began. This continues with us all the time. Our Centre is pure essence – formless, spaceless, timeless – in everything yet containing everything.

4. *Colours of the Centre*: BLUE/GREEN; MAGENTA/VIOLET

Colour is our awareness of a state of being characterised by a rate of vibration which fully expresses its unique existence as part of a harmonious whole. Colour enables us to perceive qualities of existence and differentiate between them.

In the Centre Blue is above, Green below, Magenta before and Violet behind.

Blue is the infinitude of being. It is the colour of the sky and the ocean. It is the height and the depths. It is the expression of the spiritual force of LIGHT.

Green is the colour of Nature and nurtures, refreshes and renews. Green is the colour of growth and of healing. It is the expression of the LIFE Force.

Magenta is a higher octave of Red. It is the colour of the driving force, the directing power being directed *ahead*. It is the expression of the organisational power – LAW.

Violet is the colour of the deep 'within'. It is that which inspires and gives purpose and reason. It is the expression of the binding force of LOVE.

5. *Kingdom*: CELESTIAL/SOUL

Mankind comprises the fourth 'kingdom' which, in evolutionary terms, is an intermediary between those 'below' and those 'above'. 'Below' are the 'Animal, Plant and Mineral kingdoms. 'Above' is a fifth kingdom which, for simplicity, I shall call the Celestial.

A human being is both mortal and divine, the 'divine-mortal' (Hu-man) possessing that which is eternal (the individuated Spirit) within that which is mortal (the physical body) and the wherewithall to be consciously aware of this.

The Celestial kingdom contains eternal beings who are limited neither by time nor space. The human being is evolving spiritually towards this 'higher' state.

Soul is the 'vehicle' through which the individuated Life Force or Spirit essence lives in conscious awareness and finds expression. It might be likened to a communications module whose function is to filter and sort out the physical, mental, emotional, spiritual and sexual experiences being undertaken by the entity. Spirit is the individuated essence, the driving life force of the individual. Soul is the vehicle through which it has expression and form and in which the record of experiences and lessons learned is stored.

The Individuality without the Soul is noumenal, it is incapable of separate phenomenal existence. The Individuality within the Soul is manifest – that is, it comes into light. The Great Spirit unmanifested is unimaginable. The Great Spirit-Life Force-Breath in manifestation is everything that is. The words Soul and Spirit are thus *not* interchangeable and mean different things.

The Spirit is the Life Force. Your Spirit is your individuality – your individualised Life Force.

There has been much speculation and theological argument about what the Soul is and where the Soul goes when a person dies. Indeed, so much has been written in an attempt to supply an answer that it would fill a whole library. The Centre reveals the answer. Simple, yet profound. The Soul goes nowhere but where the Individuality wills it to be. Your Soul is your vehicle of expression and experience. It goes nowhere but where you are. It is your complete *curriculum vitae* (record of your life and past lives).

6. *Heavenly Body of the Centre*: THE COSMOS

The Cosmos can be considered as an organised system which contains the Earth, Moon and Planets, the Sun and the Stars. It is the organised intelligence of our Universe. Cosmos is a word which also describes the whole of Creation operating in accordance with natural and sacred laws. The Cosmos is thus law-abiding, but it is also the Law itself. It is the organiser, the organisation as well as that which is organised. It is the Great Spirit. It functions in accordance with the laws that govern its own existence and expression and it evolves within the Law of its own Being as does everything within it.

According to the ancient wisdom, Cosmos was created out of Chaos (which might be defined as the unorganised state of the Void) where random laws condition existence. When the Cosmos came into being the Great Spirit limited Itself in its expression in Cosmos and these limitations are the Laws of the being of the Cosmos. Part of this must be seen as being necessary for the Cosmos to achieve the purpose of its creation and, at the same time, to set the boundaries to completely random expression. Only through particularised, directed existence could individual consciousness-Great Spirit be aware of its own evolution.

The ancient teaching was that about 20 per cent of Chaos remained within the boundaries of the Cosmos; there is also about 20 per cent of Cosmos within the remaining Chaos. Everything – you included – contains a Chaos element. When you get sick you could say that Chaos has strengthened within you. If you become too chaotic your body may no longer be able to sustain its organised life expression and you 'die'. Its law breaks down.

In effect there is Chaos within the Cosmos which is endeavouring to get out, and Cosmos outside in the Chaos which is endeavouring to get in. So the whole structure is under stress and in dynamic balance.

7. *Human Aspect of the Centre*: SEXUALITY

Sexual energies are polarised life energies inherent in all life forms, but especially significant in the human being. Sexuality is more than physical expression and gratification, or gender-oriented psychological behaviour, or even the urge to reproduce. Sexuality is concerned with the separation of vital energies and the tremendous force of attraction caused by their urge to reunite. It is a function of the initial individualisation of the Being and continued separate existence would be impossible without it since life would die out. Humans are essentially sexual beings, which is why psychologically sex plays such a prominent part in our conditioning.

In Christian fundamentalism, which has played a prominent part in the shaping of Caucasian attitudes to sex over the last thousand or more years, sex has been regarded as an inherent part of the 'original sin' in the story of the Fall, as a lack of control, and as the means of creating more beings with original sin. This influence has caused sexual attitudes within Western societies to be largely repressive, with an overriding guilt complex. In more recent times a relaxation of controls over sexual attitudes has resulted in the so-called 'Permissive Society'. Christian thought held that only unmanifest Spirit was pure. It begs the question, of course, since we would not be here to discuss it without the parental sex act responsible for each of us.

Repressive and guilt-ridden attitudes are contrary to what can be observed all around us in Nature. Sex is the means by which all forms of life reproduce themselves. No living thing can come into manifestation without an indulgence in the sex act. The flowers that adorn many an altar and bring such joy through their beauty and fragrance are, in fact, the sex organs of plants! How, then, can sex be fundamentally 'evil'? Did 'God' make a mistake by inventing it in the first place? Hardly, since everything seeks its polar opposite for completeness.

The problem about sex is not sex but what we think about sex. Our thoughts are largely conditioned by the kind of society in which we live. Part of the problem today is the impact of the media and especially the use of imagery which orchestrates expectations which are rarely fulfilled. The individual is thus left with a feeling of inadequacy and frustration. Again this great gift, this great power, this expression of the completeness of the Great Spirit, is abused — to sell cars, chocolates, clothes, perfume and alcoholic drink.

Sex is an exchange of energy between two flowing energy-systems. Sex is an exchange of power — a giving of oneself and a receiving into oneself. Sexuality is an expression of that moving sexual force that permeates and absorbs, that thrusts and receives, that merges and separates. It is a process of bonding, of becoming one with another. In the Centre you are both merging at all levels and becoming one with your own High Self and that of your partner in the highest expression of the sex act. At its lowest expression it is merely physical relief. Sex should link physical, emotional, mental and spiritual bodies together in oneness. Through sexuality connection is thus made with the deep forces of feeling within us, with the Great Spirit Itself within each of us.

'It enables you to see your invisible Self in the eyes of another', Silver Bear explained to me.

'Falling in love' is thus a mirroring. It is the recognition of one's own 'other Self', one's idealised 'opposite', in another person. What is seen is a vision. It is a man seeing in his loved one a reflection of his inner 'woman', his feminine 'twin' within, and a woman seeing in her lover her inner 'man', her masculine 'twin'. Partnerships suffer and traumas break up the closeness of that union when that first exciting intensity is dispersed and replaced by mundane ordinariness. What was once treasured is taken for granted. What was given freely becomes demanded 'as of right', and what was once ecstatic degenerates into unexciting habit.

The Centre stresses the importance of taking pleasure in the *doing* rather than in the satisfaction of the result. Sexuality teaches that it is the *continuance* of the doing that brings joy, not the climax of the result. Love is ongoing — the joy of continuity. Lust is concentration on a climax and is the opposite of Love which concentrates on the union with the partner and with giving pleasure.

8. *Time period of the Centre*: TIMELESSNESS

Timelessness is stillness. It is lack of movement. In the Centre we find stillness, for the centre is the point of perfect balance. It can be likened to that instant in the swing of a pendulum which *pauses* for a brief moment as it reaches the peak of its excursion before it swings back the other way. It is infinity. It is the point of no-movement as with the stationary axle of a wheel which itself is turning against the thrust block of the axle. Without resistance or friction there is no movement. It is where being dissolves into non-being and are both at one. At the Centre there is no time – eternity.

9. *Season of the Centre*: THE YEAR

A year is the whole period of Time it takes for the Earth to complete a single revolution around the Sun and embraces all four seasons. So in the Centre we are situated in *every* season, every month or Moon, every day, every hour, every minute, every moment.

The year is a cycle – a cycle of the dynamics of Life and a cycle of manifestation. It experiences ebb and flow, growth and development, rest and renewal, and incorporates within it our own physical, psychological, sexual, emotional development and spiritual evolution. It is the Wheel. Everything comes round again and again.

At the Centre we are enabled to perceive *wholeness*. The emphasis is not on a part or a point in the cycle but on its entirety. The Centre is concerned with the entirety of our being.

10. *Number of the Centre*: FIVE (___)

Numerically, Five symbolises the eternal, pulsating rhythm that moves between Creation and Destruction, between Collection and Dispersal. Anciently, it was regarded as the number of sexual vibration, of potentialities and of regenerative power.

It is the number of the primary matrix structure of Creation – that is, a centre and four cardinal directions (the Medicine Wheel). It indicates the union of Four Primary Elements of Air, Fire, Water and Earth, with Aether.

Five is the number of commonly-known physical senses – sight, hearing, touch, taste and smell – which comprise the human being's sensory equipment for knowing the physical world. Five is thus concerned with the Tonal realm of ordinary, physical, everyday reality.

Five is formed by a union of the two forms of number – odd and even. The male, odd 1 (unity) with the female even 2 (duality) duplicated: $1 + 2 + 2$. Significantly, Five is at the centre of the body of numbers:
All add to 15 which is the number of bodies the human being has. So Five also represents the Human.

Five indicates a change of *quality*. So, though it symbolises sensory stimulation it represents the means of expanding the senses and attaining greater awareness. Since there is a five-fold pattern in Nature, Five enables you to comprehend the underlying unity of Nature. It is the apex of a pyramid, the Self-centre, the Mediator at the symbolic point where the

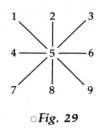

○*Fig. 29*

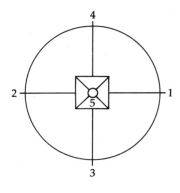

○*Fig. 30*

physical and the non-physical, the Conscious and the Unconscious meet. Five is associated with inner communication and with light (meaning the 'inner' light, or energy of the individuality), so it is the number of Expression. It is concerned with creative effort and physical motion, so is the number of Sexuality. It is also the number of the Soul Urge – the need of the Soul to express itself through physical actions and to learn.

The characteristic of Five is change, adaptability and progress.

On the 20 Count, Five is assigned the South Centre where it represents all sacred humans. It is a key to inner communication – that is, to knowledge that can be obtained shamanistically, by searching or journeying within one's own being.

11. *Enemy of the Centre*: INERTIA

As you will by now have discovered for yourself, the Centre is a comfortable place to be. It is a safe haven, a place of peace and tranquillity, where

you are not disturbed, threatened or forced onto the attack or the defens-
ive. It is a secure place to be. A reassuring place. It is being 'home'.

Having found the Centre, you have found a place you want to stay. You
want to stay where you are — and that is your 'enemy'. Inertia. Not
wanting to move. Not wanting to do anything that might disturb your
comfortableness. Not wanting to get involved.

Inertia stunts your growth, prevents you from developing, halts your
evolution. Life is for living. You have to move in older to progress. Having
discovered where and how to find your point of balance you then need to
move from it in order to create actions and reactions, remembering always
to return to it to re-establish equilibrium, for it is *dynamic* balance, not a
static one, we seek.

On our Medicine Way journey we have gone to the Centre after
exploring each Direction in order to balance and harmonise what has been
learned. Then we have taken the benefit of that knowledge with us to
another Direction and returned to the Centre again to establish equilibrium
and absorb what has been gathered. This principle is dynamic motion, an
essential teaching of the Medicine Way and a key to successful living.

12. *Manifestation of the Centre*: SPIRITUALITY

Contrary to popular opinion, spirituality does *not* mean following an
organised religion and being pious. One can be 'religious' and yet not be
even spiritually awake! Spirituality is not being the robot of someone or
something else but being guided in one's actions by the Spirit — by your
own Spirit — by the Spirit Self that is within *you*. Only then can your actions
be *determined* by the Spirit and in accord with the freedom of the Will,
rather than by the mind or emotions or by the urgings of the physical
body.

True Spirituality cannot exist without free will. The Will is the power to
determine — to make choices and decisions. Free will is the liberty to
choose. It is a primary and fundamental liberty that is essential to your own
well-being, to your own spiritual growth, development and evolution, and
that of others. That is why you must not deprive others of their free will,
otherwise your efforts will rebound to ultimately impair your own free
will. If you chain others to yourself you chain yourself to them. The Will is
not free if it is restricted by rules, laws and interpretations that limit its
movement and fetter it to a system. There is a simple Law: IF IT HARMS
NO ONE AND DOES NOT HURT YOU, THEN DO IT IF YOU WISH TO.
Remember, we are not responsible for hurt feelings in others when it is
their pride and prejudice which is offended. There are many who seek to

live our lives for us, or to live their lives through us. Do not let them. Compulsion and coercion are harmful whether done by us or to us. They may be considered necessary for the State to use to protect the weak from the strong and from 'evil'. Motive, as always, is everything. Evil is that which opposes spiritual evolution. Evil is the abuse of power and being harmful to others or yourself.

Spirituality means being guided by *principles* rather than by regulations and man-made concepts. Of course the seeker has a need for guidance or advice from a spiritual teacher or one who has trodden the Path they find inviting. However, all too often the seeker is directed into a belief system or an organisation which instead of freeing the Spirit and helping it to evolve, actually immobilises the Spirit and makes the seeker dependent on the system and on its leader. So instead of finding freedom, the seeker is led to give up freedom and to turn their power, energies and wealth over to the system and its leaders. It is the reverse of what should happen. The system or spiritual leader should *impart* power to the individual.

There are, thankfully, spiritual teachers who do allow the seeker to develop the inherent spirituality that is within, and who will lead them to find the Teacher who is true for everyone – the eternal being that dwells within. Not 'up' there. Not 'out' there. Not back there in history or beyond the now in a future that never comes even if it is called Eternity. But the Teacher who is in 'here' – in *you* – now, and who seeks nothing in return.

Look, then, for the spiritual teacher who has the power to lead you to find the Teacher on your inner planes – your own High Self who is part of your eternal being. Then you will acquire true spirituality.

Your Medicine Way journey has been a process of change and transformation. You are changing from being a robot or puppet controlled by circumstances and by others and therefore not truly responsible for what happens to you, to becoming a 'creator' and assuming responsibility for your own life.

Such a concept may be misunderstood by some. But assuming responsibility is a stage of spiritual evolution. Assuming responsibility means accepting responsibility for your own choices and decisions rather than putting the responsibility onto someone else, on conditions and circumstances, or by blaming others, or 'Fate' even 'God'.

You go to the Centre to spiral out of what you have been and spiral into what it is you want to become.

You go to the Centre to take over the controls of your own life.

You go to the Centre to make contact with your own High Self, the Spiritual Self, the Permanent Self that is your true reality.

At the Centre you 'touch' the Cosmic Mind, the Mind of the Great Everything, that knows only abundance. Anything and everything you can ever want or need is already within the Great Everything, Wakan-Tanka.

At the Centre you are the cause of your world. The place that you are in. The place where you will be. You are responsible for your world right now. If you want to change your world and your perception of it you must change your thinking – as your perception changes your world changes. You determine what shall change. You cause what shall be.

When, in Exercise No. 2, you cut an apple in two across its equator you found in the centre of the five-pointed star that is its core absolutely nothing – just emptiness. At the source of the apple there was nothing. Just invisibility. The centre of *your* being is like that.

The Source of you – where your 'I' came from – is similarly unmanifest. Why? Because it is the part of you that is part of the Creator. It might be likened to a bottle full of water which is constantly being fed from behind with water under pressure by the Great Spirit. Eventually drops fall out of the bottle, forced past the cork. Each 'I' can be thought of as one of those drops. We have been given individuality. Now we must obtain all the experience we can and learn all the lessons we can before we return to the Source – wiser, experienced and still retaining our individuality. First the 'I' became conscious of itself – consciousness, the 'I am' – then it sought to relate to all around it and learn and develop awareness.

ADVENTURER TASK NO. 6:

Developing Creative Powers

Meditation is an essential tool in awakening the inner senses and this is why the Directional 'workings' have been designed within a meditative framework. The type of meditation encouraged so far by these Units has been largely contemplative, but with this final Adventurer Task a more active form is employed to develop further the visualisation skills and to expand the consciousness.

Visualisation is not only an important meditation technique but an essential for shamanic work and is a vital key in creating for yourself the circumstances and conditions you want in life. Visualisation is the creation of a mental picture, an object, situation or location. It is thinking in pictures rather than words, which is the language of the Subconscious Mind and of the High Self. Not everyone finds this easy because it is an activity of the right side of the brain which is not exercised as much as the left side by those of us living in a modern society. It is a skill that may have to be striven for, though when it is being acquired it comes gently and naturally. Just be persistent if you are not immediately successful.

The method of meditation I am going to discuss is Creative Meditation which employs the use of what I shall call the Magikal Will. The Magikal Will is not the kind of willpower employed when a person gives up smoking or goes on a diet. That kind of willpower requires the constant exercise of the will and of checking by the Conscious Mind.

The Magikal Will is the intense application of the desire, backed by strong emotion, to bring about a desired condition or a required object, and its secret is in *letting go*. Letting go frees the emotion of the desire from the pull of the Conscious Mind and releases it to the Subconscious Mind which was described to me by Silver Bear as 'the Place of Potential Becoming'. The Subconscious Mind then sets to work to find a route for that willed thought to manifest itself in physical reality.

In this technique the Desire is coupled to the Will but is not held on to. You do not keep coming back to it. It is not a question of repetitive nagging like 'Every day in every way I am getting better and better'. You have to dismiss it – give it away. It is when such willed thoughts are not released but become stuck to the ego that the opposite of what is desired sometimes comes about. You want more money, for instance, but get more bills. You want to slim, but get unexpected invitations to eat out!

You may have realised by now that it is your High Self that supplies the energies you ask for. It is your Subconscious Mind that takes power from the High Self and directs it for you, creating whatever you have wilfully, or unconsciously, programmed it to do. Once it is given instructions it will carry them out and in so doing takes the line of least resistance in bringing them into manifestation. It does not act upon a verbal language. Words alone – whether spoken or expressed silently – will not activate it unless they are 'words of *power*' whose sonics contain an activating frequency pattern. Its language is symbolism which are patterns of mental vibrations empowered with emotive energy (belief in the outcome) and directed by the Will, and it responds to such patterns conveyed to it. Your Subconscious Mind acts robotically – like a computer. It will respond to various commands as a computer responds to functional keys. The encircled cross, which is a symbol of the basic four-directional Medicine Wheel, is one such key. Indeed it is a *master* key.

You have been setting up your own personal Medicine Wheel with the use of five directional aids – coloured stones – to impress the concepts they symbolise into your mind without the need even to be consciously aware of those concepts in detail each time. You have set it up in front of you on a number of occasions now, and have worked with it indoors and out-of-doors. But the true Medicine Wheel exists only in your mind. It is not the

Medicine Wheel of stones that gives access to your Subconscious but the Medicine Wheel that the physical representation impregnates in your imagination that has the real power.

The Medicine Wheel, as you have discovered, represents the Four Primary Elements and everything in manifestation contains these elements. The pattern of the four elements dictates the characteristics of physical matter and since everything in existence is an energy pattern, the four elements are linked in a symbolic way with every energy pattern. The Medicine Wheel thus 'contains' all Creation within it, and also within it is everything that is possible. Within it you can design the choreography of your life. In the past you have been creating the circumstances of your life largely unconsciously and without deliberate intent. The quality of your life is thus dependent to an extent on the quality of your thought. If your thoughts have been scattered, diffused and uncertain, then you are at the mercy of the random factor. As with an electronic game in which the computer selects a number from many that have been fed into it, so the 'computer' of your Subconscious Mind will pick at random one thought that it is drawn to and act upon it. What you are going to learn from this final Adventurer Task is how to use the Computer of Mind in a wilful and deliberate way to attain for you something you consciously desire.

RITE NO. 5:

The Rite of Creativity

The first step is to determine exactly what it is you want. Avoid thinking in terms of money. Money is a means of exchange. Rather, decide what it is money is wanted for if it is a material object you desire. It does not, of course, have to be a physical object. It could be a more harmonious relationship, a better job, a happier home, or even a change in yourself. Think it through so it is clear in your mind before you begin the meditation session. You will need:

- Your green 'marker' stone.
- Smudge mix or smudge stick and bowl. Smudging fan.
- Matches or lighter.
- White candle and candleholder.
- Your layout cloth.
- Notebook and pen.

Set up your working surface with the green 'centre' stone in front of you. Place the candle in its holder immediately behind the stone. The smudge burner and mix should be conveniently on the right.

Light the smudge mix and smudge your aura and working area to cleanse them of any negativities and adverse influences.

Now strengthen and close the aura.

Light the candle as if from your Inner Light as you have previously learned to do, indicating to your Subconscious Mind that the space and time period is 'switched on' for meditative and creative work. Say aloud words that will confirm that you are both outwardly and inwardly 'switched on':

ENDING DARKNESS BY THIS LIGHT
OPENS ME TO LOVE AND LIGHT
DIRECTS MY WILL, MY INNER MIND
ATTAINS FOR ME, SO I SHALL FIND
ALL I DESIRE – TRUTH AND LIGHT,
CANDLE AND SELF IN SIMPLE RITE.

Using words in a rhythmic and poetic form in this way as you light the candle gives the thought sonic impetus to get through the 'psychic censor' – that barrier between the Conscious and Subconscious Mind – and into the Subconscious where it can be acted upon.

Now look at the candle flame. Squint your eyes until you are able to discern rays of light stabbing out in all directions from the flame itself. The Inner Light within you is like that, sending out beams in all directions.

Imagine a shaft of light like a laser beam projecting upwards through the top of your head and another pointing downwards beneath your feet. Then, 'picture' another beam of light reaching out in front of you from your navel and behind your back. Imagine also a ray of light directed from the centre of your being to your left and another to your right – altogether, six rays of light beaming out from your central inner flame.

Imagine now a point of light at the end of the beam in front of you moving clockwise in a circular path to join up with the end of the ray to your right, moving round behind you, then to join up with the ray to your left, and returning to where it began in front of you.

Then a second circle of light starting at a point above your head and moving round behind you to a point beneath your feet and curving up in front of you to join up with the ray in front and then to the beam above your head.

Finally, imagine a third ring of light from the point above your head and curving down to your right, down under your feet, then up to your left and joining up above your head.

Erect this symbol in your mind every time you wish to meditate on any 'creative' work for this is a master symbol of the Subconscious Mind and gives you access to creative power.

Now we are going to couple creative thinking with rhythmic breathing. You have experienced the benefits of the four-fold breath method of rhythmic breathing to relax the body and mind, but let us take our understanding of this concept a stage further. Breathing in is an expression of Yin – the principle of receiving. Holding the breath is a unifying process through taking in the pranic life force. Breathing out is an expression of Yang and of the outgoing projection of the Will and intention. The pause between expelling air from the lungs and breathing in again is the neutral-isation process.

The four-fold breath is a pattern of In – Hold – Out – Pause. This fluid motion of raising power within an energy-system, of bringing it to its full potential, and then discharging it under the power of its own impetus, permeates Nature and is at the seat of all creativity.

Now, in the Mind Space you have established for yourself where you are completely relaxed and at ease, think of the object or situation you want to come into your life. Whatever it is, the possession of it must not deprive another nor in any way must it interfere with the free will of another person. Do not confuse creativity with manipulation. Manipulative methods usually rebound back in some way and what is 'gained' is compensated for by the 'loss' of something already held. Whatever is desired must benefit others as well as yourself. As you breathe in 'see' it in your mind's eye as if it already exists, not as something in the future but as being actually received now. Hold on to that 'picture' as you hold the breath, then as you breathe out, experience the pleasure and joy the receiving of it gives you. Put all your senses to work. If, for instance, it is an improved relationship, experience the delight that being together brings. If it is a better job, experience the satisfaction of doing the work and the difference it is going to make to your life. Whatever it is, truly desire it as you breathe in and *experience* it as you breathe out. Keep up this process for a few minutes.

Then, having established the thought, the next step is to activate it with the power of the Will. To stress this determination of the Will, say aloud and with authority:

> AS I HAVE DETERMINED
> SO SHALL IT BE.

The words must be emphatic. You are giving instructions to the Subconscious and they must be backed with authority. Put the emphasis in the word '*be*'. Let it explode from your lips. Let that little word contain the dynamic power of your Will.

Bear this in mind: before anything can come into manifestation it has first to exist as *thought*. Thought is energy. Indeed, thought is the most mobile form of energy there is — quicker than the speed of light! When you visualise something you are giving the thought visual form and when you energise it with the Desire and the Will it becomes a Creative Thought. In creative meditation, a thought *form* is thus created in the mind and that thought form becomes the pattern or mould for elemental energies to flow into, and for manifestation to then take place in due course on the physical plane.

In your first use of this method choose something small and simple that is within your present sphere of availability. You can do bigger things later as you gain experience and confidence. Don't be tempted by greed or by any tendency to exert power or control over another individual or to encroach on another person's 'space', because such endeavours will most surely rebound back in some adverse way.

When the meditation session is over, make a note of what you have done and the date and time. Then dismiss it from your mind. Let it go. Leave your Subconscious to work on it.

It is most important that at the end of the session you give a clear signal to your Subconscious Mind that you are 'switching off' as it were and returning to 'ordinary' consciousness, to mundane, everyday activity.

Closing down is simple. Express words along the following lines before you 'switch off' by snuffing out the candle flame:

I NOW CLOSE THIS SESSION
GIVING THANKS TO THE POWERS OF LIGHT, LIFE,
LOVE AND TRUTH
FOR WHAT HAS BEEN ACCOMPLISHED.
THIS SESSION IS NOW ENDED.

Snuff out the candle and imagine as you do so that the flame has been returned to the one inside you. Take a deep breath, stretch your arms, and then 'Earth' yourself to disperse any excess energies. This is done by imagining roots going down from the soles of your feet and into the ground. Then allow yourself to flop on the floor and just relax there for a minute or two to allow any excess energy to return to the cosmic reservoir where it can be drawn upon in the future. Stand up, take another deep breath, and the Rite is over.

You may find it helpful to record portions of this Rite on a cassette recorder so you can play it back to yourself on a headset during your meditation session.

The Way of the Peaceful Warrior

THE MEDICINE PATH WE HAVE traversed together leads us now to a clearing where we can sit and consider our future. We have completed a journey round and through the Circle. We have turned the Wheel a complete revolution. We have come the way of the shamanic Adventurer who sees life as an exciting learning experience. But this is not the end of the journey — only a new beginning. The beginning of the Way of the Peaceful Warrior. But why be a warrior?

Contrary to popular belief, the American Indian warrior was not essentially a warring man at all. He fought and killed only when he saw no alternative. His primary function was a spiritual one. There is a clear difference between the concept of warrior and that of a soldier. A soldier is a fighting man who acts under orders and looks to others to tell him what to do and where to go. A soldier needs to be led and to have clear and precise directions. A soldier takes no personal responsibility for his actions, whether in victory or defeat, since whatever he does is under the orders of another. In everyday life most of us are, in a sense, 'soldiers'.

A warrior, on the other hand, has no such limitations or constraints. A warrior is an individual unit — his own 'general', taking full responsibility for his actions. The devotion of the American Indian warrior to his tribe was of such high quality that it could not be contained within the limitations of human law. If a battle was lost, the warrior never gave up, but merged into the countryside to survive and fight another day.

So in life we, too, whether man or woman, can be identified as either a 'soldier' who needs rules and laws as a guide and others in authority to direct our actions, or as a 'warrior' with freedom, independence of action and in control of our own destiny. We can choose to be a 'soldier' and let someone or something else take responsibility or blame for our actions and circumstances, or be a 'warrior' and take full responsibility for our life, choices and decisions.

The 'soldier' battles against the tyrants and enemies that can be seen, and confronts those who obstruct his path by determination and force if necessary. The 'warrior's' enemies are unseen. They are the 'tyrants' that seek to enslave the mind and the spirit and keep the individual chained to a life of ignorance, fear, pain and suffering. The 'warrior's' battles are within the self.

The 'soldier' trains to overcome, and to win victory is his most important aim. The 'warrior' trains to be proficient at achieving mastery, not over others but over himself and the circumstances of his life. For him taking part matters most. Opposition is there to teach him. The 'soldier' learns how to subdue. The 'warrior' learns how to co-operate.

Chief Silver Bear explained it to me this way:

'A warrior is one who walks his talk along the Path with Heart. By so doing he touches his own life and the lives of others – and even the Earth itself – with beauty.'

Let us examine Silver Bear's definition of a warrior. To 'walk your talk' means to practice what you preach. Not just talk about your principles and ideals, but to actually live them in everyday life. Not just talking about what you have learned, but putting that knowledge into action.

The 'Path with Heart'? There are many, many paths. Some are the paths of religion. Some are the paths of philosophical or mystical systems. There are political paths, social paths and cultural paths. There are Western paths and Eastern paths. All make appealing promises. All claim to be 'good'. Some even claim to be the only 'true' path. So how do we know which is the 'Path with Heart'?

Don Juan, the Yaqui Indian in Carlos Castaneda's books, provided an answer in *The Teachings of Don Juan*.[1] A path with heart, Don Juan indicated, is pleasant and enjoyable and makes you strong, whereas a path without heart makes you work hard at liking it, and actually weakens you. A path without heart demands that you keep strictly to it, have your mind on it all the time and never lose your concentration or stray off it. A path without heart is hard work. But it leads nowhere! Most paths are paths without heart and lead nowhere.

And the 'Beauty', Silver Bear referred to? We might define beauty as 'a combination of qualities that cause delight and pleasure'. So to touch one's life and the lives of others with beauty is to receive and share the delight and pleasure that is brought about by coming into alignment with the Earth forces, with the natural laws of the universe and with the Self. And in both receiving and sharing that beauty, the individual resonates with the Earth, and touches it with delight and pleasure.

'Beauty', Silver Bear told me, 'is always harmonious'.

On a Path with Heart, the spiritual warrior speaks and acts from the heart, and receives wisdom from the heart – that is the essence of all the ancient wisdom from which the 'hidden' knowledge of Indian shamans sprang. Wisdom of the heart implies a caring – a caring for Mother Earth and all her children; a caring that springs from a recognition that separation is an illusion, that mankind is not separated from Nature and the Cosmos but is an integral part of it, supported by it and a necessary support to it.

The physical things we see that appear to be so solid are but swirling groups of energy. It is their cohesion rather than intrinsic solidity that gives the impression of solidness. Similarly, the material world appears to our physical senses to be composed of myriads of separate things, but again this is only an appearance. Everything is but an individual manifestation of an underlying Whole. Everything is connected, just like the strands of a spider's web. Touch one and you affect them all.

Everything in existence is thus interpenetrated by streams of living energy like nerves within the human nervous system or the veins of the circulatory system. Each object, each person, is an individual manifestation of the Whole which the American Indian called 'the Great Everything', Wakan-Tanka. Each is an individual energy system within a great ocean of interconnected and interacting energy systems.

The 'wisdom of the heart' is thus a recognition that everything is dependent on everything else — everything interlinked with everything else in an intricate network or web — everything respected because it is a part of the Everything that is Wakan-Tanka.

Nothing is independent. All are related and interconnected. Each is like a cell in the physical body, and although brain cells are different from blood cells, and bone cells are different from muscle cells, all live and move and have their being in the one body they all share. Likewise, individual human beings can be likened to a cell in the body of the Great Everything — the Great Spirit which is the Source of everything. The Source is thus not a separation either, but was and is in Creation with us, sharing Its life with us.

Some religions offer the view that the Creator is some kind of Entity outside the Creation, separated and distanced from it, and this has largely fostered an attitude that everything non-human on Earth is also separate from mankind and consists of either unattached inanimate 'things' put there to satisfy man's needs and desires as the 'lord of the Earth' — a microcosm of the 'Lord of Heaven' — or subservient creatures without souls and therefore lacking in any kind of spiritual 'worth'.

Some hold that God has created Man in His image and likeness and they return the compliment. What an exclusive club! Man thus became a reflection of the God image men have created and written about. This has been a mistake of near-fatal proportions and has led the ecology of the Planet to the brink of being destroyed.

The Indian had no scriptures or sacred writings to revere or to be interpreted. Only the Book of Nature. By looking into that, the Indian could understand the Mind of the Great Spirit. The Great Spirit was no nebulous theological concept, no elusive Being separated from physical existence by vast expanses of space, no historical figure locked in a different age among another people. The Great Spirit shared life with the Indian and the Indian lived his life in the Great Spirit.

The American Indian saw there was power in the Sun, Moon, Stars and Planets and that they had an influence on the Earth's life and, therefore, on his own because they, too, were part of the Great Spirit and expressed a thought in the mind of the Creator just as did a tree or a human.

The Earth was his Mother because the physical body was composed of the material elements which came from the Earth's body and would one day be returned to the Earth again. The Sun and the Sky were his Father because the Sun was the great life-*giver* and source of energy. The Indian recognised that the part of man that thought, and pondered and created was not physical but of a realm that was as eternal and as unfathomable as the vast and unending Sky.

When the Sun and Earth 'made love' they produced 'children' – plant children, animal children, human children. The Indian did not *worship* the Sun and Earth and other planets, but he did recognize their reality and *honoured* them. He held the Earth to be sacred because it was the cradle of all life, sustaining and living it, and rocks, plants, animals, and humans would still be unmanifest without It.

The Indian took notice of what happened around him as well as what happened to him. He noticed the rising of the Sun in the East and its setting in the West, the regular waxing and waning of the Moon, and how the seasons of the year were correlated with natural happenings – to the migration of birds and animals, to the cycle of growth of the trees, plants and flowers, to the periods of light and the periods of darkness, to warmth and cold, to rain and shine. He saw the Great Spirit at work in everything around him – in the animals and birds, in the trees and plants, in the rocks and stones, and he loved them because they touched his life with their beauty – they gave him delight and pleasure – and he would do nothing to cause them intentional harm or to threaten or despoil their beauty.

The Way of the Peaceful Warrior – the Medicine Way – is thus a path through nature – of relating to the tides, rhythms and pulse of the Earth, and of experiencing a one-ness with it and with the Source of one's being. It is a way of looking and listening. It is being alert and aware, no longer 'asleep'. It is a way of giving and of receiving. It is a way of loving and of sharing. It is a way of coming into unity with the divinity that is *within* us as well as the divinity that is all around us. It is way of expanding the consciousness and of growing into our full potential. It is a way of embracing the invisible as well as the visible.

A philosophy of life however, that merely stimulates the mind or is confined to the pages of a book, has little practical value or spiritual worth.

The journey you embarked upon when you began to read this book is not completed by a single cycle of the Medicine Wheel and by reaching the end of this book. Indeed, having reached the place where you now are, your journey has only just begun. You must decide whether to go forward, further and deeper — whether to become not just an Adventurer but a Warrior.

You do not need to have been born of American Indian blood to become a Warrior on the Medicine Way. Nor do you have to become a sort of Red Indian 'devotee' and dress like an Indian or substitute another culture for your own. The warrior's path *is* the Medicine Way and it does not require you to walk backwards in history, to take up the guise of those who have gone before, lived in a bygone age and a different culture. You don't have to look like them, only learn from them. It is a question of intention and attitude.

The Warrior's Path is an acceptance of responsibility for your own life from now on. It involves not only a desire for change but a *willingness* to initiate the changes that are necessary. The Warrior's way is to take just one step at a time, recognising that each leads only to the next step. It is a going forward, not a stepping back, and of finding satisfaction in the present.

Where does the path lead? Paradoxically, it is a journey without destination. It leads nowhere but where *you* are. It is a journey without end because the end is the journey itself. The journey itself is exciting, adventurous and pleasurable because it is a journey of knowledge. Not a gathering of information. Not of knowing useless facts. But knowledge that is necessary to you because it is knowledge about you, enabling you to live out the purpose of that knowledge.

The path of the warrior is also called the Rainbow Path because it is a way of harmonisation. It is a way of bringing harmonisation within yourself, harmonisation with others, harmonisation with the Earth, with the forces of Nature and with the universe. It is a path that does not bind you to a single teacher for you will learn from many teachers. But beware of any who may tell you that before you can receive their teaching you must be sworn to secrecy first. Most so-called 'secret' teachings can be found by the diligent enquirer on the shelves of libraries or leading bookshops. The most profound and powerful parts of the ancient wisdom are well enough protected because they cannot be comprehended unless the seeker is mentally, emotionally, psychologically and most of all *spiritually* prepared to receive them.

The true teachers on the path will be those who point you to the Teacher within and impart ways of learning shamanically. This book, for instance, is a practical outcome of shamanic learning. When I was 'commissioned' to write in a Vision Quest there was no great storehouse of written knowledge from which I could draw. I had only the driving force from an overwhelming shamanic experience, that I had to do it in order to know, and that this work was the most important single activity of my entire life so far.

The knowledge has come to me with the writing – each step of the way and at the point where it was needed. Even the structure and form of this book was not pre-determined and planned, in spite of many years' experience in disciplined journalistic endeavours. It developed over a three-year period almost, it seemed, of its own accord. Only as it has neared completion have I recognised a pattern unfolding in it.

It has been a thrilling experience and one that has confirmed to me that the ancient wisdom is not lost, but stored away in the Collective Unconscious of the Universal Mind and can be channelled back to us. The teachings I have received and which I have been inspired to share, have been conveyed to me through shamans and through shamanic inner plane teachers. The oral traditions and the teachings of the Sacred Fires have thus become entwined for reconstitution into modern idiom so they can be shared with all who are seeking with the heart. It is part of a purpose being projected and worked out with others in many parts of the world and in many different ways who, although not in liaison with one another, are 'connected' by a common purpose. That purpose, that common bond that connects them, is to bring healing to the minds, spirits and bodies of human beings of all races and kinds, to help to reawaken an awareness of the holistic nature of all living things and as a consequence bring healing to planet Earth also.

This book, together with its companion *Earth Medicine* which precedes it, is a testimony to the practicability of shamanic methods of learning. The writing of them has impressed upon me a vital and essential principle which was conveyed to me orally:

You have to *do* what it is you want to *know*. You have to *be* in your heart what it is you want to *become*. You have to experience inwardly what it is you wish to see manifested in your life outwardly. It requires the stillness of *watching* and *listening* so you can *hear* the Great Spirit in the sunrise and sunset, *see* the Great Spirit in the sound of the Earth and in the rustle of the trees, and *feel* the presence of the Great Spirit in the fragrance of the flora and in the fresh breeze of the morning. Then you will be touched with the beauty that comes from within and you will begin to perceive the world around you in a new light and experience living from the heart. Then you will touch the Earth with your beauty.

That is the Medicine Way – the beauty way, the beautiful way.

Glossary

Ancestors: The Ancestors are our predecessors and our own past lives and are present within us in our genes. Thus the cells of our bodies contain 'echoes' of our personal, family, national and racial past and have an influence on the way we are presently perceiving reality.

Archetype: A universal symbol of an energy pattern that indicates how certain forces or influences are operating. An Archetype is presented usually in human or animal form.

Aura: A cocoon-like fibrous energy-field in which a life form is immersed.

Awareness: Being alert to what goes on outside yourself. Awareness is not consciousness. You are conscious of yourself but aware of others. You can extend your awareness.

Balance: A state of steadiness and equilibrium. An equal and harmonious relationship.

Belief System: A religion or philosophy of not knowing, which rests upon faith in the word or authority of another.

Buffalo: A natural symbol of the universe to the North American Indian because the buffalo represented the totality of all that was manifested; it provided food and material for clothing, shelter, utensils, tools and weapons.

Centred: A state of calm receptivity and equilibrium in which the attention is no longer directed to meet the expectations other people have about yourself. It is a condition of being yourself.

Chakra: A sanskrit word meaning 'wheel' or 'disc'. A chakra is a wheel-like spiralling vortex or power centre located within the human auric cocoon which acts as a gateway between different levels or planes, and receives, assimilates and distributes subtle energies that are pulled into it.

Chaos: An unorganised state where random laws condition existence. A condition of untransformed power where energy moves freely and without direction in a disorderly way.

Cosmology: A system of comprehending the geography of the non-ordinary reality of existence.

Cosmos: The organised intelligence of the universe and of the whole of Creation operating in accordance with natural and sacred laws. The cosmos is thus law-abiding. It functions within the law of its own being as does everything within it.

Death: A transition from one state of being to another in a continuous cycle of change.

Earth Medicine: A system of personality profiling, of self-discovery and personal empowerment based upon Medicine Wheel principles and determined by the time of the year of one's birth.

Earthing: A method of ensuring that after any shamanic work or meditative exercise one is fully restored to ordinary reality. Earthing acts as an 'off' switch from non-ordinary reality and ensures that one is fully 'grounded'.

Elements: Components of the manifested Great Spirit which are coming into expression. Each Element has abstract qualities of expression which can best be comprehended in human terms by relating them to similar characteristics found in tangible earth, fire, air and water.

Energy: The power projected by a vibratory force.

Enlightenment: The ability to 'see in the dark' — that is, to see what others cannot see and to perceive what is hidden from others.

Feather: The feather is symbolic of the human aura because it gives out impulses of high frequency energy and its fibres are arranged in a structure similar to the threads of energy that comprise the human aura. The feather was used by shamans to align the auric fibres and as an auric healing tool.

The feather was also symbolic of a message or messenger, and was used as a badge of office.

Frequency: The vibratory rate of an energy field or entity.

Gods/Goddesses: Higher beings that operate principally through the mind. They are infinitely more powerful than humans, but are personified by humans as having human personalities.

Great Spirit: The unmanifest Source from which all originates and in which all has existence.

High Self: One's own Perfected Self or True Self. It is the Permanent Personality which is eternal.

Inner Light: The divinity within us that is an individuation of the Great Spirit. The Inner Light emanates from the centre of our Soul.

Innocence: Complete impartiality and objectivity. The reverse of subjective opinion and judgment.

Intuition: A teaching from within. An inner seeing and hearing.

Karma: Life lessons revealed by one's destiny. Karma is a law of action and change in which repetitive conditions and circumstances indicate areas of life that are not working harmoniously and which need to be put right in order for the individual to evolve spiritually.

Magik: A technique for bringing desired changes into one's life. Magik is a process of crafting and shaping our own lives as we want them to be by coming into harmony with natural laws. This is not the magic of superstition or of the clever illusionist, nor the magick of the ceremonial occultist.

Mana/Prana: A life energy that is taken in with the breath and is vital for the functioning of the subtle bodies of which the physical being is composed.

Mandala: A universal circular symbol which, as well as being an expression of the wholeness contained within the totality of life, is a symbol of the Self and the Source.

Medicine: *Power. Healing*. Knowledge. A Medicine man is thus a man enpowered to bring knowledge and healing.

Medicine Way: An adaptation of Medicine teachings and Medicine Wheel principles for modern-day use.

Medicine Wheel: A symbolic device for obtaining knowledge, especially about oneself, and of making connections at different levels of reality.

Nadis: Vertical, tubular channels located in the human Energy Body along the line of the spinal column which convey currents of energy to the chakras.

Nagual: The unknown. The 'hidden' or unseen realm of the Spirit. Nagual problems are spiritual problems.

Nature: The essential character of the Earth or of something on or in the Earth.

Personal History: A strong attachment to a pattern of life which has been impressed upon you by other people and which conditions your thoughts and actions. Personal history makes one feel obliged to explain and justify one's actions.

Pipe: A sacred tool that represents the universe and unites all the human, animal, plant and mineral kingdoms within it. The bowl represents the feminine aspect of divinity and the stem represents the masculine aspect. The tobacco and herbs are the sacred offering. The inhaled smoke is regarded as the breath of the Great Spirit – the exhaled smoke as the intentions and prayers of the one who smokes the pipe and of those in whose presence it is smoked.

Religion: An organised belief system in which the adherents are told what to believe either by verbal instruction or by written word. Most religions claim to be 'revelatory', that is, the tenets to be believed have been revealed by supernatural means.

Ritual: A method of converting thoughts into symbolic actions in order to powerfully impress the subconscious mind to act on the intention and to bring it into physical existence.

Sexuality: The expression of polarised life energies inherent in all life forms and especially significant to humans. Sexuality is a process of bonding. It is concerned with continuance – with doing that brings joy.

Shaman: A person who understands that there is life in everything, who has direct personal experience of realms of non-ordinary reality and is able to function within them. A shaman is primarily a 'harmoniser', one who 'heals' at all levels – physical, emotional, psychological and spiritual – and in a particular way.

Shamanism: The practice of the principles and techniques of shamans which involve working with the powers of Nature that exist both inside and outside the individual self as both manifest forms and unmanifest potentials. Shamanism is a way of learning by direct personal experience. Its methods transcend the intellect since they form part of the ancient Science of the Spirit.

Sitting Place: Your birthplace on the Medicine Wheel or Earth Medicine Web. The direction from which you perceive reality in accordance with the time of year at your birth.

Skull: An ancient symbol of the seat of consciousness and of the existence of other realms of conscious awareness that lie behind the material, fleshly world of appearances.

Smudging: The use of smoke to clear away negative vibrations and to attract beneficial energies to oneself and others.

Soul: The life expression system which enables the individuated Spirit within the life form to express itself at conscious, subconscious and superconscious levels. It might also be described as a data bank in which the record of life experience is held. The Soul retains what the individuated Spirit has done with the Life Force.

Spirit: The individuated essence of the Life Force – be it human, animal, plant, mineral or celestial. Spirit may be considered to be the driving force of the entity whether human or non-human. Everything has spirit.

Spirituality: Guided power. Being guided in one's actions by the Spirit within. Conditioning by principles rather than by rules or expectations. Spirituality retains the fundamental liberty of free will.

Symbols: A means of exchanging energy between different planes of reality. Symbols are links between the objective and subjective, between one level of consciousness and another.

Timelessness: A state of no movement. Stillness.

Tonal: The known. The physical realm of mundane, everyday existence. That which is seen in everyday activity. The things you are aware of and which may be causing you difficulties. Tonal problems are problems of physical life.

Totem: A symbolic sensor that serves as a link between different levels of existence, serving as an aid to comprehending non-physical powers and formative forces. Since a totem expresses the qualities of a living entity it is easier to relate to and is more effective as a learning aid than a geometric symbol.

Wakan-Tanka: The Great Spirit in manifestation. The Great Everything. The universe. All that is.

Yang: The masculine, active, positive, conceptual principle in all that manifests. Represented in some ancient cultures as the God-power behind Nature.

Yin: The feminine, passive, receptive, nurturing principle in all that manifests. Represented in some ancient cultures as the Goddess-power behind Nature.

Sources

CHAPTER ONE

1. *Gospel of the Redman*. Ernest Thompson Seton. Seton Village, Santa Fe, New Mexico, 1963.
2. *The Indian Chief*. Revd C. Van Dusen. 1867.
3. *Picture Writing of the American Indians*. Garrick Mallery. Dover Publications Inc., 1973.
4. *Letters and Notes on the Manners, Customs and Conditions of the North American Indians*. George Catlin. Edited by Marjorie Helpin. Dover Publications Inc., 1973.
5. *Land of the Spotted Eagle*. Chief Luther Standing Bear. Houghton Miffin, Boston and New York, 1933.
6. *Tatanga Mani, Walking Buffalo and the Stones*. Grant McEwan. M. J. Hurtig Ltd., Edmonton, Alberta, Canada, 1969.

CHAPTER TWO

1. *Sun Men of the Americas*. Grace Cooke. White Eagle Publishing Trust, 1975.
2. *The Crystal Skull*. Richard M. Garvin. Doubleday & Co. Inc., 1973.
3. *America BC*. B. Fell. New York Times Book Co., 1976.

CHAPTER THREE

1. *The Apogeton*. Alawn Tickhill. Sorcerer's Apprentice Press, Leeds, 1984.
2. *The Ancient Maya*. Sylvanus G. Morley. Stanford University Press, 1956.
3. *The Indian Historian*. American Indian Historical Society, June 1968 issue.

CHAPTER FIVE

1. *Earth Medicine*. Kenneth Meadows. Element Books Ltd, 1989.

UNIT ONE

1. *North American Indian Medicine*. V. J. Vogel. University of Oklahoma Press, 1970.
2. *Handbook of Bach Flower Remedies*. Philip M. Chancellor. C. W. Daniel Company Ltd., London, 1971.
3. *Earth Medicine*. Kenneth Meadows. Element Books Ltd, 1989.

UNIT TWO

1. *Earth Medicine*. Kenneth Meadows. Element Books Ltd, 1989.

UNIT SEVEN

1. *Earth Medicine*. Kenneth Meadows. Element Books Ltd, 1989.

UNIT TEN

1. *The Teachings of Don Juan*. Carlos Castaneda. Penguin, 1970.

Bibliography

America BC. Barry Fell. New York Times Book Co. 1976.
Atlantis. Ignatius Donnelly. Dover Publications Inc., New York, 1976.
Atlantis and the Seven Stars. J. Countryman. Robert Hale Ltd., London, 1979.
Black Elk Speaks. John G. Nerhardt. Washington Square Press, 1959.
Book of the Hopi. Frank Waters. Penguin Books, 1977.
Bury My Heart at Wounded Knee. Dee Brown. Picador, 1971.
Danger My Ally. F. A. Mitchell-Hedges, Elek Books Ltd., 1954.
He Walked the Americas. L. Taylor Hansen. Neville Spearman Ltd., (1963).
Indian Medicine Power. Brad Steiger. Para Research, Gloucester, Mass., 1984.
Ishi. Last of His Tribe. Theodora Kroeber. Bantam Books, 1973.
Journey to Xtlan. Carlos Castaneda. Penguin Books, 1974.
Lame Deer – Seeker of Visions. John (Fire) Lame Deer and Richard Erdoes. Washington Square Press, 1972.
Lame Deer – Sioux Medicine Man. John (Fire) Lame Deer and Richard Erdoes. Quartet Books Ltd., London, 1980.
Lifetide. Lyall Watson. Coronet Books, 1979.
North American Indian Mythology. Cottie Burland. Hamlyn Publishing Group Ltd., 1966.
Seven Arrows. Hyemeyohsts Storm. Ballantine Books, New York, 1972.
Supernature. Lyall Watson. Coronet Books, 1974.
Tapestries in the Sand. David Villasenor. Naturegraph Company, California, 1983.
The Ancient Maya. Sylvanus G. Morley. Stanford University Press, 1956.
The Apogeton. Alawn Tickhill. Sorcerer's Apprentice Press, Leeds, 1984.
The Cherokees. Grace Steele Woodward. University of Oklahoma Press, 1963.
The Crystal Skull. Richard M. Garvin. Doubleday and Co. Inc., 1973.
The Crystal Sourcebook. Compiled by Milewski Harford. Mystic Crystal Publications, Sedona, Arizona, 1987.

The Flight of the Feathered Serpent. Peter Balin. Arcana Publishing Co., Wisconsin, USA, 1978.

The Lost Continent of Mu. Col. James Churchward. C. W. Daniel Co. Ltd., 1959.

The Medicine Wheel. Sun Bear and Wabun. Prentice-Hall Inc. 1980.

The Message of the Crystal Skull. Alice Bryant and Phyllis Galde. Llewellyn Publications, 1989.

The Psychic Power of Animals. Bill Schul. Fawcett Publications Inc., 1977.

The Sacred Symbols of Mu. Col. James Churchward, C. W. Daniel Co. Ltd., 1960.

The Soul of the Indian. Charles Alexander Eastman. Houghton-Miffin, Boston, 1911.

The Teachings of Don Juan. Carlos Castaneda. Penguin, 1970.

Touch the Earth. Compiled by T. C. Luhan. Abacus, 1973.

Voices of Earth and Sky. Vinson Brown. Naturegraph, 1974.

Warriors of the Rainbow. William Willoya and Vinson Brown. Naturegraph, 1962.

For information on workshops and seminars on shamanism write to:

Kenneth Meadows,
BM Box 8602,
London WC1 3XX,
England.

Index